Transparency in International Trade and Investment Dispute Settlement

An increasing number of international trade disputes are settled through the World Trade Organization (WTO) dispute settlement (DS) procedure. In parallel, an increasing number of international investment disputes are settled through an investor-host state arbitration procedure. What does "transparency" mean in the context of international trade and investment dispute settlement? Why is enhanced transparency demanded? To what extent and in what manner should these dispute settlement procedures be transparent? The book addresses these issues of securing transparency in international trade and investment dispute settlement.

Transparency in international trade and investment dispute settlement drew the attention of international economic law scholars in the late 1990s, but most literature discusses the transparency in trade DS and investment DS separately. The book deals with the issue in a comprehensive and coherent manner, combining the analyses of the issue in both DS procedures and comparing the pros and cons to enhanced transparency in them. The main argument of the book is, firstly, that transparency in these procedures should be enhanced so that they may be accountable to a wider range of stakeholders, but, secondly, that the extent and the manner of transparency might differ in these two procedures, reflecting their structural and functional differences.

The book appeals to both scholars and students interested in international economic law and international relations, as well as lawyers and government officials who deal with international trade and investment regulation.

Junji Nakagawa is Professor of International Economic Law at the Institute of Social Science, University of Tokyo. Born in Hiroshima, Japan, in 1955, Nakagawa obtained his BA, MA and Ph.D. from the University of Tokyo. He has also taught at Tokyo Institute of Technology, City University of Hong Kong, University of Denver, Tufts University and El Colegio de México. His publications include *International Harmonization of Economic Regulation* (2011, Oxford University Press), *Multilateralism and Regionalism in Global Economic Governance* (2011, Routledge), *Anti-Dumping Laws and Practices of the New Users* (2007, Cameron May) and *Managing Development: Globalization, Economic Restructuring and Social Policy* (2006, Routledge).

Transparency in International Trade and Investment Dispute Settlement

Edited by
Junji Nakagawa

Routledge
Taylor & Francis Group
LONDON AND NEW YORK

First published 2013
by Routledge
2 Park Square, Milton Park, Abingdon, Oxon, OX14 4RN

Simultaneously published in the USA and Canada
by Routledge
711 Third Avenue, New York, NY 10017

Routledge is an imprint of the Taylor & Francis Group, an informa business

British Library Cataloguing in Publication Data
A catalogue record for this book is available from the British Library

Library of Congress Cataloging in Publication Data
Transparency in international trade and investment dispute settlement / edited by Junji Nakagawa.
p. cm.
Includes bibliographical references.
1. Arbitration and award, International. 2. Dispute resolution (Law)
3. Foreign trade regulation. 4. Investments, Foreign (International law)
I. Nakagawa, Junji, 1955-
K2400.T73 2012
382′.9—dc23
2012023856

ISBN 13: 978-0-415-52873-3 (hbk)
ISBN 13: 978-0-203-07726-9 (ebk)

Typeset in Times New Roman
by RefineCatch Limited, Bungay, Suffolk

Printed and bound in the United States of America by Publishers Graphics, LLC on sustainably sourced paper.

Contents

Contributors

Florentino P. Feliciano is a Senior Counsel at the Law Office of SyCip Salazar Hernancez & Gatmaitan. He was a former member of the WTO Appellate Body from 1995 to 2000, and a Justice of the Supreme Court of the Philippines from 1986 to 1995.

Yuka Fukunaga is a Professor at the School of Social Sciences, Waseda University, Japan.

Peter L. Lallas is the Executive Secretary of the World Bank Inspection Panel.

Chin Leng Lim is Professor at the Faculty of Law at the University of Hong Kong.

Daniel Magraw is the President Emeritus and Distinguished Scholar at the Center for International Environmental Law, Washington, DC.

Junji Nakagawa is a Professor of International Economic Law at the Institute of Social Science, University of Tokyo.

Federico Ortino is Reader in International Economic Law in the School of Law at King's College London.

Sofia Plagakis is a Policy Analyst at the OMB Watch, Washington. She was former Program Associate at the Center for International Environmental Law.

Acknowledgements

This book arose from an international joint research project funded by the Japan Society for the Promotion of Science (JSPS). The three-year project, which ran from 2008 to 2010, produced a couple of intermediary results. The first was the panel discussion on 'Transparency in International Trade and Investment Dispute Settlement' at the Society of International Economic Law Inaugural Conference in Geneva in July 2008. Nakagawa chaired the panel, and Yuka Fukunaga, Dan Magraw and Federico Ortino read their papers. Dr. Isabelle Van Damme also joined the panel and read her paper on the inherent powers of the WTO's Appellate Body. The members of the project learned a lot from the arguments of Dr. Van Damme and those who attended the panel.

The second intermediary result was the panel session on 'Transparency in International Trade and Investment Dispute Settlement' at the Asian Society of International Law 2nd Biennial Conference at the University of Tokyo in August 2009. Nakagawa chaired the panel, and Florentino Feliciano, Federico Ortino and Peter Lallas read their papers. The members of the project were grateful for the comments they received at the ensuing floor discussion, most notably from Professor Edith Brown Weiss. The results of the discussion were later reflected in each member's contribution to the book, though, of course, the final responsibility of each contribution is owed by its author.

Chin Leng Lim has been one of the most enthusiastic members of the project. Although he could not attend either of the above two panels, he and I have worked closely throughout the project. Dan Magraw kindly introduced Sofia Plagakis as the final member of the project; she has immense research and working experience on webcasting international trade and investment dispute settlement cases. I wholeheartedly appreciate these members of the project for their unflagging enthusiasm and support to the project.

Thanks are also due to Yong Ling Lam at Routledge, who has been as enthusiastic and creative as before in supporting the publication.

Finally, let me express my sincere gratitude to my wife, Akimi, for her support, encouragement and affection. Like my previous publications, this book will be dedicated to her.

Tokyo, June 2012
Junji Nakagawa

Abbreviations

AANZFTA	Australia and New Zealand FTA
ADR	alternative means of dispute resolution
AEM	ASEAN Economic Ministers' Meeting
AFTA	ASEAN Free Trade Area
APEC	Asia Pacific Economic Cooperation
ASEAN	Association of Southeast Asian Nations
BIT	bilateral investment treaty
BRIC	Brazil, Russia, India and China
CEC	Commission on Environmental Cooperation
CIEL	Center for International Environmental Law
CSR	Corporate Social Responsibility
DDA	Doha Development Agenda
DR-CAFTA	Dominican Republic–Central America-United States Free Trade Agreement
DSB	Dispute Settlement Body
DSM	WTO Dispute Settlement Mechanism
DSS	WTO Dispute Settlement System
DSU	WTO Understanding on Rules and Procedures Governing the Settlement of Disputes
EC	European Communities
ECHR	European Court of Human Rights
EPA	Economic Partnership Agreement
EU	European Union
FAO	Food and Agriculture Organization of the United Nations
FDI	Foreign Direct Investment
FTA	Free Trade Agreement
GATT	General Agreement on Tariffs and Trade
IACHR	Inter-American Commission of Human Rights
IAM	independent accountability mechanism
IBRD	International Bank for Reconstruction and Development
ICA	International Court of Arbitration
ICC	International Chamber of Commerce
ICCPR	International Covenant on Civil and Political Rights

ICJ	International Court of Justice
ICSID	International Centre for Settlement of Investment Disputes
ICTY	International Criminal Tribunal for the Former Yugoslavia
IFC	International Finance Corporation
IFI	international financial institution
IIA	International Investment Agreement
IISD	International Institute for Sustainable Development
ILO	International Labour Organization
ISO	International Organization for Standardization
ITLOS	International Tribunal for the Law of the Sea
LCIA	London Court of International Arbitration
MAI	Multilateral Agreement on Investment
MNE	multinational enterprise
NAAEC	North American Agreement on Environmental Cooperation
NAFTA	North American Free Trade Agreement
NCP	national contact point
NGO	non-governmental organization
ODA	official development assistance
OECD	Organisation for Economic Co-operation and Development
PCA	Permanent Court of Arbitration
PRC	People's Republic of China
RTA	Regional Trade Agreement
SCC	Stockholm Chamber of Commerce
TNC	transnational corporation
TOR	Terms of Reference
TPP	Trans-Pacific Partnership Agreement
UN	United Nations
UNCITRAL	United Nations Commission on International Trade Law
UNCTAD	United Nations Conference on Trade and Development
UNEP	United Nations Environment Program
WTO	World Trade Organization

1 Introduction

Transparency in international trade and investment dispute settlement

Junji Nakagawa and Daniel Magraw

An increasing number of international trade disputes are settled through the World Trade Organization (WTO) dispute settlement procedure.[1] Also, disputes between foreign investors and host states are increasingly being submitted to international arbitration.[2] Although these dispute settlement processes differ in the characteristics of the parties (the former being state to state, and the latter being private investor to state) and their applicable laws, they share the same function of judging the lawfulness of a wide range of domestic regulations and measures of states under international law. When the disputed domestic regulations and measures have some bearing on non-trade/investment issues such as environment and public health, settlement of such disputes can have serious economic and social impacts on the disputing state parties. Thus, more and more stakeholders are speaking out for enhanced transparency in these dispute settlement procedures (cf. Knahr 2007).

What does "transparency" mean in the context of international trade and investment dispute settlement? Why is enhanced transparency strongly asserted? Conversely, why is transparency strongly resisted by some? To what extent and in what manner should these dispute settlement procedures be transparent, and why is it so? This book aims at analyzing the theoretical and practical issues of securing transparency in these dispute settlement procedures.

Call for transparency in the WTO dispute settlement procedure

The issue of transparency in international trade dispute settlement first drew worldwide attention in the late 1990s, when the WTO dispute settlement procedure took up the case concerning the US trade restriction of shrimps to protect sea turtles (cf. Mavroidis 2002). The panel received amicus curiae briefs from two environmental non-governmental organizations (NGOs), but it declined to take them into consideration.[3] It reasoned that while a panel had the authority to seek information from any source under Article 13.1 of the WTO Understanding on Rules and Procedures Governing the Settlement of Disputes (DSU),[4] it had not sought information from the NGOs that submitted the briefs.[5] However, the panel suggested that if any of the party wished to put forward the briefs as part of their own submissions, they were free to do so.[6] In response, the United States designated part of one of the briefs submitted as an annex to its submission.

The WTO Appellate Body reversed the reasoning of the panel, stating that a panel had the discretionary authority either to accept and consider or to reject information and advice submitted to it, *whether requested by a panel or not* (emphasis in the original).[7] The Appellate Body further expanded the possibility of accepting non-solicited amicus curiae briefs in its Report in *United States – Lead and Bismuth II*, stating that the Appellate Body had the legal authority under the DSU to accept and consider amicus curiae briefs in an appeal when it found it pertinent and useful to do so.[8]

In *EC – Asbestos*, the Appellate Body, in anticipation of a large number of amicus curiae submissions on appeal, proposed an additional procedure to deal with such submissions in this appeal only, which provided that "(a)ny person, whether natural or legal, other than a party or a third party to this dispute, wishing to file a written brief with the Appellate Body, must apply for leave to file such a brief from the Appellate Body by noon on Thursday, 16 November 2000."[9] However, this initiative was opposed by a number of WTO Members. Egypt, on behalf of the Informal Group of Developing Countries, requested a special meeting of the General Council to discuss this additional procedure. The special meeting was held on 22 November 2000, and many developing countries raised voices against the Appellate Body's accepting unsolicited amicus curiae briefs.[10] Uruguay, for instance, stated that the practical effect of the additional procedure had been to grant individuals and institutions outside of the WTO a right that Members themselves did not possess.[11] Egypt argued that, if the procedure was implemented, a severe harm and a grave imbalance would be done to the rights of Members vis-à-vis external parties or individuals who were not even contractually committed to the obligations of the WTO system.[12] On the other hand, the United States asserted that the Appellate Body had the authority under Rule 16(1) of its Working Procedures[13] to adopt the additional procedure regarding the acceptance and consideration of amicus curiae briefs in that case. The United States added that the Appellate Body had adopted the additional procedures to manage the issue of accepting unsolicited amicus curiae briefs in appeal in a fair, legal and orderly manner, taking into account the interests of members of civil society in having their views considered, the interests of the parties and third parties in being able to review and respond to any amicus submissions, and the interests of all in resolving the dispute.[14] In its Report, the Appellate Body noted that it had received 11 applications for leave to file an amicus curiae brief, but each application was denied without further explanation.[15]

WTO Members have been discussing enhanced transparency in WTO dispute settlement procedures in the review negotiations of the DSU since 1997. Acceptance of unsolicited amicus curiae briefs has been one of the major issues. Some Members argue for a general prohibition on unsolicited briefs, which they argue would be in line with the intergovernmental nature of the WTO dispute settlement procedure. For others, regulating the timing of amicus curiae briefs, their length and the procedures to address the admissibility and contents of the briefs would ensure that appropriate guarantees are in place to manage such briefs.[16]

Opening panel and Appellate Body hearings to the public has been another important issue in the review negotiations of the DSU. A number of Members, including the US, Canada and EU, have called for enhanced transparency through opening panel and Appellate Body hearings to the public, and suggested that such openness could contribute to greater public confidence in the WTO dispute settlement procedure.[17] Other Members have expressed concern in relation to the preservation of the intergovernmental character of the WTO dispute settlement procedure, the protection of confidential information, as well as practical modalities and potential budgetary implications.[18] Some panels have recently opened their hearings to public viewing upon the request of the parties,[19] principally through the use of closed-circuit television.[20]

What were the major reasons for the recent call for enhanced transparency in the WTO dispute settlement procedure? One of the major reasons was the subject matter of some dispute cases that drew wide attention of the public. *US – Shrimps*, *EC – Asbestos* and *EC – Hormones* were prime examples, as they dealt with environmental protection (protection of endangered species) and/or protection of human life or health. These cases were widely publicized, and many NGOs expressed concerns about the allegedly pro-trade bias of the WTO law and the WTO dispute settlement procedure. They succeeded in persuading some WTO Members to call for enhanced transparency in the WTO dispute settlement procedure to ensure that the procedure would strike a balance between trade interests and broader public interest such as environmental protection and protection of human life or health.

On the other hand, many WTO Members, including most developing Members and some developed Members, expressed concern that enhanced transparency might erode the intergovernmental character of the WTO dispute settlement procedure.[21] Though it is not necessarily clear what they meant by the term *intergovernmental character*, it is safe to assume that it implies that the WTO dispute settlement procedure, in spite of its judicialized characteristics, still takes on a character of government-to-government, or diplomatic, settlement of disputes, where confidentiality and flexibility are needed.[22] It has also been asserted that strictly confidential information, mainly business information, should be protected in the WTO dispute settlement procedure and that this cannot be accomplished with increased transparency.[23]

A call for transparency in investor–state arbitration

In the late 1990s, transparency also became an issue in the practice of investor–state arbitration under the North American Free Trade Agreement (NAFTA) Chapter Eleven, with respect to the public access to arbitral awards and other documents (cf. Van Harten 2007: 162–163; also see Knahr and Reinisch 2007). While Article 1137.4 of the NAFTA provides a rule in favor of public access to arbitral awards when Canada or the United States is the party,[24] it leaves open the possibility that other documents may not be open to the public without the consent of both the host state and the investor. Applicable arbitration rules appeared to support a presumption in favor of confidentiality. For instance, Article 32(5) of the United Nations Commission on International Trade Law (UNCITRAL) Arbitration Rules provided that the award may be made public only with the consent of both parties. Applying this rule, the tribunal in *S.D. Myers, Inc.* v. *Government of Canada* declined to publish documents without the consent of the disputing parties.[25] The NAFTA member states, however, intervened in 2001 in favor of enhanced transparency by announcing that they would publish all documents submitted to, or issued by, NAFTA Chapter Eleven arbitral tribunals.[26]

A NAFTA tribunal went further by accepting amicus curiae briefs from NGOs. The tribunal in *Methanex Corporation* v. *United States of America* found that it had the power to accept amicus curiae briefs from NGOs under the UNCITRAL Arbitration Rules.[27] The tribunal based its decision on Article 15(1) of the UNCITRAL Arbitration Rules, which grants to the tribunal a broad discretion as to the conduct of arbitration.[28] It pointed out two additional reasons for accepting amicus curiae briefs. First, there was a public interest in the arbitration that arose from its subject matter.[29] Second, there was a broader argument, as suggested by the respondent (the United States) and Canada, that the Chapter Eleven arbitral process could benefit from being perceived as more open and transparent, or conversely be harmed if seen as unduly secretive.[30] On the other hand, the tribunal declined the NGO's request to attend hearings and to receive copies of all submissions and materials without the consent of the parties.[31]

The NAFTA member states later clarified the rules and procedures for the acceptance of written submissions by non-disputing parties.[32] Although this clarification seemed to imply the NAFTA member states' unwillingness to open the Chapter Eleven arbitral hearings to the public, the *Methanex* tribunal opened its hearing to the public in June 2004,[33] and the NAFTA member states' Joint Statement of 16 July 2004 welcomed the fact that Mexico had joined the United States and Canada in their support of open hearings in the Chapter Eleven arbitral procedure.[34]

These developments under the NAFTA Chapter Eleven arbitration seemed to have stimulated other forums for investor–state arbitration to take steps for enhanced transparency. For instance, the tribunal in the *Suez-Vivendi* case, the first International Centre for Settlement of Investment Disputes (ICSID) tribunal to deal with amicus curiae submissions, admitted that it had the power to accept amicus curiae briefs. Based on Article 44 of the ICSID Convention,[35] which is similar to Article 15(1) of the UNCITRAL Arbitration Rules, the tribunal stated that "like the *Methanex* tribunal, the Tribunal in the present case finds that acceptance of amicus submissions is a procedural question that does not affect a disputing party's substantive rights since the parties' rights remain the same both before and after the submission."[36] Subsequent to this case, the ICSID Secretariat suggested changes to the ICSID Rules and Regulations that would expressly provide for submissions of non-disputing parties.[37] These changes were adopted in 2006. Rule 37(2) of the new Rules of Procedure for Arbitration Proceedings provides that, after consulting both parties, the arbitral tribunal may allow a non-disputing party to file a written submission with the tribunal regarding a matter within the scope of the dispute.[38] Rule 32 was also changed to give a broader power to the tribunal to open up the oral procedure to the public.[39]

The UNCITRAL Arbitration Rules were revised in 2010, but the language of Article 17(1), which provides for general provisions for arbitral proceedings, is quite similar to that of its predecessor, namely, Article 15(1) of the original 1976 version. It provides that "the arbitral tribunal may conduct the arbitration in such manner as it considers appropriate, provided that the parties are treated with equality and that at an appropriate stage of the proceedings such party is given a reasonable opportunity of presenting its case."[40] As there is no specific rule concerning transparency such as acceptance of non-solicited amicus curiae briefs, opening the hearings to the public and disclosure of arbitral awards and other documents, a tribunal under the 2010 UNCITRAL Arbitration Rules will make specific arrangements for such transparency measures by resorting to the new Article 17(1).

At the same time, however, UNCITRAL's highest body declared that there is a need for greater transparency in disputes involving states and directed the same working group that prepared the 2010 amendments to ensure transparency in cases involving states. The working group is intensely engaged in that process as this book goes to press. Every government involved in those negotiations professes to favor transparency; but many of those countries follow such statements with the word "but", and the detailed positions of some countries belie any such pro-transparency views.

ICSID, UNCITRAL and the WTO are not the only bodies that engage in, or whose rules are used in, international economic dispute settlement, of course. It is also important how transparency will be treated in the rules of the Permanent Court of Arbitration (PCA), the Stockholm Chamber of Commerce (SCC), the International Chamber of Commerce (ICC), and the London Court of International Arbitration (LCIA), among others, as well as in international economic treaties such as bilateral investment treaties.

The need for transparency in international trade and investment dispute settlement

The preceding two sections briefly traced the recent developments in international trade and investment dispute settlement toward enhanced transparency. These developments can be explained by a number of factors that are pertinent to international trade and investment dispute settlement, including the subject matter of the dispute and the involvement of states in the disputes. When the disputed domestic regulations and measures have some bearing on non-trade/investment issues such as environment and public health, settlement of such disputes can have serious economic and social impacts on the disputing state parties. Enhanced transparency is needed in these cases, as they involve important public interests. Similarly, these cases can involve large financial claims, raising an obvious public interest. Also, the involvement of a state, through the government, a ministry or a state body, in these dispute settlement procedures has led to the call for enhanced transparency based on the public's right to know, particularly since cases against states invariably include a charge that the state violated international law (cf. Delaney and Magraw 2008: 723–724). Additionally, the fact that these cases are adding significantly to the body of international economic law implicates that public's interest in them. Finally, the human right of access to information presumably requires some degree of transparency.

On the other hand, enhanced transparency in international trade and investment dispute settlement cannot be achieved without costs. In general, the disadvantages of enhanced transparency fall into the following categories (cf. Delaney and Magraw 2008: 762–763):

Costs: The process of making information public, for instance, entails some financial costs. The cost might become substantial if the hearings are broadcast.

Delay: Transparency can entail delay, for instance, in posting information on a website or in translating documents. Also, accepting amicus curiae briefs and analyzing them can entail delay in the dispute settlement procedure.

Confidentiality and privacy: Transparency results in a decrease in the confidentiality of business information and state secrets.

Party autonomy and flexibility: Transparency may erode party autonomy in the settlement of disputes.

While the first three disadvantages can be compensated by logistical arrangements,[41] the last disadvantage deserves special consideration, as it touches upon what some observers view as the intrinsic value of these dispute settlement procedures. First, the WTO dispute settlement procedure, even in its highly judicialized setting, contains elements of diplomatic negotiation (Roberts 2004: 415). For example, consultation between the parties shall be confidential (Article 4.6 of the DSU). Even during the panel procedure, the parties to the dispute may develop a mutually satisfactory solution, in which case the report of the panel shall be confined to a brief description of the case and to reporting that a solution has been reached (Article 12.7 of the DSU). Negotiated solution between the parties is encouraged, and so is party autonomy and flexibility in the settlement of disputes. Enhanced transparency might be detrimental to such values in the WTO dispute settlement procedure. Secondly, investor–state arbitration has been acclaimed by foreign investors and their home governments as a means of disassociating an investment dispute from the domestic legal system of the host country.[42] Party autonomy and flexibility in the settlement of disputes have been regarded as part of the disassociated nature of investor–state arbitration (cf. Franck 2005: 1541–1542). Enhanced transparency might erode party autonomy and flexibility, and might discourage foreign investors.

A recent development is the acknowledgement of the international human right of access to information associated with the freedoms of opinion and expression – a development that has profound implications for transparency in trade and investment disputes.[43] This book does not address that set of issues. For a discussion of the human right of access to information with respect to investment disputes, see Marcos Orellana's analysis of that topic.[44]

This leads us to the need of considering the appropriate design of international trade and investment dispute settlement procedures, taking into account sometimes conflicting values and policy concerns. A number of issues should be seriously considered: What kind of transparency is asserted by which stakeholder, and on what grounds? What are the major obstacles to securing transparency in each dispute settlement procedure, and how can they be overcome? On what ground and to what extent should transparency be limited in each dispute settlement procedure, including what should the exceptions be for confidential information? Are there any alternatives to one or the other means of enhanced transparency? This book is the result of a joint research project in tackling these issues on account of transparency in international trade and investment dispute settlement.

The structure of the book

Following on from this introduction, the book consists of six chapters that deal with a wide range of issues regarding transparency in international trade and investment dispute settlement. Chapter 2, prepared by Justice Florentino Feliciano, tries to strike a proper balance between confidentiality and transparency in international trade and investment dispute settlement. He begins by tracing the history of international arbitration and points out that the motivation of party autonomy was the main reason for the emphasis on confidentiality in international arbitration. He then describes the recent move toward enhanced transparency in international arbitration rules (UNCITRAL Arbitration Rules, ICSID Arbitration Rules, etc.), and moves on to propose a balance between confidentiality and transparency in international arbitration. He argues that the line of equilibrium is a moving one, and its particular location and shape are functions of differing factors including the kind of international arbitration proceeding involved and the nature of the subject matter of the dispute. In international investment arbitration where one of the parties is a sovereign state, he argues, it seems clearly improper to assume that confidentiality duties override reasonable securing of those important sovereign interests. His argument is, however, modest here. Rather than claiming a general transparency requirement, he argues for expanding the exception to confidentiality to the disclosure and access to arbitration documents for enforcement of local criminal and anti-corruption laws. On the other hand, in international trade arbitration[45] and more judicialized dispute settlement procedures of the WTO, where the parties are two sovereign states, Justice Feliciano argues that there is material accommodation of the interests of transparency and the necessity of developing coherent and consistent case law in interpreting and applying the covered WTO agreements.

The following two chapters try to elucidate the proper position of transparency in international trade dispute settlement by expanding the context of such dispute settlement. In Chapter 3, Yuka Fukunaga focuses on the role of the domestic stage of international trade dispute settlement process in ensuring the transparency of such dispute settlement to the public. After discussing the possible merits and costs of enhanced transparency in the WTO dispute settlement proceedings, she discusses the role of the domestic stage in ensuring transparency in the three temporal sequences, namely, prior to, during, and post WTO dispute settlement proceedings. First, the stage prior to the reference of a dispute to the WTO dispute settlement system involves domestic discourse between the government and private parties, normally businesses who have encountered trade-related problems with a foreign government. While dealing with business complaints, she argues, the government can also engage in talks with citizens and take into account their interests and concerns in deciding how to address the business complaints. Second, at the stage during the WTO proceedings, the domestic discourse between the government and businesses often continues. The government should also be encouraged to maintain contact with citizens during the WTO proceedings, especially when a dispute is closely linked with the interests and concerns of citizens. The third stage ensues after the panel and Appellate Body review is completed and their recommendations are adopted by the Dispute Settlement Body (DSB). Because the DSB recommendations do not specify what measures should be taken, the responding party makes such determinations within its territory. Fukunaga emphasized that the discretion left to the government of the responding party enables it to take into account citizens' non-economic interests and concerns in determining how to domestically implement the DSB recommendations and to ensure that the implementation would not unduly harm the interests of citizens.

In Chapter 4, Chin Leng Lim takes up another important issue about transparency in international trade dispute settlement that has hardly been discussed; that is, transparency in dispute settlement in Regional Trade Agreements (RTAs), focusing on those in the East Asian region. Should parties to the RTAs in the region choose "closed" or "open" models of trade dispute settlement, especially in light of the debate on increasing the transparency of WTO dispute settlement? To answer this question, he first reviews some of the main arguments in favor of having an "open" model of trade dispute settlement. They are (1) the WTO dispute settlement system is a law court, (2) there is a trend towards greater transparency, (3) democracy and cosmopolitanism are international legal ideals, (4) a transparent model of dispute settlement is more likely to be perceived as being legitimate, and (5) democratic nations must push for democratic dispute regimes. He argues that (1) the WTO dispute settlement system still contains elements of a diplomatic model of dispute settlement, (2) we cannot extrapolate from the wishes of a few members the pattern of things to come, (3) East Asian nations are less likely to justify their policies along democratic lines but are more likely to talk about anticipated trade and commercial gains, (4) transparency is important but is unlikely to address the WTO's legitimacy crisis, and (5) the evidence thus far goes plainly against it. He thus neutralizes the arguments in favor of having an "open" model of trade dispute settlement. He then analyzes the actual treaty behavior of

East Asian nations. After an extensive survey of treaty practice in the region, he observes that there is an emerging intra-East Asian model of "closed" trade dispute settlement, whereas individual agreements with the United States demonstrate elements of an "open" model, which has also been adopted under the Trans-Pacific Partnership Agreement (TPP).[46] He concludes that East Asian nations interact on equal, sovereign terms (which leads to a "closed" model), while making small exceptions only as pragmatism might suggest, such as the perceived need under the TPP to have institutional arrangements which trans-continental partners would find more attractive.

In contrast to the preceding two chapters, Sofia Plagakis argues for enhanced transparency in international trade and investment dispute settlement in Chapter 5. Her focus is on the use of webcasting, a method of broadcasting live audio and visual to audiences via the Internet. She argues that webcasting has already been used successfully in a variety of domestic and international settings, including at the International Court of Justice (ICJ), and that webcasting international trade and investment dispute settlement proceedings is an excellent tool for expanding public access to information that affects public interest (e.g. health, safety and environmental information). Following a brief overview of the various institutions in the world that webcast their dispute proceedings, she discusses the advantages and concerns associated with webcasting international non-economic and domestic court proceedings. Among the former is an improved transparency and public awareness, increased accessibility, time and cost savings and accuracy in reporting. She argues that these will contribute to the enhancement of democracy in judicial proceedings. On the other hand, concerns associated with webcasting involve financial costs including one-off investment and operating costs, quality of the image and audio transferred, protecting personal identification and privacy, and a risk of content manipulation.

She then analyzes the ICSID's recent experience in webcasting hearings of investor–state arbitration cases. They were all based on Article 10.21(2) of the Dominican Republic–Central America Free Trade Agreement (DR-CAFTA), which requires hearings to be "open to the public". It was reportedly almost as costly as closed circuit broadcasting. To protect confidentiality, webcasts were interrupted whenever confidential information was discussed. Based on these analyses, she concludes that provisions should be added to international trade and investment dispute settlement rules requiring webcasting in all public interest cases. More specifically, a rule should be adopted that would make webcasting oral hearings the norm in state arbitrations, with exceptions to protect confidential business information and information which is protected from disclosure under that party's domestic law.

The last two chapters deal with transparency in international investment dispute settlement. In Chapter 6, Federico Ortino addresses the issue of the transparency of international investment arbitral awards in a binary manner, namely by examining their external transparency and internal transparency separately. By "external transparency" he addresses the issue of whether investment arbitral awards should be made publicly available. Examination of major investment arbitration rules leads him to conclude that the general stance is the one favoring confidentiality of arbitral awards, though there are a growing number of international investment treaties that require external transparency. Based on the empirical analysis and the analysis of the discussion between those favoring confidentiality and those favoring transparency, he concludes that, given the public nature of the issues at stake in international investment arbitration, there is a growing consensus on the need to favor external transparency over confidentiality.

Ortino moves on to the issue of internal transparency, namely the clarity of the legal reasoning of arbitration tribunals in adjudicating international investment disputes. He begins with an examination of the arbitration rules provided by the major arbitration institutions as well as those found in international investment treaties with regard to the legal reasoning of arbitral awards. He then explains the importance of the internal transparency of investment arbitral awards, as it strengthens the legitimacy of the system of international investment law and arbitration. He finally analyzes some of the instances where the legal reasoning of investment arbitral awards lacks clarity, which were caused by (1) abuse of precedents, (2) lack of internal consistency, or by (3) the lack of adequate justification supporting tribunals' legal findings.

Finally, in Chapter 7, Peter Lallas addresses an important issue of transparency in international investment law that has rarely been discussed, namely, whether the normative framework relevant to foreign direct investment (FDI) is fostering sustainable FDI, with transparency and accountability for locally affected people. At the outset, he poses an open question: given that there are nearly 3000 international investment agreements with strong legal norms and rights of recourse to protect the interests of foreign investors, why do such agreements not contain similarly strong norms and rights of recourse to protect the interests of local communities and the environment which may be affected by such investment activities? He then examines some leading examples of an emerging trend addressing this issue, including: the accountability mechanisms at international financial institutions (such as the World Bank Inspection Panel); the public submission procedure of the North American Agreement on Environmental Cooperation (NAAEC); and the complaint procedure available to NGOs, workers and other stakeholders under the Organisation for Economic Co-operation and Development (OECD) Guidelines for Multinational Enterprises. He argues that giving locally affected people an avenue for recourse and accountability under international law can provide an important means to identify and resolve adverse social and environmental impacts associated with international investment activities.

Notes

1 As at March 2012, 434 requests for consultations were submitted to the WTO dispute settlement procedure. See WTO, Chronological list of disputes cases, available at http://www.wto.org/english/tratop_e/dispu_e/dispu_status_e.htm. Last visited 30 March 2012.

2 The total number of known cases of investor–state arbitration reached 390 by the end of 2010. See UNCTAD 2011: 101.

3 Panel Report, *United States – Import Prohibition of Certain Shrimp and Shrimp Products*, WT/DS58/R and Corr.1, adopted 6 November 1998, as modified by the Appellate Body Report, WT/DS58/AB/R, para. 3.129.
4 Article 13.1 of the DSU provides that "Each panel shall have the right to seek information and technical advice from any individual or body which it deems appropriate."
5 The Panel stated that "(a)ccepting non-requested information from non-governmental sources would be, in our opinion, incompatible with the provisions of the DSU as currently applied." Supra n.3, para. 7.8.
6 *Idem.*
7 Appellate Body Report, *United States – Import Prohibition of Certain Shrimp and Shrimp Products*, WT/DS58/AB/R, adopted 6 November 1998, para. 108.
8 Appellate Body Report, *United States – Imposition of Countervailing Duties on Certain Hot-Rolled Lead and Bismuth Carbon Steel Products Originating in the United Kingdom*, WT/DS138/AB/R, adopted 7 June 2000, para. 42.
9 *European Communities – Measures Affecting Asbestos and Products Containing Asbestos*, Communication from the Appellate Body, WT/DS135/9, 8 November 2000, para. 2.
10 See WTO General Council, *Minutes of Meeting of 22 November 2000*, WT/GC/M/60, 23 November 2000.
11 Ibid., para. 7.
12 Ibid., para. 18.
13 Rule 16(1) of the Working Procedures for Appellate Review provides that "(i)n the interests of fairness and orderly procedure in the conduct of an appeal, where a procedural question arises that is not covered by these Rules, a division may adopt an appropriate procedure for the purposes of that appeal only, provided that it is not inconsistent with the *DSU*, the other covered agreements and these Rules." See WT/AB/WP/1, 15 February 1996. Although the Working Procedures have since been revised six times, the current version of the Working Procedures contains the same rule.
14 Supra n.10, para. 74.
15 *European Communities – Measures Affecting Asbestos and Products Containing Asbestos*, Report of the Appellate Body, WT/DS135/AB/R, adopted 5 April 2001, para. 56.
16 See WTO Special Session of the Dispute Settlement Body, *Report by the Chairman*, JPB(08)/81, 18 July 2008, reproduced as Appendix A to the WTO Special Session of the Dispute Settlement Body, *Report by the Chairman, Ambassador Ronald Saborío Soto, to the Trade Negotiations Committee*, TN/DS/25, 21 April 2011, p. A-38.
17 Ibid., p. A-37.
18 *Idem.*
19 For instance, the compliance panel for the *EC – Bananas III* (DS27) agreed to open its hearings of 6 and 7 November 2007 for observation by WTO Members and the general public. See WTO News Item, 29 October 2007. Available at http://www.wto.org/english/news_e/news07_e/dispu_banana_7nov07_e.htm.
20 For instance, in the *US – Hormones (Continued Suspension)* case (DS320) and *Canada – Hormones (Continued Suspension)* case, the panels allowed broadcasting the hearings through closed-circuit television. For details, see the explanation of Sofia Plagakis in infra pp. 91–92.
21 See supra n.16, pp. A-37–A-39.
22 See the argument of Chin Leng Lim in infra p. 54.
23 See supra n.16, pp. A-37–A-38.
24 Annex 1137.4 provides that, where Mexico is the disputing party, the applicable arbitration rules apply to the publication of an award.
25 See *S.D. Myers, Inc.* v. *Government of Canada*, Procedural Order No. 11, 28 October 1999, para. 2, which provides that "(a)ll transcripts and other records taken

of hearings (except those documents mentioned in Procedural Order No.3, paragraph 1, namely the Notice of Intention , Notice of Arbitration, Statement of Claim and Statement of Defense) shall be kept confidential". Available at http://www.naftaclaims.com/Disputes/Canada/SDMyers/SDMyers-AllProceduralOrders.pdf.

26 See NAFTA Free Trade Commission, Notes of Interpretation of Certain Chapter 11 Provisions, 31 July 2001, para. 1a. Available at http://www.international.gc.ca/trade-agreements-accords-commerciaux/disp-diff/nafta-interpr.aspx?lang=en&view=d.

27 See *Methanex Corporation* v. *United States of America*, Decision of the Tribunal on petitions from third persons to intervene as amici curiae, 15 January 2001, paras 24–47. Available at http://www.state.gov/documents/organization/6039.pdf. See ibid., para. 26.

28 See ibid., para. 26. Article 15(1) provides that "(s)ubject to these Rules, the arbitral tribunal may conduct the arbitration in such manner as it considers appropriate, provided that the parties are treated with equality and that at any stage of the proceedings each party is given a full opportunity of presenting his case". The decision was adhered to by a tribunal on *United Parcel Services of America* v. *Canada*, in its decision on Petitions for Intervention and Participation as Amici Curiae, 17 October 2001, which also found that it was within the scope of Article 15(1) of the UNCITRAL Arbitration Rules for the tribunal to accept amicus curiae submissions. Available at http://www.state.gov/documents/organization/6033.pdf.

29 The arbitral tribunal dealt with a California ban on the use or sale in the State of California of the gasoline additive MTBE. See US Department of State, *Methanex Corp.* v. *United States of America*. Available at http://www.state.gov/s/l/c5818.htm.

30 See supra n.27, para. 49.

31 The tribunal based its decision on this matter on Article 25(4) of the UNCITRAL Arbitration Rules, which provides that "(h)earings shall be held in camera unless the parties agree otherwise". See ibid., paras 41–42.

32 See Statement of the Free Trade Commission on non-disputing party participation, 27 October 2003. Available at http://www.international.gc.ca/trade-agreements-accords-commerciaux/assets/pdfs/Nondisputing-en.pdf.

33 See OECD 2005: para. 29. Note that the *Methanex* tribunal was not the first NAFTA Chapter Eleven arbitral tribunal to open its hearings to the public. The tribunal of the *United Parcel Services of America* v. *Canada* opened its hearings to the public by broadcasting live on 29 to 31 July 2002, as the parties to the dispute had agreed to make the hearings open to the public. See ICSID News Release, *United Parcel Service of America, Inc.* v. *Government of Canada* NAFTA/UNCITRAL Arbitration Rules Proceeding, 28 May 2001. Available at http://icsid.worldbank.org/ICSID/FrontServlet?requestType=CasesRH&actionVal=OpenPage&PageType=AnnouncementsFrame&FromPages=NewsReleases&pageName=Archive_Announcement6.

34 See NAFTA Free Trade Commission, Joint Statement, 16 July 2004. Available at http://www.international.gc.ca/trade-agreements-accords-commerciaux/agr-acc/nafta-alena/JS-SanAntonio.aspx?lang=eng&view=d.

35 Article 44 of the ICSID Convention provides that "(i)f any question of procedure arises which is not covered by this Section or the Arbitration Rules or any rules agreed by the parties, the Tribunal shall decide the question."

36 See *Aguas Argentinas, S.A., Suez, Sociedad General de Aguas de Barcelona, S.A. and Vivendi Universal, S.A.* v. *Argentine Republic*, Order in Response to a Petition for Transparency and Participation as Amicus Curiae, ICSID Case No. ARB/03/19, 19 May 2005, para. 14.

37 See ICSID 2005.

38 Rule 37(2) provides that the tribunal shall consider, in determining whether to allow such a filing, the extent to which:

(a) The non-disputing party submission would assist the tribunal in the determination of a factual or legal issue related to the proceeding by bringing a perspective,

particular knowledge or insight that is different from that of the disputing parties;
(b) The non-disputing party submission would address a matter within the scope of the dispute;
(c) The non-disputing party has a significant interest in the proceeding.

39 The new Rule 32(2) provides that "(u)nless either party objects, the Tribunal, after consultation with the Secretary-General, may allow other persons, besides the parties, their agents, counsel and advocates, witnesses and experts during their testimony, and officers of the Tribunal, to attend or observe all or part of the hearings, subject to appropriate logistical arrangements."

40 Jan Paulsson and Georgios Petrochilos, who commented on the revision of the UNCITRAL Arbitration Rules, highlighted flexibility in the conduct of the proceedings and reliance on the expertise of the arbitrators, which were embodied in the original Article 15(1) and the new Article 17(1), as two of the hallmarks of arbitration. See Paulsson and Petrochilos 2006: 64.

41 See, for instance, the procedures for dealing with the non-disputing party submission in the NAFTA Chapter Eleven arbitration, in supra n.32.

42 See the argument of Justice Feliciano in infra pp. 15–16.

43 See UN Human Rights Committee (International Covenant on Civil and Political Rights) (2011).

44 See Orellana (2011).

45 Article 25 of the Understanding on Rules and Procedures Governing the Settlement of Disputes (DSU) provides that "(e)xpeditious arbitration within the WTO as an alternative means of dispute settlement can facilitate the solution of certain disputes that concern issues that are clearly defined by both parties."

46 Signed by New Zealand, Chile and Singapore on 18 July 2005 and by Brunei on 2 August 2005, entered into force for New Zealand and Singapore on 1 May 2006, for Brunei provisionally from 12 June 2006 and came into full force in July 2009, and for Chile on 8 November 2006. According to Section 21 of its Model Rules of Procedure for Arbitral Panels, the disputing parties may decide that the hearings of the arbitral tribunals be open to the public.

Bibliography

Delaney, J. and Magraw, D. (2008), "Procedural Transparency", in Peter Muchlinski, Federico Ortino and Christoph Scheuer eds, *The Oxford Handbook of International Investment Law*, Oxford: Oxford University Press, 2008, pp. 721–788.

Franck, S. (2005), "The Legitimacy Crisis in Investment Treaty Arbitration: Privatizing Public International Law through Inconsistent Decisions", 73 *Fordham Law Review* 1521.

ICSID (2005), "Suggested Changes to the ICSID Rules and Regulations", *Working Paper of the ICSID Secretariat*, 12 May 2005. Available at http://icsid.worldbank.org/ICSID/FrontServlet?requestType=ICSIDPublicationsRH&actionVal=ViewAnnouncePDF&AnnouncementType=archve&AnnounceNo=22_1.pdf.

Knahr, C. (2007), *Participation of Non-State Actors in the Dispute Settlement System of the WTO: Benefit or Burden?* Frankfurt am Main: Peter Lang.

Knahr, C. and Reinisch, A. (2007), "Transparency versus Confidentiality in International Investment Arbitration – The *Biwater Gauff* Compromise", 6 *The Law and Practice of International Courts and Tribunals* 97.

Mavroidis, P. (2002), "Amicus Curiae Briefs before the WTO: Much Ado about Nothing", *Jean Monnet Working Paper 2/01*. Available at http://www.worldtradelaw.net/articles/mavroidisamicus.pdf.

Mourre, A. (2006). "Are Amici Curiae the Proper Response to the Public's Concerns on Transparency in Investment Arbitration?", 5 *The Law and Practice of International Courts and Tribunals* 257.

OECD (2005). "Transparency and Third Party Participation in Investor–State Dispute Settlement Procedures", OECD *Working Paper on International Investment* Number 2005/1, Paris: OECD. Available at http://www.oecd.org/dataoecd/25/3/34786913.pdf.

Orellana, M. (2011). "The Right of Access to Information and Investment Arbitration", 26(2) *ICSID Review* 59.

Paulsson, J. and Petrochilos, G. (2006). "Revision of the UNCITRAL Arbitration Rules", available at http://www.uncitral.org/pdf/english/news/arbrules_report.pdf.

Roberts, A. (2004). "A Partial Revolution: The Diplomatic Ethos and Transparency in Intergovernmental Organizations", 64(4) *Public Administration Review* 410.

UN Human Rights Committee (International Covenant on Civil and Political Rights) (2011). General Comment No. 34, CCPR/C/GC/34, 12 September 2011.

UNCTAD (2011). *World Investment Report 2011*, Geneva: UNCTAD.

Van Harten, G. (2007), *Investment Treaty Arbitration and Public Law*, Oxford: Oxford University Press.

2 The *Ordre Public* dimensions of confidentiality and transparency in international arbitration

Examining confidentiality in the light of governance requirements in international investment and trade arbitration

Florentino P. Feliciano[1]

Confidentiality as a perspective in international arbitration

Arbitration, often considered as an alternative to regular court proceedings, capitalizes on being a less public venue than the latter, thereby lending support to the general perception that confidentiality is important for the sustainability of arbitration across national borders. The concern for confidentiality was in fact not the main impetus for the establishment of arbitration as a valuable mode of settling disputes. Rather, recourse to cross-border arbitration was moved by the ability to disassociate oneself from a given domestic judicial system and the insistence on party autonomy in determining the rules of law that would govern the relationship between the disputing parties and the resolution of their dispute.

Modern arbitration finds its roots in the capitulation system prevalent in Egypt and other parts of the Ottoman Empire during the eighteenth century, where European residents in Egypt were exempt from the jurisdiction of the domestic judicial system and subject only to their own consular courts. This was frequently problematic in situations where a dispute involved an Egyptian subject to the domestic judicial system, and a foreigner exempt from the reach of the same system. This was sought to be remedied by the establishment of Mixed Courts in the late 1800s, which had jurisdiction in civil cases involving Egyptians and foreigners, or foreigners of different nationalities. The Mixed Courts had both foreign and Egyptian judges, who administered codes based on French law.[2]

The factors that led to the rise and development of international arbitration as the preferred mode of contemporary dispute resolution are multiple and complex. One of these factors was the concern of Western multinational corporations over subjection to the jurisdiction of the courts of foreign sovereigns which would of course be applying the law of the foreign sovereign.[3] International arbitration offers the possibility of insulating the foreign corporation, to some degree, from the jurisdiction of the foreign sovereign in whose territory the corporation is operating, by offering an alternative to such jurisdiction.

Confidentiality is now assumed to be a common feature and advantage of international arbitration, and has basically existed for the comfort and convenience of one or both parties in an arbitral proceeding. It prevents the disclosure of allegations made by a party which may be distressing or even offensive to the other. It allows a party to make arguments in private which it may hesitate to make in a forum open to public access.

The privacy of arbitral proceedings has facilitated and encouraged recourse to arbitration. Privacy means that only the parties, arbitrators, administrator, parties' counsel, and witnesses have right of access to the proceedings, documents, and awards rendered.[4] In this context, confidentiality pertains to the right to know of the existence of an arbitration proceeding, and the place of arbitration, the identities of the parties, the subject matter of the dispute, the identities of the arbitrators, nature of the dispute, criteria of resolution (applicable law or *ex aequo et bono*), orders and awards, and the presumed expertise of the arbitrators. Further, it means that testimony, documents, and witnesses, among others, are available only to the parties, arbitrators, and other persons designated by common consent of the parties.

Under the present setup of arbitral proceedings, arbitrators have a general duty to observe confidentiality,[5] while the duty of disputing parties to maintain confidentiality depends upon the existence of an express agreement, the arbitration tribunal, the applicable law and procedures, as well as the type of information at issue and the manner in which such information may be used.[6] The duty to observe confidentiality may likewise bind certain third parties, such as lay and expert witnesses, under specific contractual obligations.[7] This system of requiring and maintaining confidentiality is especially valuable for firms or States which place a high premium on business or government secrets and reputation.[8] The confidential nature of arbitral proceedings is likewise seen as a positive factor in the facilitation of settlement and in reducing tension between disputing parties.[9]

Actually, few countries, such as the United Kingdom, France, and the Philippines, recognize a general duty of confidentiality in international arbitration. Other countries such as the United States, Australia, and New Zealand reject the notion of a general duty of confidentiality, unless established by applicable law or the *lex arbitri* or by common consent of the parties.

Nevertheless, even where a general duty of confidentiality is recognized in a particular country, such duty is never absolute. In the Philippines, the applicable law allows for certain exceptions, i.e. arbitration proceedings,[10] including the records, evidence and the arbitral award, are considered confidential[11] and should not be published, *except* with the consent of the disputing parties or *for the limited purpose of disclosing to the court of relevant documents in cases where resort to the court is allowed.*[12]

Where a general duty of confidentiality is widely recognized, certain exceptions or limitations of such duty are also commonly recognized. Notwithstanding the mutual consent of the parties, confidentiality is limited where a legal norm or a regulatory requirement demands the disclosure of facts or evidence that would otherwise be regarded as covered by confidentiality. For instance, documents or other evidence tending to show criminal or illegal activity should be disclosed to law enforcement authorities. The requirements of *ordre public* clearly take precedence over confidentiality in this situation.

Confidentiality is likewise limited where disclosure is essential in the "interests of justice", such as where injustice to a party in the same or in another case is sought to be prevented.

In national or international arbitration, disputes are resolved by applying one of two possible standards – (a) *ex aequo et bono*, which are generally difficult to reduce to specific and detailed statements and probably best kept concealed or confidential; or (b) a system of applicable law, either agreed upon by the parties or indicated by the conflicts rules of a relevant system of law. Confidentiality seems reasonably appropriate in case (a). However it may hinder the ascertainment of whether or not the applicable law agreed upon by the parties was indeed properly applied by the arbitrators in a particular case if insisted upon too strictly in case (b).

A point of considerable irony should not escape notice: confidentiality is of greater importance in international arbitration processes, while in domestic judicial or quasi-judicial dispute resolution processes, transparency and accessibility have significantly greater scope than confidentiality, at least in national communities characterized by republican and liberal constitutional structures. The Philippines, while a small and developing country, is a good example of the point we here seek to make.[13]

Confidentiality under institutional arbitration rules

United Nations Commission on International Trade Law (UNCITRAL)

The 1976 Arbitration Rules of the UNCITRAL ("1976 Rules") seem to contain the most restrictive confidentiality provisions, where it is often impossible to gain access to documents, while awards and other arbitration-related documents are rarely made public.[14] For instance, Article 25(4) of the 1976 Rules provides that "hearings shall be held *in camera* unless the parties agree otherwise," while Article 32(5) provides that "[t]he award may be made public only with the consent of both parties."

However, the 1976 Rules were amended in 2010 ("2010 Rules") to meet changes in current arbitral practice by "enhancing the efficiency of arbitration". Notable is the amendment of Article 32(5) of the 1976 Rules, now Article 34(5) of the 2010 Rules, such that an award may now be made public not only upon the consent of all the parties, but also "where and to the extent disclosure is required of a party by legal duty, to protect and pursue a legal right or in relation to legal proceedings before a court or other competent authority".

Nevertheless, there is still nothing in the 2010 Rules relating to the publication of the minutes of meetings, the pleadings of disputing parties, and the orders of the arbitral tribunal. The absence of provisions here could imply that the matter of their publication is to be decided by the parties or to be determined by the discretion of the arbitral tribunal in a particular case.[15] Furthermore, there is still no express mechanism under the UNCITRAL Arbitral Rules for third-party submissions, although it has been held that the broad discretion bestowed on tribunals to conduct the procedural aspects of the arbitration in Article 15(1) of the 1976 Rules (now Article 17(1) of the 2010 Rules) encompasses the power to admit amicus curiae briefs.[16]

International Centre for Settlement of Investment Disputes (ICSID)

Under the ICSID regime, the Centre and the arbitrators are obliged to maintain confidentiality. The Convention on the Settlement of Investment Disputes between States and Nationals of Other States ("ICSID Convention") provides that the Centre should publish "excerpts of the legal reasoning" of the arbitral tribunals,[17] but it should not publish an arbitral award without the consent of the parties to the arbitration.[18] Reports of Conciliation Commissions, minutes, and other records of proceedings may likewise be published with the consent of both parties,[19] while general information about the operation of the Centre, including registration of all requests for conciliation or arbitration, may be published unilaterally by the Secretary-General.[20] Further, Rule 6(2) of the ICSID Arbitration Rules requires arbitrators to sign a declaration obligating themselves to keep confidential all information they come to learn as a result of their participation in an arbitration proceeding. Deliberations of an arbitral tribunal are likewise kept private,[21] and only members of the arbitral tribunal are allowed to take part in such deliberations unless the arbitral tribunal decides otherwise.[22] The arbitral tribunal, after consultation with the Secretary-General, may allow persons other than the parties, their agents, counsel and advocates, witnesses and experts during their testimony, and officers of the tribunal, to attend or observe all or part of the hearings.[23] After consultation with the parties, the arbitral tribunal may also allow third parties to submit amicus curiae briefs subject to certain conditions.[24]

It is not clear from the ICSID rules or regulations whether parties are allowed to disclose any documents to the public during or after the arbitral proceedings, but some tribunals have made pronouncements regarding this matter.[25] Some writers have noted the absence of any express prohibition against parties publicly disclosing briefs and other submissions in the ICSID rules.[26]

London Court of International Arbitration (LCIA)

The new Arbitration Rules of the London Court of International Arbitration ("LCIA Rules")[27] also contain various provisions relating to confidentiality. All meetings and hearings are held in private unless otherwise agreed by the parties or directed by the Arbitral Tribunal.[28] A more extensive clause on confidentiality is Article 30, which generally requires the parties to keep confidential all awards in their arbitration, together with all materials in the proceedings created for the purpose of the arbitration, and all other documents produced by another party in the proceedings not otherwise in the public domain – *save and to the extent that disclosure may be required of a party by legal duty, to protect or pursue a legal right, or to enforce or challenge an award in bona fide legal proceedings before a State court or other judicial authority*, and unless the parties expressly agree in writing to the contrary.[29]

The deliberations of the Arbitral Tribunal are likewise confidential, save and to the extent that disclosure of an arbitrator's refusal to participate in the arbitration is required of the other members of the Arbitral Tribunal.[30] Finally, the LCIA Court does not publish any award or any part of it without the prior written consent of all parties and the Arbitral Tribunal.[31]

International Chamber of Commerce (ICC)

Article 20(7) of the 1998 Rules of Arbitration of the International Chamber of Commerce ("ICC Rules") allows an arbitral tribunal to take measures for protecting trade secrets and confidential information, while Article 21(3) of the same Rules excludes from the proceedings all persons who are not involved therein, unless allowed by the arbitral tribunal and the parties. Further, Article 6 of the Statute of the ICC's International Court of Arbitration (ICA) and Articles 1 and 3(2) of the ICA's Internal Rules emphasize the confidential nature of the work of the ICA, its Committees, and its Secretariat. For instance, the sessions of the ICA are open only to its members and to the Secretariat,[32] and all documents and correspondence submitted by the parties or the arbitrators may be destroyed unless a party or an arbitrator requests in writing for the return of such documents.[33] ICA members are likewise obliged to keep confidential any information concerning individual cases with which they have become acquainted in their capacity as such members.[34]

The ICC has, however, been unilaterally publishing redacted versions of arbitral awards in its various publications, where the names of the parties and other identifying data are removed. Nevertheless, if a party objects to such publication, then even a redacted version of an arbitral award would not be published.[35]

Confidentiality v. transparency: the tension dynamic

The increasing level of recognition of the importance of good governance[36] has brought about more insistent calls for transparency, which in international arbitration generally takes the form of disclosure to third parties or of third-party participation in arbitral proceedings.[37] More and more writers and counsel challenge the idea that all aspects of international arbitration should always be confidential for arbitration to be valuable.[38] Some disputing parties may not value confidentiality as highly as others or may even decide to waive it entirely.[39]

Confidentiality and transparency are both values in international arbitration. They are, however, *competing* values which need to be accommodated and adjusted one to the other in specific cases. A constant or fixed amount of both values in each and every case is probably not necessary. The line of actual contact and equilibrium between the two desiderata is a moving one, and its particular location and shape are functions of differing factors. Some of these factors include the kind of international arbitration proceeding involved as well as the nature of the subject matter of the dispute sought to be resolved, matters which we discuss below.

Confidentiality and transparency in international investment arbitration

The level of public interest in arbitration proceedings is normally higher in investment arbitration than in ordinary commercial arbitration, not only because States and enterprises providing public services are frequently parties in investment arbitration, but also because the subject matter of investment disputes usually involve governmental measures.[40] The tension between confidentiality and transparency is especially highlighted where substantial public interest underlies a certain arbitral proceeding, such as where what has been made confidential demonstrates some misconduct or where unlawful activity had been resorted to by public officers or by officials of foreign multinational corporations and sometimes by stockholders and other stakeholders in the domestic corporate partners or joint ventures of the foreign corporation. This is a concern more sharply at stake in international investment arbitration, where the parties' interest in maintaining privacy and confidentiality often clash resoundingly with the general public interest in knowledge of economic development activities and accountability of public officers of the host state and officials of foreign corporations and sometimes the officials and equity owners of the local partners or associates of the foreign corporation.[41]

Some writers[42] argue that there are instances where an agreement requiring confidentiality may be unenforceable due to public policy interests or mandatory law requirements, such as where the agreement requires a party to violate securities disclosure requirements or competition law provisions.[43] A party may publicize arbitral awards or perhaps even other aspects of arbitral proceedings where reasonably necessary to comply with a legal obligation.[44]

For instance, where, in the course of the arbitral proceeding, a party or any other entity may be found to have engaged or participated in corruption in any aspect of the obligation or contract that is the subject of the proceeding, may the other party disclose information relating to such finding to comply with a legal obligation, i.e. the duty to prosecute illegal activity as in the case of a State party?

Almost by definition, international dispute resolution through arbitration involves the relocation and re-adjustment of the line of contact and equilibrium between the interests of the claimant and the respondent. What factor or factors may rationally be taken into account in the course of such relocation and re-adjustment by the independent tribunal before which one or the other party seeks the enforcement of a putative duty of confidentiality or a confidentiality agreement, or of a claimed duty of disclosure of some information or production of some documents or other materials? We turn now to at least a general consideration of this complex issue.

The first factor that almost projects itself is the kind of international arbitral proceeding in the context of which a right to receive certain information or a duty to keep certain information confidential is asserted. Is the arbitration proceeding one between two or more privately owned business companies, each asserting an individual or private commercial interest, or is it one between a private investor company and a respondent host state in whose territory an investment is claimed to have been made? If the parties to the arbitration case are both simply private business vehicles, there would seem little basis for presuming that duties in the nature of good governance *inter se* were established and that confidentiality was meant to be waived wholly or partially. Where one of the parties to the arbitration is a sovereign state with territory and a human population to secure and take care of by appropriate measures, it seems clearly improper to assume that confidentiality duties override reasonable securing of those important sovereign and public law interests. Where a private claimant seeks to escape criminal liability by asserting confidentiality duties against a sovereign respondent who could not have known about illegalities deliberately and consistently concealed by the claimant, it is not casually to be supposed that an investor's right to confidentiality and privacy override the sovereign's duties, qua sovereign, to its own people.

Confidentiality and transparency in international trade arbitration

Although dispute settlement under the international trading system of the World Trade Organization (WTO) is more often akin to litigation, the WTO Understanding on Rules and Procedures Governing the Settlement of Disputes (DSU) does provide for arbitration as an alternative means of dispute settlement.[45] Arbitration in the international trade context may be preferred in certain situations, such as where parties desire an expeditious yet binding solution to the dispute, to ensure stricter confidentiality, or where the dispute would not otherwise be directly enforceable under the DSU.[46]

The concept of confidentiality is likewise present in the WTO system, is recognized both in the arbitration and "litigation" aspects of dispute settlement, and is applicable in all stages of a dispute. Panel deliberations and Appellate Body proceedings are confidential, and opinions expressed in the Panel report by individual panelists are anonymous,[47] although parties in a number of recent cases have decided to open up the hearings of Panels and the Appellate Body to the public.[48]

Furthermore, a Panel is precluded from revealing confidential information obtained from any individual or body within the jurisdiction of a WTO member without formal authorization from the individual, body, or authorities of the WTO member providing such information.[49] Written submissions to a Panel or Appellate

Body are confidential, but will be made available to the parties to the dispute.[50] Also, any information submitted by a WTO member to a Panel or Appellate Body that such WTO member has designated as confidential will be treated as confidential information.[51]

However, a party to a dispute may publicly disclose statements of its positions or provide non-confidential summary of information contained in its written submissions.[52] On the other hand, panelists, members of the Appellate Body, arbitrators, experts participating in the dispute settlement, or members of the Secretariat or Appellate Body support staff are required to maintain the confidentiality of dispute settlement deliberations and proceedings, as well as any information identified by a party as confidential.[53] They are likewise precluded from making any statements on such proceedings or the issues in dispute in which they are participating, until the Panel or Appellate Body report has been de-restricted.[54]

Most WTO documents are made generally available, and all unrestricted WTO documents are made accessible online in the official WTO languages.[55]

Third parties having a substantial interest in a matter before a Panel and which have notified the Dispute Settlement Body (DSB) of such interest may also make written submissions to the Panel.[56] Note however that the concept of a "third party" under the DSU pertains to WTO members who are *not* the parties to the dispute. Furthermore, third parties may not appeal a Panel report, although they may make written submissions to and be given an opportunity to be heard by the Appellate Body.[57]

Private counsel were previously not allowed to represent parties in trade disputes. Some attribute this reluctance to the WTO's roots in the General Agreement on Tariffs and Trade (GATT), which had a less formal means of settling disputes that was more of a diplomatic resolution of misunderstandings and less of an adjudication of legal issues.[58] The issue of retaining private counsel emerged with the formulation of the DSU during the Uruguay Round, which transformed the nature of dispute settlement in the trading system to a rule-based adjudication process. Many opposed the move, citing access to sensitive government documents that would be revealed in the course of proceedings that are closed to the public, and the absence of any suitable WTO rule regulating such private counsel especially for breaches of obligations of confidentiality. These concerns did not prevent the Appellate Body in *EC – Bananas*[59] from overruling the Panel and holding that there is "nothing in the [WTO Agreement], the DSU or the Working Procedures, nor in customary international law or the prevailing practice of international tribunals, which prevents a WTO member from determining the composition of its delegation in Appellate Body proceedings" and that "it is for a WTO member to decide who should represent it as members of its delegation in an oral hearing of the Appellate Body."[60]

The retention of private counsel is just one step towards greater transparency in the WTO. Another is the possibility for non-governmental organizations (NGOs) to file amicus curiae submissions to both Panel and the Appellate Body.[61] This strategy has been vigorously opposed by developing countries, which frequently perceive NGOs to be representative of developed country interests owing to the belief that most NGOs are funded by developed countries – a view that has obviously not been subjected to careful research and analysis. Note that the body to which the amicus curiae briefs are submitted have the authority to determine the usefulness of such briefs, and thus their admissibility.

It should also be noted that the WTO website has included an NGO page containing information relevant to NGO participation in WTO activities and in sessions of the Ministerial Conference.[62] While attendance of NGOs in the formal plenary meetings of the Ministerial Conference is now well-established, NGO participation in these meetings has not yet been formalized.[63]

Still, the impetus for increasing transparency in the WTO is inevitable, given the continuing evolution of WTO dispute settlement into a rule-oriented system with an increasingly juridical nature. Some opine that the lack of internal transparency, i.e. non-party WTO members' access to information during and after a dispute, weaken the legal strength of developing and least developed country members which now constitute the vast majority of the WTO Members. On the other hand, the lack of external transparency, i.e. the extent that outsiders to the WTO system such as the academia, media, NGOs, individuals, and businesses or industries are able to observe dispute proceedings or access information relating to disputes, threaten the legitimacy of the WTO dispute settlement system as perceived by an increasingly vigilant international civil society.[64]

Summary of transparency mechanisms in international arbitration

As has already been touched upon above, several transparency mechanisms exist in international arbitration. The orders and awards of arbitral tribunals may be published in certain circumstances. For instance, the consent of both parties is needed to publish orders and awards of the ICSID and the ICC, except for excerpts of such orders and awards.

Participation of non-disputing parties as amicus curiae is not as difficult as it once was, with the decision of the ICSID tribunals in *Aguas Argentinas*[65] and *Aguas Provinciales*,[66] as well as the recent amendments to the ICSID Arbitration Rules. On the other hand, the issue on the disclosure of decisions and pleadings to the public, specifically through publication, is not as easily sorted out, although the discussion by the ICSID tribunal in *Biwater Gauff* v. *Tanzania*[67] would perhaps pave the way for its more substantial resolution.

Third party members with substantial interests are also allowed to participate, with some limitations, in international dispute settlement proceedings in a manner analogous to a right to intervene. They are also allowed to file submissions to the WTO Panels and Appellate Body, but they cannot initiate appeals. They also have the right to receive copies of awards, and the right to bring private counsel in Panel hearings and Appellate Body proceedings. This is in contrast with the practice that prevailed during the early years of WTO dispute settlement, where member countries could only bring their internal government counsel to oral hearings in Geneva. Finally, third parties may file amicus briefs, but the Panels and the Appellate Body will determine whether or not to accept such briefs.

In the North American Free Trade Agreement (NAFTA), a non-disputant member has the right to receive copies of all submissions of the parties and of the orders and awards in a dispute. The United States and Canada have stated that they will post on their respective websites all their written submissions in Chapter Eleven proceedings that they participate in. Mexico has likewise stated that it will follow the pertinent provisions in the Arbitration Rules governing the particular proceeding it may be participating in. Under a special mechanism, the Fair Trade Commission – where all members are represented – has the right to render written interpretations of provisions of the NAFTA, even while arbitration proceedings are ongoing.

Closing Remarks

In a quest to disassociate one from the rightful jurisdiction of domestic judicial authorities, confidentiality has risen as a value in international arbitration. It reinforces the notion of party autonomy, whereby parties are ideally given a choice of the applicable law to govern their relation. For instance, two private parties who are both Filipino citizens in the Philippines ideally have the choice of applying French or Spanish law to govern the conduct of their relation. Thus, when a dispute arises, French or Spanish law is applied in the facilitation of its resolution, and there is no way of making certain that the non-Philippine law was in fact applied correctly in their case as the proceedings are required to be confidential. Such a situation is untenable where the dispute involves a State party and the public interest at stake is substantial. If there is no way that the dispute is resolved in accordance with the ordinary law of comity or the ordinary norms of public conduct, or there is no way to gauge if these norms have actually been correctly enforced, it may very well be that the outcome of the dispute will be determined by who is more powerful, more influential, or wealthier because confidentiality shields the resolution of the dispute from the critical eye of the community.

It is thus clear that confidentiality and transparency are both values in international arbitration. It is equally clear they are also competing values which need to be accommodated and adjusted to the other in each specific case. It also seems clear that confidentiality tends to be a "wasting asset" and may be declining utility.

For instance, an international commercial proceeding between two private persons or entities involving a construction dispute as to whether specifications of materials or equipment to be used or installed have been met will probably be regarded as appropriately accorded a higher or larger scope of confidentiality. The interests involved are more likely to be essentially private in character, not involving any important community-wide or public interests that need protection through transparency mechanisms, save perhaps the coherent development of the relevant provisions of the applicable law (i.e. the *lex causae* or the *lex contractus*).

On the other hand, an international investment arbitration between an investor and the host State presents a different context. In ICSID proceedings, a sovereign State is a disputing party. Thus, public funds may well have been spent and exercises of authority by public officials may well have been undertaken, and may need careful scrutiny to determine conformity with the applicable law. In this kind of international arbitration proceedings, the interests of the host State are intensely involved. Hence, the need for transparency practices – such as access to documents and other evidence of potential criminal acts or corrupt practices, and the ability to use such documents and evidence in separate proceedings brought by the host State or third parties – is clear and pressing. The scope of the universal exception to confidentiality of documents generated in the course of the proceedings will tend to expand, and disclosure and access to such documents for enforcement of local criminal and anti-corruption laws tend to become enormously important.

Further, in an international trade arbitration or in a Panel or Appellate Body proceeding of the WTO, the parties in dispute are two sovereign States. Both proceedings are regarded as confidential and private, but not in the absolute sense. There is material accommodation of the interests of transparency and the necessity of developing coherent and consistent case law in interpreting and applying the covered WTO agreements. Over the last decade, there has been appreciable movement toward greater transparency values, especially in the development of a coherent system of international trade law that is enforceable within the WTO system. There is a trend towards a greater degree of judicialization – adjudication of disputes in accordance with law that is understood by every member state and applied and enforced in a consistent and rational manner.

There are many kinds of situations where disclosures of and open access to materials acquired or generated in the course of such proceeding significantly outweigh the convenience and economy of effort that confidentiality and privacy make possible. In principle, the demands of transparency are frequently more important and more insistent – from longer term perspectives – for both developed and developing countries, than the efficiencies and economies that confidentiality might otherwise afford.

Notes

1 Senior Associate Justice, Supreme Court of the Philippines (ret.); Former Member and Chairman, Appellate Body, WTO; Senior Counsel, SyCip Salazar Hernandez & Gatmaitan (Manila).

The extensive assistance rendered by May Ann R. Rosales, Nelson T. Antolin and Jose Florante M. Pamfilo, all of SyCip Salazar Hernandez & Gatmaitan, is gratefully acknowledged. I must also express my appreciation to Jane E. Yu and Rebecca E. Khan, both of the Office of the Solicitor General of the Philippines. These young professionals read this piece and made helpful comments.

2 For a more detailed background, see Gabriel M. Wilner, "The Mixed Courts of Egypt: A Study on the Use of Natural Law and Equity" (1975), available online at http://digitalcommons.law.uga.edu/fac_artchop/210/; see also http://www.britannica.com/EBchecked/topic/180382/Egypt/22385/From-the-French-to-the-British-occupation-1798-1882.

3 One or both parties in an international arbitration case may have some hesitation in relying totally upon the domestic court system of the respondent state. See William H. Knull, III and Noah D. Rubins, "Betting the Farm on International Arbitration: Is it Time to Offer an Appeal?", 2 *American Review of International Arbitration* 4 (2000), 5.

4 See, for instance, Loukas Mistelis, "Confidentiality and Third Party Participation: UPS v. Canada and Methanex Corp v. United States", in Todd Weiler ed., *International Investment Law and Arbitration: Leading Cases from the ICSID, NAFTA, Bilateral Treaties and Customary International Law*, London: Cameron, May, 2005, pp.169–199, p.171.

5 See ICSID Arbitration Rules, Rule 6.

6 Cindy G. Buys, "The Tensions between Confidentiality and Transparency in International Arbitration", 14 *American Review of International Arbitration* 121 (2003), p.124.

7 Ibid., pp.123–124; Colin YC Ong, "Confidentiality of Arbitral Awards and the Advantage for Arbitral Institutions to Maintain a Repository of Awards", 1(2) *Asian International Arbitration Journal* 169 (2005).

8 Hans Bagner, "The Confidentiality Conundrum in International Commercial Arbitration", 12(1) *ICC International Court of Arbitration Bulletin* 18 (2001); Buys, supra n.6, p.123.

9 Christina Knahr and August Reinisch, "Transparency versus Confidentiality in International Investment Arbitration – The Biwater Gauff Compromise", 6 *The Law and Practice of International Courts and Tribunals* 97 (2007), pp.109–110.

10 This covers both domestic arbitration proceedings and international commercial arbitration proceedings. See REP. ACT NO. 9285, sections 23 and 33.

11 Note that "confidential information" covers the following: (1) oral or written communication made in a dispute resolution proceeding, including any memoranda, notes or work product of the neutral party or non-party participant; (2) oral or written statements made or which occur during mediation or for purposes of considering, conducting, participating, initiating, continuing or reconvening mediation or retaining a mediator; and (3) pleadings, motions, manifestations, witness statements, reports filed or submitted in an arbitration or for expert evaluation. See REP. ACT NO. 9285, sec. 3(h).

12 REP. ACT NO. 9285, sec. 23. The court in which the action or the appeal is pending may even issue a protective order to prevent or prohibit disclosure of documents or information containing secret processes, developments, research and other information where it is shown that the applicant will be materially prejudiced by an authorized disclosure thereof.

13 Thus, the Constitution of the Philippines lays great stress on the right of the people to be informed on matters of public concern. Article III (7) of the 1987 Philippine Constitution provides that:

> (t)he right of the people to information on matters of public concern shall be recognized. Access to official records and to documents and papers pertaining to official acts, transactions, or decisions, as well as to government research data used as basis for policy development, shall be afforded the citizen, subject to such limitations as may be provided by law.

The case law of the Supreme Court of the Philippines is to the effect that this provision of the Constitution is "self-executing" and that what may be provided by the legislature are *reasonable* conditions and limitations upon the access to be afforded, which access must be consistent with the declared State policy of "full public disclosure of transactions involving public interest." See, e.g. *Legaspi v. Civil Service Commission*, G.R. No. 72119, 29 May 1987, 234 Phil. 521, and *Gonzales v. Narvasa*, G.R. No. 140835, 14 August 2000, 392 Phil. 521.

Philippine Administrative law includes the following noteworthy statutory provisions: (i) Book VII (Administrative Procedure), Chapter 3, (Adjudication),

Section 16(1) of the Revised Administrative Code of 1987 provides: "Every agency shall publish and make available for public inspection all decisions or final orders in the adjudication of contested cases." Further, Section 5(e) of Republic Act No. 6713, entitled "the Code of Conduct and Ethical Standards for Public Officials and Employees" (promulgated 20 February 1989) states: "All public documents must be made accessible to, and readily available for inspection by, the public within reasonable working hours."

At the same time, the Internal Rules of the Supreme Court of the Philippines promulgated on 4 May 2010, (A.M. No. 10–4-20-SC) prohibits the disclosure of: (a) the result of the raffle of cases to the individual members of the Supreme Court [Rule 7, Section 3] and the result; (b) the actions taken by the Court on each case included in the agenda of the Court's sessions [Rule 9(2) and (4); and (c) the deliberations of the members during the sessions of the Court on cases and matters before it [Rule 10(2)].

14 Knahr and Reinisch, supra n.9, p.98.

15 Some have noted in connection with the 1976 Rules that the UNCITRAL Model Law on Arbitration deliberately refrained from regulating the issue of confidentiality. According to the UNCITRAL Model Law Working Group in paragraph 101 of the Report of the Secretary-General on possible features of a model law on international commercial arbitration (A/CN.9/207), "it may be doubted whether the Model Law should deal with the question whether an award may be published. Although it is controversial since there are good reasons for and against such publication, the decision may be left to the parties or the arbitration rules chosen by them." See Knahr and Reinisch, supra n.9, p.99. Even in *S.D. Myers Inc.* v. *Canada*, the tribunal found that "whatever may be the position in private consensual arbitration between commercial parties, it has not been established that any general principle of confidentiality exists in an arbitration such as that currently before this tribunal." See *S.D. Myers Inc.* v. *Canada*, Procedural Order No. 16 of 13 May 2000, para. 8.

16 Gary Born and Ethan Shenkman, "Confidentiality and Transparency in Commercial and Investor-State International Arbitration", in Rogers, Catherine A. and Alford, Roger P. eds, *The Future of Investment Arbitration*, Oxford: Oxford University Press, 2009, pp.5–42, p.30, citing *Methanex Corporation* v. *United States*, Decision of the Tribunal on Petitions from Third Persons to Intervene as Amici Curiae, January 15, 2001; *United Parcel Services of America* v. *Government of Canada*, Decision of the Tribunal on Petitions for Intervention and Participation as Amici Curiae, October 17, 2001; *Glamis Gold Ltd.* v. *United States*, Decision on Application and Submission by Quechan Indian Nation, 16 September 2005.

17 ICSID Arbitration Rules, Rule 48(4). It must be noted that prior to the 2006 amendments to the ICSID Arbitral Rules, the ICSID was not obliged to do so.

18 ICSID Convention, Chapter IV, Section 4, Article 48(5); available online at http://icsid.worldbank.org/ICSID/StaticFiles/basicdoc/CRR_English-final.pdf. This is reiterated in Rule 48(4) of the ICSID Rules of Procedure for Arbitration Proceedings ("*ICSID Arbitration Rules*"), available online at http://icsid.worldbank.org/ICSID/StaticFiles/basicdoc/CRR_English-final.pdf.

19 ICSID Administrative and Financial Regulations, Regulation 22(2). See *Giovanna a Beccara and others* v. *Argentine Republic*, ICSID Case No. ARB/07/5, Procedural Order on Confidentiality (27 January 2010), para. 153.

20 *Idem*, Regulation 22(1). In fact, these information are currently published on ICSID's website.

21 ICSID Arbitration Rules, Rule 15(1).

22 ICSID Arbitration Rules, Rule 15(2).

23 *Idem*, Rule 32(2). In such cases, the arbitral tribunal will have to establish procedures for the protection of proprietary or privileged information.

24 *Idem*, Rule 37(2).

25 See *Amco Asia Corporation and others* v. *Republic of Indonesia*, ICSID Case No. ARB/81/1, Decision on Provisional Measures, 9 December 1983. In this case, the Respondent requested provisional measures to prevent the Claimant from publishing a newspaper article containing statements that would be detrimental to the Respondent. However, the tribunal refused to grant such by arguing that the said article could not have harmed the Respondent nor could it have exacerbated the dispute. It may thus be said that *Amco* v. *Indonesia* supports the approach that parties are in principle free to publish documents or awards unless they have explicitly agreed on confidentiality. Still, the tribunal stated that there may be situations where the parties may have to refrain from making public certain information so as not to aggravate or exacerbate their dispute.
26 Born and Shenkman, supra n.16, p.29.
27 Adopted to take effect for arbitrations commencing on or after 1 January 1998.
28 LCIA Rules, art. 19.4.
29 LCIA Rules, art. 30.1.
30 LCIA Rules, art. 30.2.
31 LCIA Rules, art. 30.3.
32 ICA Internal Rules, Article 1(1); available online at http://www.iccwbo.org/uploadedFiles/Court/Arbitration/other/rules_arb_english.pdf. However, the ICA Chairman may invite other persons to attend in exceptional circumstances, but these persons are also bound by the provisions on confidentiality. See ICA Internal Rules, Article 1(2).
33 ICA Internal Rules, art. 1(7).
34 ICA Internal Rules, art. 3(2). However, the ICA members may communicate specific information to their respective National Committees when requested by the ICA Chairman or Secretary General.
35 Born and Shenkman, supra n.16, p.20.
36 Mabel I. Egonu, "Investor-State Arbitration Under ICSID: A Case for Presumption Against Confidentiality?", 24(5) *Journal of International Arbitration* 487 (2007).
37 Knahr and Reinisch, supra n.9, p.110.
38 See Buys, supra n.6, p.121.
39 Mistelis, supra n.4, p.171, citing *Andersen Consulting Business Unit Member Firms and Arthur Andersen Worldwide Societe Cooperative*, ICC Case No. 9797/CK/AER/ACS of 28 July 2000. The parties in the much discussed cases *CME/Lauder* v. *Czech Republic* also decided to have the awards widely published.
40 See Knahr and Reinisch, supra n.9, p.113.
41 Mistelis, supra n.4, p.170.
42 Jack J. Coe, Jr., "Transparency in the Resolution of Investor-State Disputes – Adoption, Adaptation and NAFTA Leadership", 54 *Kansas Law Review* 1339 (2006), pp. 1361–1362; Ong, supra n.7, pp.174–175; Steven Kouris, "Confidentiality: Is International Arbitration Losing One of Its Major Benefits?", 22(2) *Journal of International Arbitration* 127 (2005), p.127; J. Anthony Van Duzer, "Enhancing the Procedural Legitimacy of Investor-State Arbitration through Transparency and Amicus Curiae Participation", 52 *McGill Law Journal* 681 (2007), p.685.
43 Born and Shenkman, supra n.16, p.9.
44 *Idem*, p.24.
45 DSU, art. 25; available online at http://www.wto.org/english/docs_e/legal_e/28-dsu_e.htm.
46 Jan Bohanes and Hunter Nottage "Arbitration as an alternative to litigation in the WTO: Observations in the light of the 2005 Banana Tariff Arbitrations", in Yasuhei Taniguchi, Alan Yanovich and Jan Bohanes eds, *The WTO in the Twenty-First Century*, Cambridge: Cambridge University Press, 2007, pp.212–247, p.227.
47 DSU, arts. 14, 17(10) and 17(11). See, generally, Florentino P. Feliciano, "Dispute Settlement Under the Aegis of the World Trade Organization," in *Odyssey and Legacy: The Chief Justice Andres R. Narvasa Centennial Lecture Series* (Supreme Court of the

Philippines and the U.P. College of Law: 1998) pp. 179–203; Florentino P. Feliciano and Peter L.H. Van den Bossche, "The Dispute Settlement System of the World Trade Organization: Institutions, Process and Practice", 75 PHIL L. J. 2 (2000).

48 See Debra P. Steger, "Introduction to the Mini-symposium on Transparency in the WTO", 11(4) *Journal of International Economic Law* 705 (2008), p.709.

49 DSU, art. 13.

50 *Idem*, art. 18(2).

51 *Idem* The panel in *EC – Export Subsidies on Sugar* has clarified this to mean that parties and other WTO members have the responsibility of ensuring that no member of their delegation will disclose to any person outside of the delegation any information designated as confidential.

52 DSU, art. 18(2).

53 Rules of Conduct for the Understanding on Rules and Procedures Governing the Settlement of Disputes, WT/DSB/RC/1 (11 December 1996), Clause VII(1) in relation to Clause IV(1); available online at http://www.wto.org/english/tratop_e/dispu_e/rc_e.htm#top.

54 *Idem*, Clause VII(2).

55 Peter Van den Bossche. "NGO Involvement in the WTO: A Comparative Perspective", 11(4) *Journal of International Economic Law* 717 (2008), p.732.

56 DSU, art. 10.

57 *Idem*, art. 17(4).

58 Priscilla McCalley, "The Dangers of Unregulated Counsel in the WTO", 18(3) *Georgetown Journal of Legal Ethics* 975 (2005).

59 *EC – Regime for the Importation, Sale and Distribution of Bananas*, WT/DS27/AB/R (1997).

60 *EC – Bananas*, para. 10.

61 *US– Import Prohibition of Certain Shrimp and Shrimp Products*, WT/DS58/AB/R (1998); *EC – Measures Affecting Asbestos and Asbestos-Containing Products*, WT/DS135/AB/R (2001).

62 Van den Bossche, supra n.55, p.733.

63 *Idem*, p.727

64 Eliyahu E. Wolfe, "Shining Sunlight on Dispute Settlement: Strengthening the Multilateral Trading System Through Enhanced Transparency in the WTO Dispute Settlement System", 2009, available online at http://works.bepress.com/eliyahu_wolfe/1/.

65 *Aguas Argentinas S.A., et al.* v. *Argentine Republic*, ICSID Case No. ARB/03/19, Order in Response to a Petition for Transparency and Participation as amicus curiae, 19 May 2005, available online at http://ita.law.uvic.ca/documents/AguasArgentinas Vivendi-OrderAmicusCuriae.pdf.

66 *Aguas Provinciales de Santa Fe S.A., et al.* v. *Argentine Republic*, ICSID Case No. ARB/03/17, Order in Response to a Petition for Transparency and Participation as amicus curiae, 17 March 2006, available online at http://icsid.worldbank.org/ICSID/FrontServlet?requestType=CasesRH&actionVal=showDoc&docId=DC512_En&caseId=C18.

67 *Biwater Gauff (Tanzania) Ltd.* v. *United Republic of Tanzania*, ICSID Case No. ARB/05/22, Procedural Order No. 3, 29 September 2006, available online at http://ita.law.uvic.ca/documents/Biwater-PONo.3.pdf.

3 Transparency and the role of domestic process

Connecting citizens to the WTO dispute settlement

Yuka Fukunaga[1]

Introduction

International disputes are often settled through diplomatic channels behind closed doors – or at least they were in the past. Secrecy was considered essential for effective dispute resolution, and international trade disputes were no exception. Trade officials of the disputing countries talked, negotiated, and compromised in government buildings unknown to the public. The indispensable stakeholders in international trade disputes were governments and businesses, and the goal of dispute settlement was a resolution that would satisfy these stakeholders. Citizens had no idea how, when, and by whom international trade disputes were settled. The participation of citizens in the dispute settlement was neither ensured nor requested.

However, the situation has changed. As international trade expands, international trade disputes have greater impact on citizens' daily lives and citizens have developed a keener interest in their resolution. Having become one of the most important stakeholders in international trade disputes, citizens are now demanding higher transparency in the way these disputes are settled. In response to this growing demand for transparency, efforts have been made to make the dispute settlement process more transparent to the public. Among others, the World Trade Organization (WTO) dispute settlement system has contributed significantly to making the settlement process more public. Now when a trade dispute is referred to the WTO dispute settlement system, citizens can learn how and when the dispute is raised, settled, and resolved.

Ironically, the increasing visibility of this process has fueled criticism among citizens about the lack of transparency in the WTO dispute settlement system. In fact, this criticism is often targeted towards the most visible phase of the WTO dispute settlement proceedings, i.e. the panel and Appellate Body proceedings. Despite the full disclosure of panel and Appellate Body reports, critics denounce the secrecy of the panel and Appellate Body reviews, such as the closed panel and Appellate Body hearings and the involvement of faceless bureaucrats of the Secretariat (see, e.g. McRae 2003).

Interestingly, the criticism about the lack of transparency addresses is not limited to the issue of visibility. The demand for higher visibility is often accompanied by a demand for higher participation of the public in the panel and

Appellate Body proceedings. While the former is concerned only with the procedural involvement of citizens in the proceedings, the latter requires more substantive citizen participation.[2] That is, the latter is a demand to allow citizens to express their interests and concerns during WTO dispute settlement proceedings, and have them reflected in the findings rendered by panels and the Appellate Body. The hope is that the participation of citizens would promote the reflection of non-trade concerns in the findings of panels and the Appellate Body and thereby eliminate their trade bias (see, e.g. Schultz 1995).

In response to criticism, several specific proposals have been made to enhance the transparency of the WTO dispute settlement system. Among others, critics propose to increase visibility by opening panel and Appellate Body hearings and allowing citizens to attend and observe them. They have also proposed to allow the participation of citizens in the panel and Appellate Body review process by accepting and taking into account unsolicited amicus curiae briefs filed by citizens. One of the objectives of this chapter is to review these proposals and to analyze both the actual and potential consequences associated with them. In particular, this chapter raises concerns about the potential costs of higher public participation, which could outweigh the potential benefits.

The other objective of this chapter is to shift focus from the WTO dispute settlement proceedings and to discuss the transparency of dispute settlement in a wider context. Seen in a wider light, WTO dispute settlement proceedings are only a part of the broader process of international trade dispute settlement. The argument of this chapter is that the appropriate degree and nature of transparency naturally differs at each stage of the broader dispute settlement process. While ensuring the transparency to citizens at one stage may produce benefits that outweigh potential costs and risks, ensuring the same level of transparency at another stage may be burdensome and produce little benefit. Thus, this chapter assumes that the lack of transparency at one stage does not necessarily have to be resolved at that stage but rather could, or even should, be compensated for with higher transparency throughout other stages. In other words, transparency to citizens could be ensured collectively in multiple stages of the broad process of dispute settlement.

On the basis of the above assumption, this chapter focuses on the role of the domestic stage of the dispute settlement process in ensuring the transparency of the international trade dispute settlement to the public. The domestic process of dispute settlement plays an indispensable role in settling international trade disputes. For example, the government considers and decides how to tackle the trade restrictive measures of a foreign government through domestic discourse with private interested parties. In addition, panel and Appellate Body findings of violations and their recommendations cannot resolve an international trade dispute on their own, unless they are implemented within the domestic process of the responding party. Considering the importance of the domestic process, a question arises as to whether the transparency demand needs to be satisfied within the WTO proceedings, or alternatively, can be fulfilled at the domestic process of dispute settlement.

I argue that the transparency criticism is blinded by the more visible process of panel and Appellate Body review, while overlooking the less visible but more important domestic process of dispute settlement. The alleged lack of transparency to the public of the WTO dispute settlement proceedings can and should be compensated for by transparency in the domestic process of the international trade dispute settlement (cf. Keohane et al. 2001; Koh 1997; Koh 1996).

This chapter is constituted as follows. The following section first reviews the background of WTO transparency criticism. It then analyzes specific transparency-related proposals and their actual impacts on the dispute settlement practice and the Understanding on Rules and Procedures Governing the Settlement of Disputes (DSU) review negotiations in the Doha Development Agenda (DDA). The section also discusses the potential benefits of the proposals may be outweighed by their potential costs. Next, the role of the domestic process in the settlement of WTO-related disputes is discussed. It is argued that the transparency in the domestic process can compensate for the alleged lack of transparency to the public of the WTO dispute settlement proceedings. The final section concludes the chapter.

Transparency demands and their consequences

Background of transparency demands

Traditionally, the international law process, including the settlement of international trade disputes, involved the utmost secrecy and lay far beyond the reach of democratic control by citizens. This does not necessarily imply that states stubbornly rejected the involvement of citizens; rather, citizens themselves tended to be indifferent to the international law process that was mainly concerned with interstate relationships. Nor was the settlement of international trade disputes a matter of major concern to citizens who were mostly self-sufficient in the local or domestic economy (McGinnis and Movsesian 2000). In this context, citizens did not have a strong incentive to involve themselves in the international law process.

However, the situation has changed. Citizens' enthusiasm for opening the international law process is growing and states' monopoly over the process is being eroded by awakened citizens (cf. Keohane and Nye 2001). This change underlies the demand that the WTO dispute settlement proceedings become more transparent to citizens.

There are both practical and theoretical reasons behind the growing enthusiasm for transparency. In terms of practical reasons, as the transnational flow of goods, people, and companies expands, citizens are more exposed to the international law process, which has increasing impact on their lives, and as a result, they have come to pay more attention to it. This trend is most prominent in the case of international trade law. The strengthened rules and dispute settlement procedures in international trade have begun to affect the daily lives of citizens either directly or indirectly (Charnovitz 2000). For example, we have repeatedly witnessed situations wherein reports of WTO panels and the Appellate Body affected our diets including bananas and genetically modified foods. It is a natural consequence that citizens have become more interested in the process of international trade dispute settlement. The transparency criticism is the result of this change in situation and the growing interest of citizens.

From a theoretical perspective, it is noticeable that citizens' growing enthusiasm for transparency is consistent with the idea of a cosmopolitan democracy (Held 1995) or global democracy (Slaughter 2000). Recently, the concept of cosmopolitan/global democracy has stimulated discussions on democracy in international law scholarship in a number of different ways (Stein 2001). Although democracy is far from an established rule of international law, its significance is increasingly being acknowledged (see UN 2005). For example, the construction of democracy is becoming a key element in the recognition of new states[3] and in the post-conflict peace-building.[4] Moreover, the cosmopolitan/global democracy purports to refer to not only the promotion of democracy within states, which has been a central concern in international law (cf. Crawford 1993; Franck 1992), but also the democratization of the international law process itself, which is only recently being recognized. The latter argument criticizes the international law process, which has been closed to the public, for its "democratic deficit", and demands that it be "democratized" by allowing citizens to participate in its decision making. The argument is gaining ground particularly in the WTO. Enthusiasm for the enhanced transparency to the public in the WTO dispute settlement proceedings constitutes a part of a more comprehensive attempt to achieve cosmopolitan/global democracy (Petersmann 2011; Charnovitz 2002; see also Schneider 1998).

Enthusiasm for transparency also resonates with the controversy over legitimacy. While the issue of legitimacy is repeatedly debated in legal scholarship (Weber 1978), the most influential work in international law is undoubtedly that of Thomas Franck. Noting that the legitimacy of a rule or an institution may encourage voluntary compliance with that rule or institution's decision, Franck highlights the critical importance of legitimacy in international law which lacks effective enforcement tools (Franck 1990). His argument has stimulated the legitimacy debate in international law, particularly in the context of the WTO dispute settlement system (see, e.g. Cass 2005 and Zampetti 2003).

There are different aspects to legitimacy,[5] and what is most relevant in the transparency debate is the legitimacy as perceived by citizens (Fukunaga 2008: 97–100; see also Howse 2000: 36–42). It is argued that the WTO dispute settlement system's lack of transparency to the public could harm citizens' confidence in the findings and recommendations of panels and the Appellate Body and thereby undermine the legitimacy of the dispute settlement system as perceived by citizens. This could give rise to a sense of distrust among the citizens of the responding party and induce them to pressure their government to not comply with the findings and recommendations rendered by the system (Jacobson and Weiss 1995; see also Bodansky 1999: 610–611). Thus, it is argued that, in order to overcome distrust and noncompliance, the legitimacy of the dispute settlement system, as perceived by citizens, should be secured by enhancing the transparency to the public of the dispute settlement system (Fukunaga 2008: 97–100).

While the above mentioned theoretical underpinnings of the transparency criticism have been attracting wide attention, it should be noted that they are not without drawbacks. For example, in light of its diversity and its fragile sense of community, it is far from clear whether the international community has matured enough and has met the necessary conditions to adopt the global/cosmopolitan democracy. The hasty democratization of international institutions, without first meeting the necessary conditions, could even be detrimental to citizens (Fukunaga 2007; see also Weiler and Motoc 2003: 69–71; Howse and Nicolaïdis 2001: 241–243; Dahl 1998: 37–38). There are also doubts about the relationship between the legitimacy of the dispute settlement system and its transparency to the public. Although the transparency to the public is surely one source of legitimacy of the dispute settlement system, it is not the only one. There are several other sources of legitimacy including independence, authority, and effectiveness. They could compensate for the lack of others, but they might also be in conflict with each other. What ensures the overall legitimacy of the system is a delicate balance of many different sources of legitimacy. The value of transparency to the public needs to be evaluated in consideration of both its positive and potential negative effects on legitimacy (Fukunaga 2008: 89–97).

Having said that, this chapter does not deny that citizens have growing interests and a larger stake in international trade disputes, nor does it deny that the process of international trade dispute settlement needs to be more transparent to the public. The question addressed in this chapter is whether the transparency to the public needs to be ensured within the WTO dispute settlement system or if it could be compensated for at the domestic stage of the international trade dispute settlement process. The next section reveals the potential costs ensuing from the enhanced transparency to the public of the WTO dispute settlement system.

Transparency proposals and their impact on dispute settlement practice and the DDA

This section discusses proposals put forth by the transparency criticism and the consequences that would result from such proposals. In particular, it aims to point out the potential costs of the transparency proposals which could outweigh their potential benefits.

To begin with, it is worth noting that, compared to the General Agreement on Tariffs and Trade (GATT) dispute settlement system, the WTO dispute settlement system has significantly contributed to increasing the transparency of the international trade dispute settlement. In particular, the publication of relevant documents has become more extensive and more immediate, making the WTO dispute settlement proceedings more visible to the public. For example, a request for consultations filed by the complaining party clarifies, at least in part, the nature and the scope of a dispute (DSU, Art. 4.4), while a notification by the parties describes a mutually agreed solution reached between them (DSU, Art. 3.6). Moreover, when a dispute is referred to the panel and Appellate Body review process, panel and Appellate Body reports are published immediately after the issuance to reveal the relevant facts and legal findings of the dispute in detail (DSU, Art. 12.7). In some cases, the disputing parties disclose to the public their own submissions filed to the panel and the Appellate Body (DSU, Appendix 3[3]). Progress in the implementation of Dispute Settlement Body (DSB) recommendations can be confirmed, though often briefly, in status reports provided by the responding party (DSU, Art. 21.6). These documents can now be easily downloaded from the WTO website.

Despite the increased visibility, criticism is mounting over WTO dispute settlement, with claims that the transparency to the public is seriously limited. Ironically, the criticism is often addressed to the most visible stage of the WTO dispute settlement proceedings, i.e. the panel and Appellate Body review stage. Needless to say, criticism does by no means imply that citizens should be given full-fledged access to the panel and Appellate Body review process. Instead, the transparency criticism often demands two specific improvements: One is even higher visibility to citizens and the other is the participation of citizens in the dispute settlement proceedings.

Although the focus of this chapter is on the participation of citizens in the dispute settlement proceedings, it is worth mentioning the proposal regarding higher visibility. According to this proposal, panel and Appellate Body meetings with the parties should be open to the public.[6] More specifically, advocates of this proposal argue that citizens should be allowed to attend and observe panel and Appellate meetings with the parties. In the same vein, some developed Members have proposed in the DDA the opening of meetings,[7] while some developing Members are objecting to the proposal.[8]

Considering that the review process of panels and the Appellate Body is quite similar to the judicial process of courts and that most international courts open their hearings to the public,[9] it seems reasonable to also open panel and Appellate Body meetings. In fact, the transparency to the public is considered essential to ensuring the legitimacy of judicial review (Weiler 2002: 191).

However, the transparency to the public of the international trade dispute settlement process may need to be limited in some cases. For example, certain safeguard measures would need to be in place when a dispute involves highly confidential business information. In addition, due regard should be paid to the nature of the WTO dispute settlement system, which is designed as a "government-to-government" process.[10] While these considerations do not totally negate the need for the transparency to the public, a cautious approach should be taken to balance the interests of citizens against the interests of governments and business enterprises.[11]

The current practices of some panels and the Appellate Body provide guidance on a practical approach towards addressing the above-mentioned concerns. For example, panels and the Appellate Body have opened their meetings only when one of the parties requested it, and all the parties have agreed.[12] In addition, opening meetings does not mean that citizens are allowed to be physically present in the meeting room. Instead, citizens are given a separate room within the WTO Secretariat and the meetings are broadcast through closed-circuit television

(WTO News 2010). Any amendments to the DSU, if any are to be made at all, should reflect the current practice of the dispute settlement system. That is, while it would be advisable to amend the DSU to encourage panels and the Appellate Body to open their meetings, agreement between the disputing parties should be a prerequisite; further, due considerations should be paid to secure the interests of both governments and businesses.

Turning to the second aspect of the transparency to the public, the participation of citizens could create a more serious problem than the opening of meetings. This proposal is specifically concerned with the treatment of unsolicited amicus curiae briefs. These are opinion briefs filed by non-Member non-governmental entities, such as individuals and non-governmental organizations (NGOs), to panels or the Appellate Body, in the absence of a request by the panels or the Appellate Body. In some WTO disputes, especially those related to the environment, citizens filed unsolicited amicus curiae briefs.[13] This practice raised the question of whether or not such briefs may be accepted and taken into consideration by panels and the Appellate Body. Although Article 13.1 of the DSU authorizes a panel to seek on its own initiative information and technical advice from any individual or body that it deems appropriate, the DSU remains silent on the treatment of unsolicited information filed by individuals or NGOs.

In *US – Shrimp*, the treatment of unsolicited amicus curiae briefs became a major issue between the disputing parties. While the panel in this case found that accepting unsolicited information from NGOs would be incompatible with Article 13 of the DSU, which gives a panel the initiative to seek information and the authority to select the information source (PR, *US – Shrimp* [7.7–7.8]), the Appellate Body reversed the findings of the panel. The Appellate Body acknowledged that, while only Member State parties have a legal right to make written submissions to a panel and a panel is obliged by law to accept and consider such submissions, a panel is vested with the discretionary authority under Article 13 of the DSU either to accept and consider or to reject information and advice submitted to it regardless of whether or not the information or advice is requested by the panel (ABR, *US – Shrimp* [101–110]).[14] In a later case, the Appellate Body also confirmed that it has legal authority under the DSU to accept and consider amicus curiae briefs (ABR, *US – Lead and Bismuth II* [39–42]).

Since *US – Shrimp*, a number of amicus curiae briefs have been submitted to panels and the Appellate Body from private parties.[15] However, panels and the Appellate Body remain reluctant to take into account unsolicited amicus curiae briefs, though they do not deny that they have a right to do so. In many of these cases, panels and the Appellate Body rejected considering them by finding it is not "necessary to rely on" them in rendering their findings.[16] Against this background, the transparency criticism demands that panels and the Appellate Body accept and take into account unsolicited amicus curiae briefs to ensure that the panel and Appellate Body findings reflect the interests and concerns of citizens.

The treatment of unsolicited amicus curiae briefs is also one of the most controversial issues in the DSU review negotiations in the DDA. In the DDA, the issue is not limited to whether unsolicited amicus curiae briefs should be accepted and considered by panels and the Appellate Body. In the view of some WTO Members, the findings of the panels and the Appellate Body already allow that the current DSU authorizes panels and the Appellate Body to accept and take into account such briefs despite the absence of an explicit provision. Based on this assumption, the more important issue for these Members is how such briefs should be handled. For example, the European Union (EU) proposes to better define the framework and conditions for allowing such briefs in order not to cause a delay in the proceedings or substantial additional burdens for developing Members, while ensuring sufficient time for citizens to make submission and for the parties, panels, and the Appellate Body to review the briefs.[17] In contrast to the EU proposal, some developing Members suggest that the findings of the panels and the Appellate Body regarding unsolicited amicus curiae briefs are "totally unexpected and unintended" interpretations of Article 13 of the DSU, and raise doubts as to the right of panels and the Appellate Body to receive unsolicited information.[18]

This chapter does not discuss whether or not the interpretations of Article 13 of the DSU by the panels and the Appellate Body were correct. Instead, it examines whether or not the panels and the Appellate Body should accept and consider unsolicited amicus curiae briefs. In assessing the appropriateness of the proposal regarding unsolicited amicus curiae briefs, an important difference between this proposal and the one regarding open meetings should be noted. While the latter seeks only to enhance the public visibility of the panel and Appellate Body proceedings, the former seeks to get citizens more involved in the proceedings and to have them exert influence over their outcome. Such extensive involvement of non-party citizens in the proceedings cannot be justified merely by the judicial nature of the panel and Appellate Body review. Moreover, there are not only practical difficulties but also systemic concerns[19] associated with the extensive involvement of citizens through amicus curiae briefs.

First, it is questionable that amicus curiae briefs can have citizens' interests reflected fully and properly in the proceedings of the panels and the Appellate Body. Two problems are outlined out here. One is the problem of representation, which means that the interests and concerns of only a few citizens can be represented through amicus curiae briefs given the gaps in capacities and resources among citizens. That is, most of the citizens in the international community are not capable of making submissions to panels or the Appellate Body and the interests of those unrepresented citizens could be undermined by the acceptance and consideration of amicus curiae briefs filed by others (Fukunaga 2008: 122–124). The other is the problem of coordination, which means that the interests and concerns of citizens, even if fully represented in the WTO dispute settlement proceedings, cannot be coordinated in a way that is satisfactory to all of them. Considering the wide variety of citizens' interests and concerns, coordinating them to reach a single decision is almost an impossible task.[20] The question also arises as to whether or not panels and the Appellate Body are suitable bodies for such a task.

Second, the excessive involvement of non-party citizens could make it difficult for the party governments to resolve a dispute effectively. The dispute settlement system provides for procedures between a party, whose benefits under the WTO Agreement are allegedly impaired or nullified, and another party, whose measures are alleged to violate the WTO Agreement. The involvement of those whose rights or obligations are not directly provided for in the WTO Agreement could complicate the procedures.[21] This is even more compelling given that citizens could be adequately represented in the dispute settlement proceedings, though indirectly, through the intervention of the government, as long as their interests are meaningfully taken into account by the government.[22] At this point, it is noteworthy that international courts handling intergovernmental disputes have also been reluctant to accept and consider unsolicited amicus curiae briefs by citizens.[23] For example, the Practice Direction XXII, Paragraph 1, of the International Court of Justice (ICJ), as amended 20 January 2009, explicitly states "[w]here an international non-governmental organization submits a written statement and/or document in an advisory opinion case on its own initiative, such statement and/or document is not to be considered as part of the case file."[24]

Having pointed out the problems ensuing from the enhanced participation of citizens through amicus curiae briefs, this chapter now broadens the focus from the WTO dispute settlement proceedings to discuss the transparency to the public within a wider context. The next section focuses on the role of domestic process in ensuring the transparency to the public of the international trade dispute settlement.

Role of domestic process in international trade dispute settlement

The process of international trade dispute settlement becomes more visible when it comes to the international arena, especially the WTO dispute settlement system. What happens in the WTO dispute settlement system tends to become the focal point for attention and criticism. However, a closer look reveals that a dispute often arises from interactions at the domestic stage, such as interactions between the government and exporters having complaints against a foreign government. Often a dispute also ends through interactions at the domestic stage, such as interactions between the government taking measures to implement the DSB recommendations and domestic producers competing with foreign exporters.

This section argues that the WTO dispute settlement proceedings are only a part of the broader international trade dispute settlement process, and that their lack of transparency to the public can be compensated for with enhanced transparency at the domestic level of the process. Specifically, it is argued here that citizens, even if they cannot participate directly in the WTO dispute settlement proceedings, can have their interests and concerns reflected in the proceedings through domestic interactions with their government.

It should be remembered that the proposal regarding citizens' participation in the dispute settlement proceedings represents a substantive, rather than procedural demand that citizens' interests and concerns should be reflected in the outcome of the proceedings. As long as citizens' interests and concerns are taken into account by their government at the domestic stage, and represented, though indirectly, by their government during the dispute settlement proceedings, their direct participation in the proceedings would become unnecessary (Bolton 2000: 217–218).[25] Moreover, the problems associated with the direct participation of citizens in the WTO dispute settlement proceedings, such as the representation and coordination problems would not arise, or at least be less serious, if the considerations of citizens' interests and concerns took place within the domestic process (cf. Fukunaga 2008: 116).

This section discusses the role of domestic process in the following three temporal sequences, i.e. prior to, during, and post WTO dispute settlement proceedings. In the author's view, the post WTO dispute settlement proceedings stage plays a critical role in reflecting the interests and concerns of citizens in the outcome of the dispute settlement. The rest of this section discusses chronologically how transparency to the public can be secured in the three stages of domestic process, with a focus on the last stage.

First, the stage prior to the reference of a dispute to the WTO dispute settlement system involves domestic discourse between the government and private parties, i.e. normally businesses who have encountered trade-related problems with a foreign government, or possibly against foreign competitors. Some WTO Members, such as the United States (US) and the EU, have the domestic legal instruments that channel businesses' complaints regarding trade practices of a foreign country to the government.[26] Although other WTO Members, such as Japan, do not have such legal instruments, the trade ministries normally have routine contacts with businesses, through which the government can recognize complaints businesses have against a foreign country.

While these domestic interactions are primarily concerned with business interests, they have the potential to ensure the transparency to the public (Bogdandy 2006: 235–236; see also Nichols 2004; Jackson 2003). That is, while dealing with business complaints, the government can also engage in talks with citizens and take into account their interests and concerns in deciding how to address the business complaints. In fact, the legal instruments of the US and the EU have provisions requiring the consideration of citizens' interests and concerns.[27] These instruments help government decide how to handle business complaints from a broader perspective.

Second, at the stage during the WTO dispute settlement proceedings, especially during the panel and Appellate Body review, the domestic discourse between the government and businesses often continues in order to reflect the interests and concerns of businesses in the oral and written submissions of the government. Such discourse is naturally required given that business interests are most likely to be affected by the outcome of the proceedings.

The government should also be encouraged to maintain contact with citizens during the WTO dispute settlement proceedings, especially if a dispute is closely linked with the interests and concerns of citizens. For example, the government may reinforce its position in proceedings by seeking input from citizens who have factual information that cannot be accessed by the government, or who support the government's position from a different point of view. In this regard, it is noteworthy that some panels have decided to consider views expressed in unsolicited amicus curiae briefs as long as the disputing parties or third parties decided to adopt the views in their own submissions and arguments to the panels (see, e.g. European Communities Panel Report 2007: 12–13). The practice of these panels suggests that citizens would be able to reflect their interests and concerns in the proceedings through the written and oral submissions of the government parties even if the citizens cannot directly participate in the proceedings.

The third and final stage ensues after the panel and Appellate Body review is completed and their recommendations are adopted by the DSB. It involves the process of domestic implementation of the DSB recommendations. The DSB recommendations request the responding party to bring the measures that have been found to violate the WTO Agreement into conformity with it; their implementation normally requires the adoption of certain domestic measures. Because the DSB recommendations do not specify what measures should be taken, the responding party makes such determinations within its territory (Fukunaga 2006: 383, 399).[28] Therefore, the domestic process of the responding party plays a critical role in implementing the DSB recommendations and bringing the measures concerned into conformity with the WTO Agreement.

The domestic implementation process of the DSB recommendations is also critical from the point of view of protecting the interests of citizens. In disputes involving non-economic interests and concerns of citizens, the implementation process of the DSB recommendations requires the reconciliation of two seemingly conflicting objectives – compliance with the WTO Agreement and protection of non-economic interests. More specifically, when a dispute concerns measures that aim at protecting non-economic interests such as environment and human rights that are found to violate the WTO Agreement, bringing the measures into conformity with the WTO Agreement could harm the non-economic interests protected by such measures. The government of the responding party needs to take extra caution, in determining appropriate implementation measures through its domestic process, in order to achieve both the objectives of securing compliance with the WTO Agreement and protecting non-economic interests in a reconcilable manner.

It is worth recalling, at this point, that the transparency criticism is concerned with the fact that the WTO dispute settlement proceedings prevent a state from taking domestic measures to protect non-economic interests of citizens. The criticism unconsciously (and erroneously) assumes that the outcome of the WTO dispute settlement proceedings directly influences the domestic policies and measures of the responding party (Fukunaga 2009: 1042–1043).[29] However, in reality, the DSB recommendations do not automatically permeate into the domestic legal order of the responding party, and the government retains discretion on how to implement recommendations.

The discretion left to the government of the responding party enables it to take into account citizens' non-economic interests and concerns in determining how to domestically implement the DSB recommendations and to ensure that the implementation would not unduly harm the interests of citizens. In fact, in the past disputes where the panels and the Appellate Body found that measures protecting non-economic interests of citizens violated the WTO Agreement and were not justified, the responding party often succeeded in resolving disputes without sacrificing indispensable non-economic interests. For example, in *US – Gasoline*, while the Appellate Body found that the US regulation on gasoline, purporting to improve air quality in the US, violated Article III:4 of the GATT and was not justified under Article XX of the GATT (PR, *US – Gasoline*), the US was not required to (and did not) revoke the regulation. Instead, the US successfully resolved the dispute by merely amending the regulation and adding flexibility to it.[30] In the words of the US government, the amendment does not prevent the US from maintaining its policies that "fully protect public health and the environment, and at the same time are consistent with the obligations of the United States under the WTO."[31]

Moreover, the domestic implementation process of DSB recommendations opens the possibility for citizens to directly participate in the dispute settlement process. Such a possibility is indicated by some of the past disputes where the government of the responding party, in implementing the DSB recommendations, engaged in talks at least with domestic producers. For example, in a series of disputes where Japan's quarantine measures were repeatedly found to violate the SPS Agreement (PR, *Japan – Agricultural Products*; ABR, *Japan – Agricultural Products*; PR, *Japan – Apples*; ABR, *Japan – Apples*), deliberative discussion between the government and agricultural producers enabled the modification of the measures that satisfied both the producers and the complaining party (Oyane 2005). Considering that the national government is obviously more accessible for citizens than the WTO dispute settlement system, the domestic process is expected to take into account and reflect the wider range of citizens' interests and concerns. In short, the domestic process of DSB recommendations can serve as the final line of defense for citizens.

To sum up this section, the domestic process of international trade dispute settlement can reflect interests and concerns of citizens more effectively and with lesser disadvantages than the WTO dispute settlement proceedings. Transparency to citizens can be better ensured domestically than in the WTO. The high level of transparency to citizens in the domestic process can compensate for the lack of transparency in the WTO dispute settlement proceedings and enhance transparency to citizens in the international trade dispute settlement process as a whole.

Conclusion

In light of the growing impact of international trade disputes on citizens, the demand for transparency toward citizens in the international trade dispute settlement process and the need to respond to it are reasonably justified and not denied in this chapter. However, the transparency demand often focuses exclusively on the WTO dispute settlement proceedings and overlooks the importance of the domestic process in international trade dispute settlement.

This chapter critically examined proposals seeking to enhance transparency to citizens in the WTO dispute settlement proceedings, and pointed out the difficulties of the proposals. It then shifted focus from the WTO dispute settlement proceedings and highlighted the critical role of the domestic process in ensuring the transparency to citizens in the international trade dispute settlement process.

If higher transparency toward citizens is required, efforts should first be made to improve the domestic process to make it more accessible and responsive to the needs of citizens.

Notes

1 Professor, Waseda University. A part of this chapter is developed from a conference paper submitted to the inaugural conference of the Society of International Economic Law. The author would like to acknowledge Farzan Sabet of the Graduate Institute of International and Development Studies for assistance in editing this text.

2 There are several ways for citizens to participate in the dispute settlement proceedings. (See Esty 1998).

3 See, e.g. European Community: Declaration on Yugoslavia and on the Guidelines on the Recognition of New States, 31 *I.L.M.*1485 (1992). (Also see Crawford 2006: 150–155, cautioning that a democratic national government is not a legal prerequisite for statehood).

4 See, e.g. High-Level Panel on Threats, Challenges, and Change, Report of the Secretary General's High-Level Panel on Threats, Challenges, and Change, A More Secure World: Our Shared Responsibility (2004).

5 In the early work, the author distinguishes objective legitimacy and subjective legitimacy. While the former follows from the actual properties of a rule or institution, the latter arises from the perceptions of a rule or institution by those affected by the rule or institution. The latter depends on the perceptions of the government, businesses and citizens respectively. (Fukunaga 2008: 87–97).

6 Interestingly, although the consultations or DSB meetings are even less transparent than the panel and Appellate Body review stage, the former is hardly criticized. This is probably because consultations and DSB meetings are considered as political in nature and should not be easily opened up to citizens.

7 See, e.g. Contribution of the European Communities and its Member States to the Improvement of the WTO Dispute Settlement Understanding: Communication from the European Communities [EU Proposal], TN/DS/W/1 (13 March 2002), at 6–7; Contribution of the United States to the Improvement of the Dispute Settlement Understanding of the WTO Related to Transparency: Communication from the United States [US Proposal], TN/DS/W/13 (22 August 2002), at 1–2; Contribution of Canada to the Improvement of the WTO Dispute Settlement Understanding: Communication from Canada, TN/DS/W/41 (24 January 2003), at 6.

8 See, e.g. Negotiations on the Dispute Settlement Understanding: Proposal by the African Group [African Group Proposal], TN/DS/W/15 (25 September 2002), at 6.

9 See, e.g. Statute of the International Court of Justice, Art. 46, 26 June 1945, 59 Stat. 1055, 33 *U.N.T.S.* 993; Statute of the International Tribunal for the Law of the Sea (Annex VI of the United Nations Convention on the Law of the Sea), Art. 20.2.

10 See Contribution by the Separate Customs Territory of Taiwan, Penghu, Kinmen and Matsu to the Doha Mandated Review of the Dispute Settlement Understanding (DSU):

Communication from the Separate Customs Territory of Taiwan, Penghu, Kinmen and Matsu [Taiwan Proposal], TN/DS/W/25 (27 November 2002), at 1–2.

11 Compare with Contribution of the United States on Some Practical Considerations in Improving the Dispute Settlement Understanding of the WTO Related to Transparency and Open Meetings: Communication from the United States, TN/DS/W/79 (13 July 2005), at 3.

12 See, e.g. Communication from the Chairman of the Panels, United States – Continued Suspension of Obligations in the EC – Hormones Dispute (WT/DS320), Canada – Continued Suspension of Obligations in the EC – Hormones Dispute (WT/DS321), WT/DS320/8, WT/DS321/8 (2 August 2005).

13 Among the earliest disputes in which unsolicited amicus curiae briefs were filed to panels were *US – Gasoline* and *EC – Hormones*, though the panels refused to acknowledge the submission of the briefs. Charnovitz 2000: 182. See PR, *US – Gasoline*; PR, *EC – Hormones*.

14 For more details, see Fukunaga 2007: 114–117.

15 Private parties submitting amicus curiae briefs include not only individuals and NGOs but also industrial associations. For example, in *Mexico – Soft Drinks*, the Appellate Body received an amicus curiae brief from the National Chamber of the Sugar and Alcohol Industries of the responding party (ABR, *Mexico – Soft Drinks* [8]).

16 Most recently, an unsolicited amicus curiae brief was rejected by the Appellate Body to be relied on in *China – Autos* for such a reason (ABR, *China – Autos* [18]).

17 EU Proposal, supra note 7, at 7. See also US Proposal, supra note 7, at 2–3; Contributions towards the Improvement and Clarification of the WTO Dispute Settlement Understanding: Communication from Jordan, TN/DS/W/43 (28 January 2003), at 7–8.

18 African Group Proposal, supra note 8, at 5. See also Taiwan Proposal, supra note 10, at 2.

19 Below, mainly systemic concerns are discussed. The practical difficulties associated with accepting amicus curiae briefs include an increase in burden for the parties, especially developing country parties as well as the panels and the Appellate Body.

20 Fukunaga 2008: 122–128 (discussing the problems of representation and coordination of private parties' interests).

21 Compare with Negotiations on the Dispute Settlement Understanding: Proposals on DSU by Cuba, Honduras, India, Malaysia, Pakistan, Sri Lanka, Tanzania and Zimbabwe, TN/DS/W/18 (7 October 2002), at 2–4.

22 Compare with Howse 2002: 94, 114.

23 For the practice of international courts, see Ruth Mackenzie, Cesare P.R. Romano, and Yuval Shany with Philippe Sands, Manual on International Courts and Tribunals, paras 1.33, 2.30, 3.24, 4.24, 5.24, 6.30, 7.28, 8.24, 10.2.18, 10.3.13, 11.23, 11.25 and 12.31 (2010). As implied from the book, amicus curiae briefs by non-governmental entities may be accepted and considered without imposing serious problems in international courts that handle disputes involving non-governmental parties.

24 Note that states and intergovernmental organizations presenting written and oral statements in the case may refer to such documents in the same manner as publications in the public domain. Practice Direction XXII, Paragraph 2.

25 In fact, the direct participation of citizens in the WTO dispute settlement proceedings could even become redundant if their interests and concerns are fully taken into account in the domestic process.

26 In the US, an interested party may file a petition with the US Trade Representatives (USTR) requesting an investigation of a practice of a foreign country in accordance with Section 301 of the Trade Act of 1974. Section 301 of the Trade Act of 1974 as amended, 19 U.S.C. §2411. As for the EU, the Trade Barriers Regulation (TBR) gives European businesses a tool to file a complaint against foreign government's trade restricting measures. Council Regulation (EC) No.3286/94 of 22 December 1994,

laying down Community procedures in the field of the common commercial policy in order to ensure the exercise of the Community's rights under international trade rules, in particular those established under the auspices of the World Trade Organization (OJ L 349, 31.12.1994, at 71), as amended by the Council Regulation (EC) No.356/95 of 20 February 1995 (OJ L 41, 23.2.1995, at 3) and Council Regulation (EC) No.125/2008 of 12 February 2008 (OJ L 40 14.2.2008, at 1) [Council Regulation (EC) No.3286/94]. See also Shaffer 2003.

27 The Trade Act of 1974 provides that the USTR, before taking any action under Section 301, "shall provide an opportunity . . . for the presentation of views by interested persons, including a public hearing if requested by any interested person". 19 USCS §2414(b)(1)(A). In the EU, the TBR provides that the Commission shall initiate an examination procedure when there is sufficient evidence to justify initiating the procedure and the procedure "is necessary in the interest of the Community". Council Regulation (EC) No.3286/94, Art. 8.1.

28 The Second Sentence of Article 19.1 of the DSU provides that a panel or the Appellate Body may suggest ways in which the responding party could implement the recommendations, but they rarely make such suggestions.

29 The author argues, in a previous work, that the transparency criticism stands on a premise that the WTO dispute settlement system reinforces the continuity between the domestic legal orders and the WTO Agreement in the sense that the WTO Agreement directly determines the content of the domestic law of WTO Members without allowing them to craft their policies autonomously.

30 Regulations of Fuels and Fuel Additives, 40 C.F.R. §80.94 (2008).

31 62 Fed. Reg. 45533, 45535 (1997).

Bibliography

Bodansky, D. (1999), "The Legitimacy of International Governance: A Coming Challenge for International Environmental Law?", 93 *American Journal of International Law* 596.

Bodansky, D. (2006), "Constitutionalism in International Law: Comment on a Proposal from Germany", 47 *Harvard International Law Journal* 223.

Bogdandy, A. von (2006), "Constitutionalism in International Law: Comment on a Proposal from Germany", 47 *Harvard International Law Journal* 223, 235–236.

Bolton, J.R. (2000), "Should We Take Global Governance Seriously?", 1 *Chicago Journal of International Law* 205.

Cass, D.Z. (2005), *The Constitutionalization of the World Trade Organization: Legitimacy, Democracy, and Community in the International Trading System*, Oxford: Oxford University Press.

Charnovitz, S. (2000), "Opening the WTO to Nongovernmental Interests", 24 *Fordham International Law Journal* 173.

Charnovitz, S. (2002), "WTO Cosmopolitics", 34 *NYU Journal of International Law and Politics* 299.

Crawford, J. (1993) "Democracy and International Law", 64 *British Year Book of International Law* 113.

Crawford, J. (2006), *The Creation of States in International Law*, Oxford: Clarendon Press.

Dahl, R.A. (1998), *On Democracy*, New Haven: Yale University Press.

Esty, D.C. (1998), "Non-Governmental Organizations at the World Trade Organization: Cooperation, Competition, or Exclusion", 1 *Journal of International Economic Law* 123.

Franck, T.M. (1990). *The Power of Legitimacy Among Nations*. Oxford: Oxford University Press.

Franck, T.M. (1992). "The Emerging Right to Democratic Governance", 86 *American Journal of International Law* 46.

Fukunaga, Y. (2006), "Securing Compliance through the WTO Dispute Settlement System: Implementation of DSB Recommendations", 9 *Journal of International Economic Law* 383.

Fukunaga, Y. (2007), "Participation of Private Parties in the WTO Dispute Settlement Processes: Treatment of Unsolicited Amicus Curiae Submissions", 4 *Soochow Law Journal* 99.

Fukunaga, Y. (2008), "Civil Society and the Legitimacy of the WTO Dispute Settlement System", 34 *Brooklyn Journal of International Law* 85.

Fukunaga, Y. (2009), "Discontinuity in the Internalization of the World Trade Organization Rules: Assessing the Democratic Deficit Critique against the World Trade Organization Dispute Settlement System", 46 *Alberta Law Review* 1039.

Held, D. (1995), *Democracy and the Global Order: From the Modern State to Cosmopolitan Governance*, Stanford: Stanford University Press.

Howse, R. (2000), "Adjudicative Legitimacy and Treaty Interpretation in International Trade Law: The Early Years of WTO Jurisprudence", in J.H.H. Weiler ed., *The EU, the WTO and the NAFTA: Towards a Common Law of International Trade*, Oxford: Oxford University Press.

Howse, R. (2002), "The Boundaries of the WTO: From Politics to Technocracy – and Back Again: The Fate of the Multilateral Trading Regime", 96 *American Journal of International Law* 94.

Howse, R. and Nicolaïdis, K. (1998), "Legitimacy and Global Governance: Why Constitutionalizing the WTO is a Step Too Far", in R.B. Porter, P. Sauvé, A. Submanian and A.B. Zampetti eds., *Efficiency, Equity, and Legitimacy: The Multilateral Trading System at the Millennium*, Washington, DC: Brookings Institution Press.

Jackson, J.H. (2003), "Sovereignty-Modern: A New Approach to an Outdated Concept", 97 *American Journal of International Law* 782.

Jacobson, H.K. and Weiss E.B. (1995), "Strengthening Compliance with International Environmental Accords: Preliminary Observations from a Collective Project", 1 *Global Governance* 119.

Keohane, R.O. and Nye, J.S. Jr. (2001), "The Club Model of Multilateral Cooperation and Problems of Democratic Legitimacy", in R.B. Porter, P. Sauvé, A. Submanian and A.B. Zampetti eds, *Efficiency, Equity, and Legitimacy: The Multilateral Trading System at the Millennium* ,Washington, DC: Brookings Institution Press.

Keohane, R.O., Moravcsik, A. and Slaughter, A.M. (2001), "Legalized Dispute Resolution: Interstate and Transnational", in J. Goldstein, M. Kahler, R.O. Keohane and A.M. Slaughter eds., *Legalization and World Politics*, Cambridge: The MIT Press.

Koh, H.H. (1996), "Transnational Legal Process", 75 *Nebraska Law Review* 181.

Koh, H.H. (1997), "Why Do Nations Obey International Law?", 106 *Yale Law Journal* 2599.

Mackenzie, R., Romano, C.P.R. and Shany, Y. with Sands, P. (2010), *Manual on International Courts and Tribunals*, Oxford: Oxford University Press.

McGinnis, J.O. and Movsesian, M.L. (2000), "The World Trade Constitution", 114 *Harvard Law Review* 511.

McRae, D. (2003), "Trade and the Environment: Competition, Cooperation or Confusion?", 41 *Alberta Law Review* 745.

Nichols, P.M. (2004), "Extension of Standing in World Trade Organization Disputes to Nongovernment Parties", 25 *University of Pennsylvania Journal of International Economic Law* 669.

Oyane, S. (2005), "Compliance with International Norms and Domestic Politics: A Constructivist Analysis of Japan – Agricultural Products", in T. Kawase and I. Araki eds, *Implementation System under the WTO Dispute Settlement Mechanism*, Tokyo: Sanseido. (In Japanese)

Petersmann, E.U. (2001), "Human Rights and International Economic Law in the 21st Century: The Need to Clarify Their Interrelationships", *4 Journal of International Economic Law* 3.

Schneider, A.K. (1998), "Democracy and Dispute Resolution: Individual Rights in International Organizations", 19 *University of Pennsylvania. Journal of International Economic Law* 587.

Schultz, J. (1995), "The GATT/WTO Committee on Trade and the Environment – Toward Environmental Reform", 89 *American Journal of International Law* 423.

Shaffer, G.C. (2003), *Defending Interests: Public-Private Partnerships in WTO Litigation*, Washington, DC: Brookings Institution Press.

Slaughter, A.M. (2000), "Building Global Democracy", 1 *Chicago Journal of International Law* 223.

Stein, E. (2001), "International Integration and Democracy: No Love at First Sight", 95 *American Journal of International Law* 489.

United Nations (UN) (2005), World Summit Outcome, G.A. Res. 60/1, para.73, UN Doc. A/Res/60/1, 24 October.

Weber, M. (1978), *Economy and Society: An Outline of Interpretive Sociology*, Berkeley: University of California Press.

Weiler, J.H.H (2002), "The Rule of Lawyers and the Ethos of Diplomats: Reflections on the Internal and External Legitimacy of WTO Dispute Settlement", 13 *American Review of International Arbitration* 177.

Weiler, J.H.H. and Motoc, I. (2003), "Taking Democracy Seriously: The Normative Challenges to the International Legal System", in S. Griller ed., *International Economic Governance and Non-Economic Concerns*, Wien: Springer.

Zampetti, A.B. (2003), "Democratic Legitimacy in the World Trade Organization: The Justice Dimension", 37 *Journal of World Trade* 105.

Website

WTO opens panel proceeding to public for the first time, WTO News (12 September 2005) Online. Available at http://www.wto.org/english/news_e/news05_e/openpanel_12sep_e.htm (accessed: 25 December, 2011).

WTO Panel and Appellate Body Reports

Panel Report, *Japan – Measures Affecting the Importation of Apples* [*Japan – Apples*], WT/DS245/R (15 July 2003).

Panel Report, *Japan – Measures Affecting Agricultural Products* [*Japan – Agricultural Products*], WT/DS76/R (27 October 1998).

Panel Report, *United States – Import Prohibition of Certain Shrimp and Shrimp Products* [*US – Shrimp*], WT/DS58/R (15 May 1998).

Panel Report, *European Communities – Anti-Dumping Measure on Farmed Salmon from Norway*, WT/DS337/R (16 November 2007).
Panel Report, *European Communities – Measures Concerning Meat and Meat Products (Hormones)* [*EC – Hormones*], WT/DS26/R, WT/DS48/R (18 August 1997).
Panel Report, *United States – Standards for Reformulated and Conventional Gasoline* [*US – Gasoline*], WT/DS2/R (29 January 1996).
Appellate Body Report, *United States – Definitive Anti-Dumping and Countervailing Duties on Certain Products from China* [*China – Autos*], WT/DS379AB/R (15 March 2011).
Appellate Body Report, *Mexico – Tax Measures on Soft Drinks and Other Beverages* [*Mexico – Soft Drinks*], WT/DS308/AB/R (6 March 2006).
Appellate Body Report, *Japan – Apples*, WT/DS245/AB/R (26 November 2003).
Appellate Body Report, *United States – Imposition of Countervailing Duties on Certain Hot-Rolled Lead and Bismuth Carbon Steel Products Originating in the United Kingdom* [*US – Lead and Bismuth II*], WT/DS138/AB/R (10 May 2000).
Appellate Body Report, *Japan – Agricultural Products*, WT/DS76/AB/R (22 February 1999).
Appellate Body Report, *US – Shrimp*, WT/DS58/AB/R (12 October 1998).

WTO, Government, and Other

62 Fed. Reg. 45533, 45535 (1997).
Communication from the Chairman of the Panels, *United States – Continued Suspension of Obligations* in the *EC – Hormones* Dispute (WT/DS320), *Canada – Continued Suspension of Obligations* in the *EC – Hormones* Dispute (WT/DS321), WT/DS320/8, WT/DS321/8 (2 August 2005).
Contribution by the Separate Customs Territory of Taiwan, Penghu, Kinmen and Matsu to the Doha Mandated Review of the Dispute Settlement Understanding (DSU): Communication from the Separate Customs Territory of Taiwan, Penghu, Kinmen and Matsu [Taiwan Proposal], TN/DS/W/25 (27 November 2002).
Contribution of Canada to the Improvement of the WTO Dispute Settlement Understanding: Communication from Canada, TN/DS/W/41 (24 January 2003).
Contribution of the European Communities and Its Member States to the Improvement of the WTO Dispute Settlement Understanding: Communication from the European Communities [EU Proposal], TN/DS/W/1 (13 March 2002).
Contribution of the United States on Some Practical Considerations in Improving the Dispute Settlement Understanding of the WTO Related to Transparency and Open Meetings: Communication from the United States, TN/DS/W/79 (13 July 2005).
Contribution of the United States to the Improvement of the Dispute Settlement Understanding of the WTO Related to Transparency: Communication from the United States [US Proposal], TN/DS/W/13 (22 August 2002).
Contributions towards the Improvement and Clarification of the WTO Dispute Settlement Understanding: Communication from Jordan, TN/DS/W/43 (28 January 2003).
Council Regulation (EC) No.125/2008 of 12 February 2008 (OJ L 40 14.2.2008).
Council Regulation (EC) No.356/95 of 20 February 1995 (OJ L 41, 23.2.1995).
European Community: Declaration on Yugoslavia and on the Guidelines on the Recognition of New States, 31 *I.L.M.* 1485 (1992).
High-Level Panel on Threats, Challenges, and Change, Report of the Secretary General's High-Level Panel on Threats, Challenges, and Change, A More Secure World: Our Shared Responsibility (2004).

Negotiations on the Dispute Settlement Understanding: Proposal by the African Group [African Group Proposal], TN/DS/W/15 (25 September 2002).

Negotiations on the Dispute Settlement Understanding: Proposals on DSU by Cuba, Honduras, India, Malaysia, Pakistan, Sri Lanka, Tanzania and Zimbabwe, TN/DS/W/18 (7 October 2002).

Regulations of Fuels and Fuel Additives, 40 C.F.R. §80.94 (2008).

Statute of the International Court of Justice, Art. 46, 26 June 1945, 59 Stat. 1055, 33 U.N.T.S.

Statute of the International Tribunal for the Law of the Sea (Annex VI of the United Nations Convention on the Law of the Sea).

Understanding on rules and procedures governing the settlement of disputes (DSU) 1994.

World Trade Organization (OJ L 349, 31.12.1994).

4 Why should there be public knowledge and understanding of East Asia's regional trade disputes?

Chin Leng Lim[1]

Introduction

In the last ten years, there has been a proliferation of Regional Trade Agreements (RTAs)[2] in the East Asian region.[3] Parties to RTAs are free to choose between various models of dispute settlement, but we might also ask what sort of trade dispute settlement model East Asian countries should adopt. Should they choose "closed" or "open" models of trade dispute settlement design, especially in light of the debate on increasing the transparency of WTO dispute settlement? Should trade dispute proceedings be open to the public, and should arbitral tribunals and panels receive unsolicited amicus curiae briefs? East Asia – comprising the Northeast and Southeast Asian sub-regions – deserves our attention because this vast region promises to be a melting pot of ideas about trade rule design in light of the emergence in recent years of "trans-continental" RTAs between the United States (US) and Asian nations, as well as the entry of Canada, Australia, the European Communities (EC) and others into the RTA race in the wider Asia-Pacific.

US RTAs, for example, have conformed to an open model.[4] Others, such as Australia's FTAs, have been more equivocal and have adopted both transparent and closed regimes. This, presumably, is a result of individual negotiating dynamics and possibilities as much as it involves questions about Australia's foreign policy priorities. On the other hand, the Association of Southeast Asian Nations (ASEAN) has resisted an open model, either in the dispute settlement system for the ASEAN Free Trade Area (AFTA),[5] or under the various ASEAN 'Plus One" FTAs with China (the China-ASEAN FTA),[6] Korea (the Korea-ASEAN FTA),[7] Japan (the Japan-ASEAN FTA, hereafter "Japan-ASEAN"),[8] and with Australia and New Zealand ("AANZFTA").[9] Many ASEAN and East Asian countries are also the ones arguing against further transparency in Geneva's dispute settlement system (e.g. regarding public submissions, open proceedings and amicus curiae briefs). They argue that transparency threatens the intergovernmental nature of the system, making East Asia and the wider Asia-Pacific region an important site in which such debate now takes place.

The second section addresses some of the main arguments for having greater transparency in trade dispute settlement. The third section discusses developments in East Asia and the Asia-Pacific. The fourth section evaluates the likelihood of greater transparency in East Asian trade dispute settlement design as these nations begin to integrate their economies between themselves, and also with their trading partners within the broader Asia-Pacific and beyond. An argument against resorting to cultural and democratic explanations of (and prescriptions for) East Asian treaty behavior in favor of a pragmatic understanding which accepts both the entrenchment of an East Asian, "closed" model of trade dispute settlement and the limited success of democratic arguments thus far in modifying the treaty behavior of these nations, is put forward. Democratically-informed scholarship is more likely to have an impact on East Asia's current and future trans-continental trading partners although this chapter does not claim that "Western" FTAs are prime exemplars of cosmopolitanism. There is simply a greater likelihood of receptivity to cosmopolitan ideals in the diplomatic and trade treaty-related behavior of a number of Western trading nations. As we will go on to see, the United States and the EU have championed greater transparency in WTO trade dispute settlement.

In any event, what we are seeing today is the emergence of a new, "for export" model of trade dispute settlement design within East Asia where East Asian nations sometimes find themselves negotiating trans-continental deals with Western nations. Taken alongside East Asia's own "closed" treaty model, we are therefore beginning to see two different treaty models of trade dispute settlement emerge from within the Asian region. While this new phenomenon seems real enough, its causes may be harder to explain. Could it be that some East Asian trading nations now believe that trade agreements ought to conform to cosmopolitan ideals? Can the "West" now expect this of East Asia? This chapter argues against the view that there has been any significant change in fundamental beliefs within East Asian policy circles. East Asia's own closed model is almost invariably employed when East Asians enter into intra-regional treaties. The more cosmopolitan arrangement under the Trans-Pacific Strategic Partnership Agreement, which we will discuss further below,[10] may be explained precisely on the basis that it is meant to form the basis of a cross-Pacific deal with trading partners for whom, presumably, cosmopolitanism is something more than a convenience.

Five contemporary arguments for having greater transparency in trade dispute settlement

A brief overview of some of the main arguments in favor of having an "open" model of trade dispute settlement may be useful, before looking at the current forms of East Asian treaty behavior.

1. "*The WTO Dispute System is a Law Court*". The first argument relies on the fact that the WTO's dispute settlement system already resembles a judicial process.[11] According to this argument, if the WTO dispute system *is* a judicial system, or is closely akin to one, then it should be "open" in the same way that judicial proceedings elsewhere, both domestically and internationally, are both public and transparent.[12] Insofar as many East Asian RTAs have

adopted the WTO as a "benchmark", these RTA systems should therefore be judged against a WTO/judicial standard of openness. The argument turns on the nature or true character of the WTO system – whether the WTO model is truly a judicial model today, or still resembles a "diplomatic" model of trade dispute settlement. We will see that it contains elements of both.

2. "*The Trend Today is for the World Trade Court to Become More Open*". A second argument has to do with the perception that there is now a *trend* towards having more transparency in WTO dispute settlement. According to this argument, if the WTO system is becoming more transparent,[13] then closed RTA dispute systems which mimic or copy the WTO dispute settlement system are increasingly in danger of being inconsistent with that which they had set out to copy.[14]
3. "*Democracy and Cosmopolitanism as International Legal Ideals*". A third, related argument has to do with debate about what the WTO system (and RTA dispute systems) *should*, ideally, become. WTO dispute settlement *should* continue to move towards an open model and become more transparent. "Closed" models should be avoided. One reason for saying this is that there is an emerging international law principle of democratic governance which, in turn, is related to cosmopolitan ideals. In this chapter, however, we will refer to two meanings of cosmopolitanism which have been adapted to the trade policy context. The first refers to a theory of politics founded upon the notions of individual freedom, choice and autonomy (i.e. normative individualism, or the idea that our moral concepts refer, in the last analysis, to individual rights). According to this first meaning, the State qua treaty actor should act in ways which respect and promote individual freedom, choice and autonomy.[15] A basic requirement of sovereign trade treaty behavior therefore is that such behavior should be known to individual citizens in the first place, without such knowledge the citizen will be unable to exercise freely a consumer choice. [16] In such a case, the State acts illegitimately. Typically, such choices will relate to particular trade policy outcomes, including the outcomes of trade disputes. Secondly, "cosmopolitics" – a term coined by Pascal Lamy – has now become a term of art. It refers to a counter-Statist view of the world trading order; one which embraces non-governmental, non-sovereign participation and debate.[17] In the first sense, the State's internal legitimacy is at stake, while the second sense of the term "cosmopolitanism" implicates the legitimacy of the world trading system.
4. "*Legitimacy is Functionally Important*". A fourth argument is that an undemocratic or anti-democratic dispute settlement system lacks popular legitimacy, feeds the globalization backlash, and threatens the functioning, health and long-term viability of both the global trading system and regional trading systems.[18] This argument responds to the various criticisms of the WTO following events in Seattle in 1999.[19] These range from dissatisfaction over the loss of jobs (e.g. Ross Perot's reference to a "giant sucking sound going South"),[20] to the environmental impact of economic globalization, as well as human and labor rights concerns over the proliferation of Third World

sweatshops. Friends of the WTO generally believe tragic misunderstanding underlies these criticisms about what the WTO is and what it does. They argue that such doubt can be dispelled if only there were greater knowledge about the WTO – i.e. greater transparency in what it does,[21] and better understanding of how its dispute settlement system works.[22] Their arguments are not confined to saving the WTO system. Perot was talking about NAFTA.[23]

5. "*Democratic Nations Must Push for Democratic Dispute Regimes*". A fifth argument has to do with the need for "policy coherence" between the domestic political regimes of individual RTA countries and the supra-national RTA systems they create. Thus democratic nations should advocate open, democratic trade dispute settlement in their RTA negotiations or risk undermining democracy both at home and abroad.[24] While admitting that trade policy probably cannot be used internationally to promote periodic elections,[25] such proponents argue that it can nonetheless be used to promote ancillary values – e.g. accountability, openness and transparency.

These arguments merit a closer examination, even if they require rehearsal of some old debates.

Is there a World Trade Court?

A judicial system?

The WTO dispute settlement system (DSS) today represents a far more "judicialized" regime than the GATT regime of old which evinced a "nuanced diplomatic style of adjudication".[26] It is argued that the WTO dispute settlement system should, therefore, be just as transparent. To quote Zimmermann:[27]

> It is held that the lack of transparency in WTO dispute settlement emanates from the 'old' diplomatic model of dispute settlement where compromise was encouraged and confidentiality played an important role. In the litigation setting of a more judicial dispute settlement system, withholding litigation documents would no longer be appropriate. By contrast, opponents to more transparency argue that the government-to-government nature of the WTO should be preserved. Enhanced transparency would only lead to increased public pressure on negotiators and thereby preclude mutually agreed settlements.

Likewise, Mercurio and Laforgia have argued that:[28]

> It should come as no surprise that . . . the GATT was, and the WTO is, a member-driven organization . . . Moreover . . . the dispute settlement process in the GATT began as conciliation . . . However, as the system moved towards an adjudicatory model, the reasons for keeping the process closed became less persuasive.

The view that the WTO system resembles adjudication is unobjectionable in itself. But it is a different matter when "adjudication" as a shorthand expression for describing WTO dispute settlement becomes a statement about what *all* trade dispute settlement should be about. In any event, the fact that the WTO has moved towards adjudication, and resembles adjudication, does not make it so in the strictest sense of the word.

Arbitration and international adjudication are distinguishable by the feature that both result in legally binding decisions or awards. Transparency is not a traditional distinguishing feature. In that sense they are no different from resort to good offices, conciliation and mediation which typically occur behind closed doors. Even as transparency increasingly becomes a feature of international adjudication and inter-state arbitration, the WTO and RTA dispute systems remain distinguishable on this score precisely because of their confidential nature. That is why WTO dispute settlement is said to contain "vestiges of the diplomatic model" of dispute settlement.[29]

There are other features to consider. First, WTO panel and Appellate Body reports are not binding awards. They require adoption by a political body – the WTO Dispute Settlement Body.[30] No court reports to a political body and seeks political approval of its judgments, and even with *adopted* panel and Appellate Body reports (i.e. those which have already been adopted by the Dispute Settlement Body (DSB)) there is still the view that they do not impose legally binding obligations as such.[31]

Second, to the extent that the WTO Dispute Settlement Mechanism (DSM) resembles arbitration, it resembles arbitration only in its archaic form. In previous times, a friendly sovereign who is asked to arbitrate a dispute between two nations might entrust the matter to experts who will then make their recommendation to that sovereign in due course. The friendly ruler "adopts" their recommendation and issues a "binding award".[32] If that sounds familiar, it is precisely what the DSB does as a body comprising all the members of the WTO. The adopted report thereby enjoys the imprimatur of the whole membership, almost all of whom are sovereigns, much like enlisting the services of a powerful monarch as arbitrator. In this respect too, WTO dispute settlement still retains the features of diplomatic settlement.

Third, the degree of control which disputing parties wish to exert over the dispute settlement process, particularly over the selection of arbitrators, distinguishes WTO panel settlement from international adjudication. One of the issues debated from time-to-time has been the proposal for the WTO to have "permanent" panelists. The European Communities have formally proposed such an arrangement, for example,[33] although the proposal goes back as far as 1998.[34] Yet, to date, the WTO does not have such a permanent set-up for panels. Instead, an ad hoc appointments system *characteristic* of arbitration currently exists and is likely to remain so on account of the current lack of support for a permanent panel body (PPB).[35] In fact, some of the arguments made against the idea of permanent panelists are reminiscent of arbitration.[36] They have to do with the extent to which the sovereign members *should* exercise some degree of control over the dispute settlement process.[37]

Fourth, consultations are secret and may occur in parallel with dispute settlement proceedings.[38] In that regard too, WTO dispute settlement continues to retain elements of diplomatic settlement. If it resembles arbitration, it again represents that "older" model which is often associated with secrecy.[39] In diplomatic arbitration, such secrecy may extend to the fact or the content of negotiations to resolve a dispute.[40] Arbitrations of such kind have probably not fallen entirely into disuse even today.[41]

It is therefore an exaggeration to say that the WTO dispute settlement is adjudicatory, and to draw from that metaphysical finding the proposition that all trade dispute settlement should represent domestic court proceedings. At most, it may be said that WTO dispute settlement resembles international adjudication in some important aspects.[42] As for the WTO system's resemblance to arbitration, there are many forms of arbitration lying along an imaginary spectrum, and the WTO system still contains significant elements which fall towards the diplomatic end of that spectrum.

Still a diplomatic body

Admittedly, saying that no court submits its ruling to the approval of a political body is not the end of the matter altogether. The adoption by the Dispute Settlement Body (DSB) of the panel or Appellate Body report is virtually automatic under the WTO's Dispute Settlement Understanding (DSU) due to the operation of a reverse consensus rule – so long as one DSB member favors adoption, the report will be adopted.[43] And however much the DSB is a political body, the Appellate Body is not,[44] and political debate in the DSB does not affect the panel and Appellate Body report adoption process as such.[45]

What truly makes the WTO Dispute Settlement System a diplomatic mechanism is that in the case of adjudication the winning plaintiff cannot *negate* a judicial ruling. In the case of the WTO, the wining plaintiff, acting with the consent of the other WTO members in the DSB, can – in principle, at least – seek the non-approval of a ruling of a panel or the Appellate Body. The WTO dispute system was designed to cure the situation where the losing party could block the adoption of a GATT panel report, but it was probably not designed to deal with the situation where the winning party, or the party which brought the claim, refuses the adoption of the report.[46] While this seems unlikely to occur often in practice, it does show that the system is unlike a domestic court. The WTO system does not fully separate political rule from judicial rule. The WTO's political branch holds sway over its "adjudicatory" system notwithstanding the fact that the DSU's "negative consensus" rule is often easily, even routinely, met.[47]

Is there a "trend" towards greater transparency?

In Geneva, the transparency debate was, first, sparked by the leakage of panel reports. This resulted in questions about whether Members could actually discuss pending cases. It was against this backdrop that debate arose about the merits of having greater transparency,[48] leading to diplomatic proposals being put forward by the United States and Canada.[49]

Among the reasons given for greater transparency has been the need to secure heightened legitimacy for the dispute settlement system, and the futility of concealing parties' arguments where panel reports will eventually become public anyway. Another factor was the wider policy argument that greater openness is generally a good thing in trade policy – it leads to a "Dracula effect" ("exposing evil to sunlight helps to destroy it").[50] This view is well captured in James Bacchus' plea:[51]

> We must open the doors of the WTO, and . . . let in the light of public scrutiny. We must let the five billion people in the world who are served by the WTO see the WTO . . . if we do not, the Members of the WTO will never secure the increased public support that will be needed worldwide to continue to maximize all the mutual gains that can be made from trade through a ruled-based world trading system.

Much depends however on what we mean by "transparency". According to Bacchus, it does not mean that panel deliberations should be exposed. He admits that no court does this. But panel proceedings, Appellate Body oral hearings, and Dispute Settlement Body meetings must be open (some of this is already beginning to happen). Likewise, unsolicited amicus curiae briefs should be accepted by panels and the Appellate Body.[52]

Others, such as the United States, go further. It has not only proposed that panel, Appellate Body and arbitration proceedings should be open to the public, but that parties' submissions too should be made public except for sections involving confidential information.[53] Canada made the same proposal,[54] while the EC has proposed a slightly different version of the argument – i.e. that within 10 days of panel establishment, the parties should agree on whether the proceedings should be open to the public in whole or in part.[55] According to the EC proposal, the first substantive hearing could also be divided into two sections – one which is open to the public, and the other closed. Amongst the Asian countries, Japan too called for parties' submissions to be made public within two weeks of each meeting.[56]

However, other Asian and developing countries such as Mexico, Malaysia, Egypt, India, Taiwan and the African Group strongly opposed this view.[57] The Asian states had previously played a notable role in resisting unsolicited amicus curiae briefs by (unsuccessfully) opposing the legal power of panels and the Appellate Body to receive them.[58] Other WTO Members have also opposed making WTO proceedings and submissions public on account of the intergovernmental nature of the WTO dispute settlement system. For example, Brazil, Chile, India, Mexico and Uruguay have voiced their opposition to the possibility of "media trials".[59] Likewise with Norway's concern with external pressure from interest groups,[60] while Switzerland has expressed the over-riding concern that public access might actually prevent settlement in individual cases.[61]

Even if in other respects there is already a trend towards greater WTO transparency (e.g. in the declassification of WTO documents, and so forth),[62] the dissenting voices amongst the Membership still need to be accounted for. One of the most significant reasons given for saying that there is now a trend towards openness ignores this fact. Much depends upon how we should view the Appellate Body's 2005 ruling in the *EC – Hormones* compliance case. There, the Appellate Body allowed proceedings to be made public through closed-circuit television. The Appellate Body reasoned that nothing in the rules precluded the parties from opening up the hearings to observers *if the parties so chose*.[63] But that ruling, precisely because it reflects only the views and agreement of the parties in that case, cannot be taken to support a more general view, that:[64]

> This decision provides further evidence that not only is the WTO moving away from the closed system, but that FTAs that narrowly interpret the mechanisms based on WTO provisions may now contradict the very system they copied.

No RTA party would disagree with the view that dispute proceedings could, or even should, be opened up *if* the parties jointly agreed to do so. It is a useful juncture to introduce a silent but significant development on the Asia-Pacific RTA scene. The Trans-Pacific Strategic Economic Partnership Agreement (currently comprising a potential treaty basis of the Trans-Pacific Partnership talks between New Zealand, Singapore, Chile, Brunei, Australia, Vietnam, Peru, the United States and Malaysia)[65] provides exceptions to the confidentiality rule should the parties to the dispute agree.[66] Even without such express treaty clauses, nothing should preclude bilateral RTA parties from opening up dispute settlement proceedings (i.e. waiving their rights by agreement) where the matter solely concerns their rights and obligations *inter se*. Presumably the explicit provisions creating the exceptions under the Trans-Pacific SEP Agreement were thought necessary because of its multilateral nature.

In the case of the *EC – Hormones* ruling, Canada, the US and the EC – the principal proponents of transparency – all agreed to open the hearings.[67] The ruling was based specifically on the joint request of the parties, and while it applies to cases in which the parties so agree, that is not the same thing as saying that the WTO dispute system as a whole is moving away from the closed model. At most, the Appellate Body did not prevent the parties from choosing to adopt a procedure which the rules do not explicitly disallow. It would have been more significant had the Appellate Body ruled that hearings should be open regardless of the views of the parties, or of one of the parties, or if WTO Members other than those very Members which have proposed greater openness were to switch towards making such joint requests in their disputes. None of this has *yet* occurred.

We might welcome the *EC – Hormones* compliance ruling. But to say that there is a "trend" towards an open model, and that RTA parties which have simply "bilateralized" and adopted the DSU in their RTAs are now bound to adopt a more open model overstates the matter. We cannot extrapolate from the wishes of a few members the pattern of things to come.

Democracy as ideal

Should RTAs perform no democratic role at all? With the demise of the Cold War, there has been increased attention since the 1990s on whether international law should uphold a right to democratic governance.[68] Such attention has been concerned with the activities of the Human Rights Committee, the European Court of Human Rights, the European Commission, and the Inter-American Commission in furthering an international law right to democratic governance.[69]

But since RTA dispute settlement bodies also resemble these other international courts, tribunals, and bodies and trade law also involves the application of international legal rules, questions have understandably arisen about whether RTA dispute settlement should promote, or at least not defeat democratic ideals.

Around the same time, fierce debate erupted over the democratic legitimacy of supra-national trade bodies such as the WTO and NAFTA.[70] There was intense scrutiny of the domestic implications of entry into the WTO in the US and the EU leading to congressional hearings in the former and litigation in the case of the latter.[71] One issue had to do with the perceived loss of sovereignty in light of common perceptions about the enormous power which the WTO dispute settlement mechanism wields over national regulatory policies.[72]

It is therefore unsurprising that having greater transparency in RTA dispute systems has also come up for debate. Perhaps the best-known argument for democratic trade decision-making is that offered by Robert Housman. According to Housman, universality may be better secured by infusing trade decision-making and regime design with democratic credentials because this "can help prevent value-based economic clashes".[73] Nonetheless, Housman admits that:[74]

> [B]ecause many of the elements of democratic governance at the national level (for example, the election of representatives in free and fair elections) are inapplicable in the statially oriented world of international trade decision-making . . . [this argument] . . . focuses narrowly on the element of democracy that is most applicable to international relations: the democratic right of citizens to have knowledge of and participate in decisions that will [affect] their interests.

Housman's proposal tries to avoid confusing domestic democratic legitimacy with international legitimacy.[75] He distinguishes the international legitimacy which supra-national trade bodies require from, for example, the kind of view expressed by the US House Majority Leader during the PRC's WTO accession talks – i.e. that trade policy is a democratic tool and "[w]e must look towards expanded trade as a significant opportunity to build greater understanding and encouragement of freedom and democracy".[76] Yet it is doubtful that such a distinction can always be maintained. In practice, an attempt to make trade decision-making and dispute settlement more participatory is just as likely to be seen by a trading partner as an encroachment into its internal affairs. Insofar as democratic arguments could therefore lead potential RTA partners towards a sense of rejection, or cause such countries to conceive the issue as a contest of moral-political values, they are likely to be self-defeating. Questions about RTA design depend ultimately on the consent of the RTA partners. Their resolution therefore involves negotiation not debate.

So how might democratic trade dispute regimes be promoted in East Asia? For many East Asian countries, legitimacy is not always a matter of addressing democratic gaps in public participation but involves the need to secure better public understanding of the intended economic benefits of trade liberalization. Various trade ministry and official RTA websites are largely directed at informing business and voters about these benefits. Why do they not focus on participation in trade policy decision-making, as opposed to commercially useful knowledge and consumer knowledge? We need to distinguish two very different senses of "transparency" – a "thick" and a "thin" sense of the term. The cosmopolitan view, which we described earlier, involves the thick sense of advocating trade policy-related public information, but there is also a thin sense of doing so. East Asian nations do not appear to question the view that members of the public (citizens, workers and consumers) will need to know something about how trade policies will affect them; even if some East Asian nations have questioned the need to introduce greater transparency into WTO trade dispute settlement.[77] So they agree that information about the aims and effects of particular trade policies may have to be communicated to the public. But while cosmopolitanism *requires* the communication of such information, East Asian nations may have entirely extraneous policy reasons to do so as part of an effort to "sell" individual policies (e.g. the benefits of having an FTA programme) to their citizenry. Impressionistically, at least, East Asian nations are less likely to justify their policies along democratic lines but are more likely to talk about anticipated trade and commercial gains. Another reason why providing public information may have nothing to do with upholding cosmopolitan ideals may be gleaned from the observation that few East Asian nations (except Japan) have agreed with the United States and Europe about the principled arguments for having greater transparency at the WTO,[78] and even fewer intra-East Asian FTAs have evinced a high degree of commitment towards fostering greater transparency in their trade dispute settlement *arrangements*.[79]

Finally, it can be counter-productive for democratic trading nations to frame trade negotiations in explicitly democratic terms. This could cause potential RTA partners to doubt the existence of a genuine commitment towards building up a trade relationship, and can backfire.

A heightened search for legitimacy through cosmopolitan engagement

Perhaps what we are searching for is a more pragmatic and attractive version of the democratic argument. One example may be the view that a transparent and accountable international trade decision-making process is more likely to be perceived to be legitimate. The argument arose from the WTO's "legitimacy crisis". It reflects James Bacchus' argument, discussed above, that if the WTO would only let in a little light, such "misunderstandings" might be resolved.[80] In short, different rules or rule-making institutions enjoy differing degrees of "compliance pull" (i.e. perceived legitimacy),[81] and "getting institutional design right" will have a likely bearing on the legitimacy of the particular international body.[82]

To be sure, the WTO as a whole has become more "transparent". Documents have been declassified, and NGO participation has increased.[83] What is less certain is that the WTO's legitimacy crisis had that much to do with transparency in the first place. Complaints about the legitimacy of WTO action are often substantive in nature, not merely procedural or political. In the aftermath of the backlash against the WTO, the current Director-General, Pascal Lamy has called for greater attention to "cosmopolitics" in giving a name to what he sees as a potential solution for the WTO's crisis. The solution furnished responds to a perceived political-procedural need to involve non-governmental stakeholders more closely in the everyday life of the WTO as an organization.[84] While that might address the poor light in which the WTO is sometimes viewed, a number of examples suffice to illustrate that the real problem is not that the WTO suffers from bad press but why it does so.

Saying that the WTO is easily misunderstood is insufficient. Where governmental regulation of the market is justified ultimately on democratic grounds, new limitations on governmental action at the supra-national level naturally leads to concerns over the possible emergence of a "democratic gap". Yet calling for greater citizen participation and accountability treats the difficulty as nothing more than a shallow political or public relations problem while genuine, substantive concerns about commercial fairness and social justice lurk in the background. To take the example of allegations of judicial activism on the part of the Appellate Body in anti-dumping cases,[85] businesses are allowed to express a legitimate concern when it comes to dumping because they are rightly concerned that a level commercial playing field should exist. When businesses that are regulated differently engage in predatory pricing, for example, their competitors are entitled to protest. But when the Appellate Body restricts the freedom of WTO members to employ trade remedies in such cases, the fear arises that unfair trade from abroad cannot be stopped by democratic national processes. In the US, the consent of business to the implementation of the GATT Tokyo Round was based precisely on the promise of having effective trade remedy rules (i.e. in exchange for allowing foreign trade competition). Business accepted more competition provided it was "fair".[86] The Appellate Body's restraints on US trade remedy action constitute the "real problem", not for lack of a better understanding of the Appellate Body. The WTO is "illegitimate" because it is (alleged) to be "unfair",[87] not because people are ignorant about what it does.

For other non-governmental actors, the problem is the reverse. For them, it is not that the WTO limits governmental acts which otherwise would favor business interests, but that it *limits* governmental action which tries to reign in the excesses of the free market. Such concerns about labor and environmental standards were admittedly a part of what Seattle was about, but while some have focused on the lack of unity amongst the Quad countries, the Clinton Administration's lack of fast-track authority or its correspondingly limited ambitions in Seattle, and the disaffection of developing countries as possible explanations,[88] others only cite NGO dissatisfaction as the cause of a crisis at the WTO.[89] Few trade negotiators think that the Seattle talks broke down "because the WTO lacks popular legitimacy". If anything, a well-known, veteran trade negotiator has criticized some developing country delegations for playing to the gallery in Cancun, instead of getting on with the task of the negotiations.[90]

The argument that some of the WTO's difficulties are attributable to an absence of transparency in the way it handles disputes is therefore something of an overstretch. Transparency is important but is unlikely to address the WTO's legitimacy crisis. Professor William Davey, who also favors greater transparency in panel and Appellate Body hearings, presents one of the more careful and considered views:[91]

> I see no problems with having more openness . . . The problem of pressure can be solved by closed-circuit TV, such that the audience can see, but will not be seen . . . the reality is that some disputes draw a great deal of attention. For these high-profile disputes, it is helpful to the credibility of the WTO system at large for those who have an interest in them to see how they are resolved.

While arguing that "given popular fears of globalization and the WTO's connection therewith, such increased credibility can be viewed as essential to ensure the future effectiveness of the WTO itself, as well as the dispute settlement system",[92] Professor Davey admits to having "no empirical evidence to support this claim". In doing so, he comes closer than most writers in asking whether legitimacy and transparency are connected. The Indian delegation has pointed out that such a connection does not exist.[93] So Davey's point is a far more modest one – "openness of this sort would [at least] eliminate an argument that has been effectively used in US newspapers", namely the "reference in full-page advertisements in US newspapers to dispute settlement as involving 'faceless GATT bureaucrats' and 'star chamber proceedings' could no longer be made".[94] His explanation accepts the "transparency" argument for what it is; *a plea for better public relations* but however well-considered, smart and apt, it may have less to do with the legitimacy crisis as such.

At the other extreme, Joseph Stiglitz is less concerned with transparency than with reform. According to Stiglitz, the WTO's legitimacy crisis requires a concerted response to environmental and labor concerns. Transparency is a *means* by which popular opinion may then be brought to bear on panelists and Appellate Body members.[95] The danger in this view is that it comes down to a prescription for panelists and Appellate Body members to decide trade disputes in light of those values which receive the loudest expression and it is difficult to see how that could be more democratic.

In sum, the transparency argument is ultimately too little or too much, depending on the version one favors. Calling for more transparency amounts to saying that the WTO needs better public relations, or that it needs wholesale reform anyway, particularly in the way the linkages are drawn between trade and environmental concerns or trade and labor concerns.[96]

The need to pursue democratically coherent trade policies

Many of these arguments are about the WTO but they also apply to RTAs; either because some RTA dispute systems are modeled after the WTO or because the arguments themselves apply to RTAs by analogy. The democracy argument reflects an ideal to which all trade policy decision-making should aspire. Connected with these arguments for greater democracy and legitimacy is the argument which Mercurio and Laforgia have adapted from Housman and applied to RTAs. Mercurio's and Laforgia's central argument is that democratic nations like Australia should pursue accountable and participatory RTA rules for the likely impact of such a policy in Southeast Asia and the wider Asia-Pacific region. Perhaps this is true. But insofar as Mercurio and Laforgia are suggesting that Australia would, or could successfully, effect a shift from a preference for closed trade dispute settlement towards a preference for open trade disputes,[97] the evidence thus far goes plainly against it.

In the next part, we will look to the actual treaty behavior of Asian members, including those which have actively resisted the US and EC proposals at the WTO.[98]

Settling East Asian trade disputes

Asia and the International Settlement of Disputes

Resort to international adjudication had a slow start in Asia, with the notable exception of India and some of the reasons for Asian conservatism are historic. Nations that are still adapting to the use of formal third-party dispute settlement, unlike other "high-end" and sophisticated users, are simply less likely to innovate and adopt progressive policies. As for the People's Republic of China, Korea and Japan, none have ever brought a case before the International Court of Justice (ICJ).

A more encouraging picture in recent years has been the willingness of Indonesia, Malaysia and Singapore to bring various territorial disputes before the ICJ – in the Indonesia-Malaysia dispute over the islands of *Sipadan* and *Ligitan*,[99] and the Malaysia-Singapore dispute over *Pedra Branca/Pulau Batu Puteh*.[100] The latter had been preceded by another Malaysia-Singapore dispute brought before the International Tribunal for the Law of the Sea (ITLOS).[101] Before that, the last Southeast Asian case which had appeared before the ICJ had involved a 1962 territorial dispute between Cambodia and Thailand.[102]

South Asia, unlike the Northeast and Southeast Asian sub-regions, has produced one case between Portugal and India,[103] and three contentious cases between Pakistan and India.[104] In none of these cases, be they in East or South Asia, was the underlying dispute economic in nature.

In contrast, WTO dispute settlement has been a resounding success in Asia. Japan, India, South Korea and China have been active participants in WTO disputes. The first case ever brought before the WTO involved a dispute between Singapore and Malaysia.[105] With the experience of Japan,[106] India, South Korea,[107] and with China's recent spate of cases,[108] the WTO has unarguably contributed to the reception of formalized dispute settlement in international affairs in Asia. Prior to the establishment of the WTO in 1995, the East Asian nations showed little interest in GATT dispute settlement, Japan being the one notable exception.[109] By mid-2006, however, Korea had emerged as the most active East Asian complainant with 13 cases, compared to 12 each for Japan and Thailand during that period,[110] and by late 2007, India had become the world's second most frequent developing country complainant after Brazil.[111] A notable feature in the last three years has been the sudden spate of cases involving China (both as complainant and respondent) with new disputes constantly emerging.[112]

At the same time, the sheer amount of RTA activity in Asia in recent years has required the greater familiarization of these East Asian nations with the *design* of formal dispute settlement systems for their bilateral and regional trade treaty regimes. Yet as one commentator points out:[113]

> While East Asia[n] countries have been involved in a substantial number of disputes in the WTO . . . they still cling to their non-litigious tradition of the past. This is evidenced by the increasing tendency to participate as co-complainants or third parties and the substantial number of disputes being resolved through consultations. In addition, the lack of expertise in WTO law, as well as the substantial legal costs . . . appear to be major obstacles . . . particularly for developing country Members.

Similarly, East Asian nations participating in the Geneva debate on reforming the WTO Dispute Settlement Understanding have tended to avoid proposals on systemic issues. Japan and Korea, for example, have focused on the so-called "sequencing" issue.[114] China has issued a proposal on increasing third-party participation, while Malaysia has a proposal on the costs of litigation for developing countries.[115]

Such conservatism is reflected in the RTA treaty behavior of these nations. By and large, they have chosen to adapt from the existing WTO dispute settlement system, sometimes wholesale. This clearly does not mean that current attempts by the EU and the US to make the WTO dispute system more transparent will be supported by the East Asian nations. Indeed, the contrary is true. We have seen that while Japan did support the call to make party submissions public, Malaysia and Taiwan have objected to the US-EU proposal. As for the unsolicited submission of amicus curiae briefs by NGOs to panels and the Appellate Body, Hong Kong, Malaysia, China, Japan, the Philippines, Singapore and ASEAN as a whole have consistently objected to panel and Appellate Body acceptance of such briefs.[116]

In the next section, we will go on to see that the design of bilateral FTAs between individual East Asian nations and countries such as the US are another matter altogether. In such cases, the individual East Asian nation are more likely to accept a "US treaty template", for example, when negotiating with the US. We will then go on to see that where East Asian nations such as Brunei and Singapore have participated in the design of regional FTAs which (as with the Trans-Pacific Strategic Partnership Agreement) have not only potential regional adherence, but also a potential trans-continental reach, that conservative intra-East Asian model has been laid aside in favor of a more cosmopolitan treaty model.

Studying East Asia's regional trade treaties

The treaties surveyed in this chapter have been carefully chosen to reflect regional, as opposed to bilateral, treaty behavior. What we are looking for is convergence in regional (i.e. region-wide) treaty behavior and, currently, no one East Asian nation is able to significantly influence or dictate FTA treaty design within the region, or is likely to be able to do so in the future. Individual bilateral treaties concluded by any individual East Asian nation, to the extent that they even exhibit any high degree of design consistency are not likely to provide much indication of region-wide behavior.[117]

In Southeast Asia, countries like Singapore, Malaysia and Thailand, and to a lesser extent Brunei, have concluded various bilateral treaties with both regional and extra-regional trading partners; most famously in the case of Singapore, which has the most extensive network of bilateral FTAs within the region.[118] Likewise, Japan's policy-makers concluded that it should not simply complete a deal with the whole of ASEAN, and proceeded to conclude FTAs with Indonesia, Singapore, Malaysia, the Philippines, Thailand, Brunei and Vietnam within Southeast Asia before concluding the larger Japan-ASEAN deal.[119] Japan had observed how China, which had imagined that it would have to negotiate with one entity – i.e. ASEAN – had ended up in ten separate bilateral negotiations at the outset. In addition, Japan negotiated FTAs with extra-regional partners. Like Japan, Korea too adopted a "simultaneous bilateral FTA policy",[120] and engaged in a host of bilaterals world-wide including bilateral agreements with individual ASEAN nations, while concluding the FTA with ASEAN as a whole. Yet in none of these cases can we see an East Asian model emerge from the specific behavior of any East Asian nation. This may also have to do with the fact that, to date, China, Japan and Korea have not yet been able to conclude a deal between themselves and have instead focused their efforts during the past ten years on concluding their respective trade treaties with ASEAN instead. That is what makes ASEAN, which has also concluded an FTA with China, Korea, and Japan, and an FTA with Australia and New Zealand, and its closed model of dispute settlement so central to any serious study of the regional treaty behavior of the East Asian nations.

Turning from bilateral to regional deals, the Southeast Asian nations were the first to evolve a sub-regional treaty (i.e. under a "closed" model) whose model the People's Republic of China was content to adopt in its FTA with ASEAN.[121] The China-ASEAN FTA is now the largest regional FTA in East Asia. The existence of a China-ASEAN trade treaty spurred Japan and Korea to complete FTAs with ASEAN. Both these treaties also employed the ASEAN model and there are many similarities in the negotiation and design of the China-ASEAN, Korea-ASEAN and Japan-ASEAN treaties.[122] Convergence between the China-ASEAN, Japan-ASEAN and Korea-ASEAN FTAs is what makes it possible to say that there is now an emerging intra-East Asian model.

A notable divergence from this emerging regional model is that provided under the dispute settlement provisions of the Trans-Pacific Strategic Economic Partnership Agreement.[123] It is for this reasons that we have chosen to focus on a comparison between this treaty and the ASEAN, China-ASEAN, Japan-ASEAN and Korea-ASEAN treaties.

Finally, as we are solely concerned with East Asian inter-state *trade* dispute settlement,[124] we will leave aside investor–state dispute settlement provisions under existing East Asian treaties.[125]

ASEAN

Much has been written about Southeast Asia's preference for diplomatic settlement according to the so-called "ASEAN Way" (i.e. via consultation and consensus, as opposed to legal settlement). Following the creation of the ASEAN Free Trade Area (AFTA) in 1991 and its "re-launch" in 1994, ASEAN however moved towards having a dispute settlement system. The result was ASEAN's Protocol on the Dispute Settlement Mechanism of 1996.[126] The most important shift in thinking was the authority given to ASEAN's meeting of Senior Economic Officials (ASEAN SEOM) to issue final and legally binding rulings by *majority* vote.[127] The 1996 Protocol was eventually superseded by the "Protocol on Enhanced Dispute Settlement Mechanism" of 2004 (2004 Protocol). The latter was part of a series of reforms designed to take ASEAN closer to the aim of having an ASEAN Economic Community.[128]

Mirroring the WTO DSM, the 2004 Protocol adopts the WTO's "negative consensus" procedure. A panel shall be established, its report (and in the case of appeals, the report of the ASEAN Appellate Body) shall be adopted unless the SEOM decides by consensus not to do so. Similarly, authorization for the suspension of concessions in case of non-compliance shall be given unless the SEOM decides by consensus not to do so.[129] As in the case of the WTO, the provisions in the Protocol governing ASEAN's panel and Appellate Body procedures are preceded by provision for consultations,[130] good offices, conciliation and mediation.[131] In short, the 2004 Protocol created a regional version of the WTO dispute settlement system.

Under Articles 8 and 12 of the 2004 Protocol, ASEAN panel and Appellate Body deliberations shall be confidential, and reports shall be drafted in the absence of the parties.[132] Article 13(2) provides that while parties' written submissions too "shall be" confidential, a party may publicly disclose its own position. Members shall treat as confidential information submitted by another Member to the panel or the Appellate Body where the information has been designated so. Upon the request of a Member State, however, a non-confidential summary "shall be" provided to such a requesting Member for public disclosure.[133]

The 2004 Protocol expressly states that the "the interests of full transparency" under this ASEAN framework simply means that "presentations, rebuttals and statements . . . shall be made in the presence of [only] the parties".[134] This, clearly, is a far cry from the democratic view of what transparency should mean in trade dispute settlement (discussed above).

Instead, ASEAN adopts a closed model for all its dispute settlement needs, including its trade dispute settlement requirements.

Trade dispute settlement in ASEAN's agreements with China, Korea, Japan, Australia and New Zealand

Introduction

The emergence of the 2004 ASEAN protocol coincided with the proliferation of East Asian RTAs.[135] It was a period during which various proposals for East Asian economic integration were also heard, including proposals for an agreement between ASEAN, China, Japan, and South Korea, and possibly extending to the inclusion of Australia and New Zealand and India as well. In addition, there have been proposals for an agreement between the 21 members of APEC,[136] and a wider proposal by Australia's erstwhile Rudd Administration to have the 21 APEC economies and India within a single "Asia Pacific Community".[137] Together with the individual, mainly bilateral, RTAs recently concluded or pursued by China, Korea, Japan, Australia, New Zealand and virtually all the individual ASEAN countries, these larger initiatives form part of a complex network of intra-regional and extra-regional, trans-continental RTAs which aim to connect the East Asian and Asia-Pacific economies with each other, as well as with East Asia's trading partners in other continents.

The first major step towards a broader, regional – as opposed to a purely bilateral – model was the China-ASEAN FTA. There had been an earlier proposal for China-Japan-Korea-ASEAN economic integration, but failing consensus at the ASEAN Economic Ministers' Meeting (AEM) in Chiengmai in October 2000, the Chair had proposed separate RTAs between ASEAN and China, ASEAN and Japan, as well as ASEAN and Korea. Between 2001 and 2009, ASEAN accordingly began concluding RTAs with China (the China-ASEAN FTA), Korea (the Korea-ASEAN FTA), Japan (Japan-ASEAN), India (AIFTA), and with Australia and New Zealand (AANZFTA).[138] In each case, the dispute settlement provisions provide for the submission of inter-state disputes to arbitration.[139]

Closed proceedings and confidential submissions in trade disputes

A "closed" dispute settlement model akin to ASEAN's 2004 Protocol was adopted in ASEAN's FTAs with China, Korea, Japan, Australia and New Zealand. All these treaties contain explicit rules requiring closed proceedings and the confidentiality of written submissions. These rules are substantially similar to those adopted in the 2004 ASEAN Protocol.[140]

Arbitrators' confidentiality obligation

There is an even closer resemblance between the China-ASEAN, Korea-ASEAN, Japan-ASEAN and ASEAN-Australia-New Zealand FTAs. Unlike ASEAN's 2004 Protocol, ASEAN's agreements with these nations provide for an arbitration tribunal. Nonetheless, there remain subtle differences even between these latter treaties. For example, the China-ASEAN FTA and the Japan-ASEAN FTA are silent where the Korea-ASEAN FTA and the AANZFTA expressly impose an obligation of confidentiality upon the "members of the arbitral panel and the persons retained by the arbitral panel", permitting only the disclosure of information which is already in the public domain.[141]

While arbitrators are generally bound by an ethical duty to maintain confidentiality notwithstanding the China-ASEAN FTA's and the Japan-ASEAN FTA's silence,[142] it is noteworthy that the Korea-ASEAN FTA and AANZFTA chose to make this a matter of express treaty obligation and to extend that treaty obligation to persons retained by the arbitral panel.

Rules governing the presence of parties and third-parties

ASEAN's trade deals with China, Korea, Japan, and with Australia and New Zealand also state – in somewhat curious language – that the parties are allowed to be present only when invited to do so by the tribunal.[143] This drafting language is derived from the ASEAN 2004 Protocol's Panel Working Procedures.[144] With the exception of the China-ASEAN Dispute Settlement Agreement, each treaty also makes express provision for third-parties to be heard.[145] However, while the Japan-ASEAN and Korea-ASEAN FTAs envisage a session being set aside during the first meeting for this purpose, and also provides explicitly for the presence of third-parties "during the entirety of this session", the AANZFTA only states that third-parties "shall have an opportunity to be heard by the arbitral tribunal at its first substantive meeting with the Parties to the dispute".[146]

The AANZFTA's more restrictive formulation seems to have been derived from the ASEAN 2004 Protocol's provision for third parties.[147] Nonetheless, any practical difference between the ASEAN 2004 Protocol and AANZFTA, or between these and the Japan-ASEAN and Korea-ASEAN FTAs would be more apparent than real. Both the AANZFTA and the ASEAN 2004 Protocol go on to provide for an entire session being set aside for third-parties in their respective tribunal and panel working procedures instead.[148]

Confidentiality of tribunal deliberations

ASEAN's 2004 Protocol,[149] and ASEAN's FTAs with China, Korea, and Japan, as well as with Australia and New Zealand state that a tribunal's internal "deliberations" shall be confidential.[150]

Notably, the AANZFTA's Annex and the Korea-ASEAN FTA contemplate the retention of assistants, interpreters and translators,[151] and while only tribunal members may "take part" in the deliberations,[152] such deliberations shall be kept confidential by tribunal members as well as persons retained by the tribunal.[153] ASEAN's 2004 Protocol, and ASEAN's FTAs with China, Korea and Japan contain express language forbidding the parties to be present during the "drafting" of the award.[154]

Keeping the existence of a dispute confidential

The more noteworthy difference between the 2004 Protocol and the China-ASEAN, Korea-ASEAN and Japan-ASEAN FTAs lies in the fact that the latter treaties require the final report of the arbitral panel to be made publicly available within 10 days of the report being presented to the parties.[155] AANZFTA contains a similar rule, stating that:[156]

> The arbitral tribunal shall provide its final report to all other Parties seven days after the report is presented to the Parties to the dispute, and at any time thereafter a Party to the dispute may make the report publicly available subject to the protection of any confidential information contained in the report.

The significance of this is that, in principle, the very existence of a dispute solely between ASEAN Members *could* be kept secret; whereas a dispute arising under ASEAN's FTAs with China, Korea, and Japan, and under the AANZFTA, must eventually be disclosed.

Enter the United States, and the Trans-Pacific Strategic Economic Partnership Agreement

Future agreements with the US, Canada and the EU could alter Asia's emerging approach towards dispute settlement. Individual agreements with the United States such as the US-Singapore FTA,[157] the US-Australia FTA,[158] and the Korea-US FTA demonstrate elements of, and adherence to, an open model.[159] But despite debate at the WTO, the intra-East Asian and Australasian RTAs have thus far demonstrated a preference for closed dispute settlement.

So East Asia now has two co-existing models for trade dispute settlement. Putting aside Singapore, Australia and Korea's FTAs with the US, the Trans-Pacific SEP Agreement, which at the time of writing is receiving considerable press attention following the Obama Administration's support for its enlargement through the Trans-Pacific Partnership talks,[160] allows its parties to agree on alternative dispute procedures. Failing such special agreement, the general procedures in Annex 15.B of the Agreement apply. Annex 15.B prescribes a closed model for panel proceedings *unless* the parties "decide" otherwise.[161] Parties' submissions may be designated confidential, but this is without prejudice to the disclosure of a party's own submissions.[162]

The Trans-Pacific SEP Agreement is at once more open and demonstrates a degree of flexibility absent in the East Asian RTAs discussed above. As a result, there are potentially two models of "East Asian" trade dispute settlement at the present time. The first is a closed model for the "internal" management of Northeast, Southeast Asian and Australasian trade relations *inter se*, and the other a flexible, "for export only" arrangement which would permit (and is intended to attract) future accession by trans-Pacific, trans-continental RTA partners.

Thus, the region has not only chosen a closed model, it has developed a dexterous mechanism in its future treaty engagements with non-regional trading partners.

Analytical limitations of the "cultural" explanation

Many if not most of the East Asian nations we have discussed have continued to resist both cosmopolitics and its legal counterpart – namely, legal rules that would support, even increase non-governmental participation in WTO dispute proceedings. For these, unless and until a WTO member consents to increased public participation, the WTO system should therefore remain a government-to-government ("G-to-G") organization.

We have also seen earlier that criticisms of this view rely on arguments about the nature and contemporary direction of the WTO; arguments which are sought to be justified by appealing to democratic theory, to the need to treat transparency as a prerequisite of legitimacy, and to the need for policy coherence on the part of democratic nations entering into FTA negotiations. In rough terms, these are anti-authoritarian arguments. Against this view, recent writings on arbitration and alternative means of dispute resolution (ADR) demonstrate a strong thread of culturally- and philosophically-oriented scholarship celebrating "Asian",[163] "Confucian", "Chinese" and other forms of cultural exceptionalism,[164] and which are sometimes inadvertently or otherwise reminiscent of the "East Asian Values" debate of the 1990s.[165]

But there is also another way of looking at the treaty behavior of the East Asian trading nations. We could simply take Asian treaty behavior as representations of longer term policy commitments. In studying these designs, we find an increasing acceptance of the importance of formal legal institutions in international economic relations, and predictable legal rules. We also find a general rejection of cosmopolitics,[166] but while cultural critiques provide some explanation for such rejection, they fall short of explaining East Asia's ready adoption of third-party settlement, at least when it comes to trade disputes, and the region's broad acceptance of the need for stable, predictable international legal rules. Culture has not caused the East Asian nations to reject liberal economic rights either. Granting foreign investors the right to bring investor–state disputes under an RTA investment chapter goes against authoritarianism, and calls for serious explanation if the cultural perspective is to be believed.

Treating an emergent "East Asian approach" as an expression of cultural difference is therefore intellectually unsatisfying if such differences are treated simply as unalterable cultural facts.[167] Confucian metaphors have made their way into trade scholarship,[168] but that picture must be measured empirically against modern developments in actual treaty behavior. The recent flurry of scholarship on the emergence of Japanese,[169] and more recently Chinese "aggressive legalism" (i.e. litigiousness) speaks to this change.[170] Aggressive legalism at the WTO on the part of the East Asian nations and strong rule-based and formalized dispute settlement mechanisms show that the East Asian nations are not averse to cultural adaptation.In ASEAN's case, where liberal democratic and non-liberal democratic nations interact closely, the acceptance of binding inter-state dispute settlement mechanisms for the management of their economic and other relations, albeit within a highly closed dispute settlement model, suggests prior deliberation and pragmatic choice, not culture. While the choice currently lies in favor of a closed model of trade dispute settlement, what underlies the acceptance of an increasing number – indeed an entire "noodle bowl" – of formal RTA rules is a broader intention to develop and complement export-oriented, investment-friendly economic strategies. As the *Jakarta Post* in Indonesia has observed:[171]

> The real aim of ASEAN in establishing a free trade area and in building an economic community of ten nations is . . . to enhance the competitiveness of the entire community, and thereby its attractiveness as an investment destination, both from within and more importantly from outside ASEAN.

This reflects Thailand's "discussion paper" outlining the original proposal for an ASEAN Free Trade Area; namely, a need to (a) prepare for greater global trade liberalization following the Uruguay Round, (b) liberalize internal trade in order to attract foreign direct investment, (c) conduct trade negotiations with external trading partners as a single entity, and (d) to do so within APEC and the East Asia Economic Group.[172] In other words, the ASEAN FTAs are motivated – at least on the Southeast Asian side – by economic, not political, considerations in the language of neo-functionalist theory.[173]

In cases where RTA dispute settlement design is likely to become a negotiating issue, there is therefore a real likelihood of accommodating some degree of pressure from external trading partners about conferring greater transparency on trade disputes. This explains the difference between the ASEAN agreements and the Trans-Pacific SEP Agreement. But in cases where the East Asian nations – the nations of ASEAN, China, Korea and Japan, and even including Australia and New Zealand – are interacting *purely* between themselves, transparency has been given a fairly low priority.

Conclusion

An East Asian view about how trade dispute settlement systems should be designed is slowly emerging. Democratically-inspired trade law scholarship and cultural explanations of the international law behavior of the Southeast and Northeast Asian trading nations have failed to capture or prescribe East Asia's regional treaty behavior. Instead, such behavior has resulted in the emergence of two different treaty models for the settlement of trade disputes. In the course of our argument, we have traced the treaty practice of the Association of Southeast Asian Nations (ASEAN), together with that of China, Korea, Japan, Australia, and New Zealand. We find two models of trade dispute settlement emerging. The first is to be found in ASEAN's 2004 dispute settlement protocol and the regimes established under the China-ASEAN, Korea-ASEAN, Japan-ASEAN, and ASEAN-Australia-New Zealand FTAs. All adopt a closed, sovereign-centric view of trade dispute settlement. The second is to be found in the Trans-Pacific Strategic Economic Partnership Agreement.

Democratic arguments supporting greater transparency in trade disputes are salient where authoritarianism is primarily at issue. But that is not the case with East Asia. Major East Asian (and Australasian) trading nations are democratic, with some of the newer democracies such as Indonesia demonstrating an even more fervent popular commitment to democratic ideals. A cultural argument (e.g. an "Authoritarian Asia" argument) would have difficulty in explaining treaty behavior which has adapted along pragmatic lines of economic strategy. On the other hand, culture would also be a poor normative argument in response to the benefits which greater transparency can bring; namely, its tendency to improve the quality of third-party decision making, reduce the risk of corruption or undue influence, and lead to a more coherent body of jurisprudence.

While East Asia has demonstrated a basic acceptance of Hans Kelsen's notion of institutionalized modes for the pacific settlement of international disputes,[174] this has not amounted to a further acceptance of "Kantian" cosmopolitanism.[175] Contemporary developments in Asian trade dispute design reflect, instead, a world-view in which the Northeast and Southeast Asian trading nations interact on equal, sovereign terms while making small exceptions only as pragmatism might suggest; such as the perceived need, under the Trans-Pacific SEP Agreement and Korea's FTA with the US, to have institutional arrangements which trans-continental partners would presumably find more attractive. In their innermost vision of an intergovernmental world trading order, the traditional modes of inter-state, classical diplomacy trump cosmopolitanism. The East Asian nations subscribe to realism in international affairs, not liberalism.[176]

Similarly, democratically-inspired trade law scholarship has had limited practical bearing, persuasive import and predictive value in relation to how the East Asian trading nations behave. Yet such scholarship speaks to the region's potential trans-continental trading partners.

Frederick Abbott once likened the rise of RTAs to that of a "new dominant trade species".[177] We can take the analogy further. East Asia now has a new, regional sub-species – an East Asian RTA dispute settlement model – following the successive conclusion of the China-ASEAN, Korea-ASEAN, and Japan-ASEAN FTAs, and the ASEAN-Australia-NZ FTA. Together with the "for export" dispute settlement model found in the Trans-Pacific SEP Agreement,[178] and to a lesser extent the US-Singapore, Australia-US, and the (as yet unratified) Korea-US bilateral deals, these two models co-exist; each occupying its own niche in East

Asia's emerging trade architecture. By this diversification of trade policy choices, East Asia's policy-makers have helped to create an environment where the two species will not be forced to compete in what resembles ecology's "niche" concept:[179]

> [I]f . . . two species are forced to compete in an undiversified environment one inevitably becomes extinct. If there is a diversification in the system so that some parts favor one species, other parts the other, the two species can coexist.

Another way of describing what now seems to be happening in the realm of trade dispute settlement design in the East Asian region is that we have one model, historically derived from ASEAN's own internal dispute settlement regime which "leans in" towards Southeast Asia, China, Korea, Japan, Australia and New Zealand, and another based on the model in the Trans-Pacific SEP Agreement (to which Singapore, New Zealand, and Brunei are founding parties), the US-Singapore, Australia-US and Korea-US FTAs which "lean outwards" to the wider Asia-Pacific.

What this means is that East Asia's trans-continental trading partners have a historic opportunity to influence the treaty behavior of the East Asian nations, and beyond that, the political-morality of East Asia. While there is the risk – following the Global Financial Crisis – that an ascendant East Asia could become more insular;[180] trade and the policies, commercial habits and public treaty arrangements which accompany it may yet hold the key to a continued engagement between East and West. When the GATT was first established, the United States was the largest economy in the world. Since then, first the European Union, then Japan, now China have also become the world's most powerful economies with national economic and political systems which are different, and in the case of China considerably different, from that of the United States, Canada and Western Europe.[181] From the social-market economy model in Europe,[182] to the steered economic liberalization of China,[183] these East Asian nations (and the great majority of nations) now embrace Adam Smith's view that as with people, nations too can trade and in that way cooperate without coercion.[184] The East Asian trading nations all accept the benefits which an international division of labor will bring. Yet the commercial societies they create within this "simple system of natural liberty" do not always adhere to democratic ideals; their governments support the workings of the market without always recognizing that just as a free market fosters individual freedom, choice and autonomy,[185] there is at least an argument to be made for fostering free markets through policies which uphold these individual values.

Justice William Brandeis of the US Supreme Court once said of the constitution of his nation:[186]

> Those who won our independence believed that the final end of the state was to make men free to develop their faculties; and that in its government the

> deliberative forces should prevail over the arbitrary . . . They believed that freedom to think as you will and to speak as you think are means indispensable to the spread and discovery of political truth . . . the greatest menace to freedom is an inert people . . . public discussion is a political duty . . . [T]hey knew that order cannot be secured merely through fear of punishment for its infraction; that it is hazardous to discourage thought, hope and imagination . . . that the path of safety lies in the opportunity to discuss freely supposed grievances and proposed remedies; and that the fitting remedy for evil counsels is good ones.
>
> Believing in the power of reason as applied through public discussion, they eschewed silence coerced by law . . .

A transnational, regional economic charter is today being formed by the treaty interactions of the East Asian nations: between themselves and with others, albeit occurring in relative silence.

It may be that what Brandeis had to say so many years ago about the constitution of his nation has little application to what is happening today in East Asia. Indeed, while there are East Asian nations which practice free speech, there are those which proclaim it only at the level of principle. Others deny it. There is also the belief that "trade" is distinct from "politics". Even so, only a minority if they exist will deny the importance of furthering commercial free speech.

Trade ministries are careful to express the merits of today's regional trade arrangements, and the national gains to be expected from the latest treaty initiative. No doubt, these statements on public websites and through press releases are intended to demonstrate the performance of the several national governments in increasing the welfare of their people. Nonetheless, the assumption must still exist that it is valuable to have a degree of public understanding of these treaties, at the very least so that commercial gain may be obtained both privately and in the furtherance of national industry while ordinary citizens may also appreciate an increase in consumer choice. By extension, that also becomes the case for imparting knowledge of the nation's trade disputes.

Another US Supreme Court Justice, Justice Blackmun, had occasion to declare in a commercial advertising case:[187]

> As to the particular consumer's interest in the free flow of commercial information, that interest may be as keen, if not keener by far, than his interest in the day's most urgent political debate . . . Those whom the suppression of prescription drug price information hits the hardest are the poor, the sick, and particularly the aged. A disproportionate amount of their income tends to be spent on prescription drugs. . . . Generalizing, society also may have a strong interest in the free flow of commercial information. Advertising, however tasteless and excessive . . . is nonetheless dissemination of information . . . So long as we preserve predominantly free enterprise economy.

Should we have to seek a principled basis for greater public knowledge and understanding of the East Asian region's trade disputes, perhaps the most basic answer lies in the need to promote both commercial knowledge and consumer choice. Some East Asian policy-makers accept that, others may reject it, and yet others may at the very least accept that "the path of safety lies in the opportunity to discuss freely supposed grievances". Still, others might think that while wider acceptance of national trade policies is valuable, greater public understanding may nonetheless challenge that acceptance, or worse the national government.

Whichever view is taken, it seems the time has now come for East Asian trade policy-makers to address the issue squarely. They will be shaping some of the most fundamental notions about how free markets should operate within the region, and how much consumers in addition to merchantmen should know of the several nations' trade policies; underpinned by some of these nations' most solemn treaty commitments.

Notes

1 Professor of Law and Chair of the East Asian International Economic Law & Policy Programme, University of Hong Kong; Visiting Professor of Law, King's College London. This chapter is a slightly revised and expanded version of an article which first appeared in the *McGill Law Journal*. I am grateful to Junji Nakagawa, Dan Magraw, Julien Chaisse, Joel Trachtman, and two anonymous reviewers of the *McGill Law Journal* for their comments. All views and errors are mine alone. Email: chin.leng.lim@post.harvard.edu.

2 This chapter uses a broader term – "RTAs" – which would include both FTAs and customs unions, unless a more specific term (e.g. "FTAs") is more appropriate in the context in which the specific term arises.

3 See C.L. Lim, "Who's Afraid of Asian Trade Regionalism, and Why?", in Ross Buckley, Richard Hu and Douglas Arner eds, *East Asian Economic Integration: Law, Trade and Finance*, Cheltenham, UK and Northampton, MA, USA: Edward Elgar, 2011.

4 See, e.g. the US-Singapore Free Trade Agreement, done in Washington, 6 May 2003, Art. 20.4(4)(d); and the US-Chile Free Trade Agreement, done in Miami, 6 June 2003, Art. 22.10(1).

5 Framework Agreement on Enhancing ASEAN Economic Cooperation, done in Singapore, 28 January 1992 ("ASEAN Framework Agreement"); Agreement on the Common Effective Preferential Tariff Scheme for the ASEAN Free Trade Area, done in Singapore, 28 January 1992 ("CEPT").

6 Framework Agreement on Comprehensive Economic Co-operation between ASEAN and the People's Republic of China, done in Phnom Penh, 5 November 2002 ("China-ASEAN"); Agreement on Dispute Settlement Mechanism Framework Agreement on Comprehensive Economic Co-operation between ASEAN and the People's Republic of China, done in Vientiane, 29 November 2004 ("China-ASEAN DSA").

7 Agreement on Trade in Goods under the Framework Agreement on Comprehensive Economic Cooperation among the Governments of the Member Countries of the Association of Southeast Asian Nations and the Republic of Korea, done in Kuala Lumpur, 24 August 2006 ("the Korea – ASEAN FTA").

8 Agreement on Comprehensive Economic Partnership among Japan and Member States of the Association of Southeast Asian Nations, April 2008 ("the Japan-ASEAN FTA").

9 ASEAN-Australia-New Zealand Free Trade Agreement, done in Phetchaburi, 27 February 2009 ("AANZFTA").

10 The Trans-Pacific Strategic Partnership Agreement is my main example here as that is where a cosmopolitan model may be found of a treaty which is intended to have broad regional application (i.e. as opposed to some of the many "small" bilaterals that are, today, scattered about East Asia).

11 See Robert E. Hudec, "The New WTO Dispute Settlement Procedure: An Overview of the First Three Years", 8 *Minnesota Journal of Global Trade* 1 (1999); Michael K. Young, "Dispute Resolution in the Uruguay Round: Lawyers Triumph over Diplomats", 29 *International Lawyer* 389 (1995); J.H.H. Weiler, "The Rule of Lawyers and the Ethos of Diplomats: Reflections on WTO Dispute Settlement", in R.B. Porter et al. eds, *Efficiency, Equity, Legitimacy: The Multilateral Trading System at the Millennium*, Washington, DC: Brookings Institution Press, 2001, p. 334; Arie Reich, "From Diplomacy to Law: The Juridification of International Trade Relations", 17 *Northwestern Journal of International Law and Business* 776 (1996–1997).

12 Thomas A. Zimmermann, *Negotiating the Review of the WTO Dispute Settlement Understanding*, London: Cameron May, 2006, p. 168; Bryan Mercurio and Rebecca Laforgia, "Expanding Democracy: Why Australia Should Negotiate for Open and Transparent Dispute Settlement in its Free Trade Agreements", 6 *Melbourne Journal of International Law* 485 (2005), p. 493.

13 See *US and Canada – Continued Suspension of Obligations in the EC – Hormones Dispute*, WTO Doc. WT/DS320/8, WT/DS321/8 (2005) (Communication from the Chairman of the Panels).

14 Mercurio and Laforgia, supra n.12, pp. 496–497.

15 Fernando R. Tesón, "The Kantian Theory of International Law", 92 *Columbia Law Review* 54 (1992).

16 Robert F. Housman, "Democratizing International Trade Decision-Making", 27 *Cornell International Law Journal* 699 (1994), p. 701.

17 Pascal Lamy, "Harnessing Globalization. Do We Need Cosmopolitics?", Lecture, London School of Economics, 1 February 2001, available at http://www.lse.ac.uk/collections/globalDimensions/lectures/harnessingGlobalisationDoWeNeedCosmopolitics/Default.htm (last accessed: 31 December, 2010).

18 Related to this are other benefits of bringing transparency to bear; namely, that transparency increases the quality of third-party decision making, reduces the risk of corruption or undue influence, and could lead to a more coherent body of jurisprudence.

19 Jeffrey J. Schott ed., *The WTO After Seattle*, Washington, DC: Institute for International Economics, 2000.

20 "The 1992 Campaign, Transcript of Second Debate between Bush, Clinton and Perot", *New York Times*, 16 October 1992.

21 James Bacchus, *Trade and Freedom*, London: Cameron May, 2004.

22 *Idem.*

23 See William Greider, "A New Giant Sucking Sound: China is Taking Away Mexico's Jobs, as Globalization Enters a Fateful New Stage", *The Nation*, 31 December 2001.

24 Mercurio and Laforgia, supra n.12, pp. 512–514.

25 Strictly speaking, nothing stops RTAs from being used to impose direct electoral obligations.

26 Hudec, supra n.11; Young, supra n.11; Weiler, supra n.11; Reich, supra n.11.

27 Zimmermann, supra n.12, p. 168.

28 Mercurio and Laforgia, supra n.12, p. 493.

29 Debra P. Steger, *Peace through Trade: Building the WTO*, London: Cameron May, 2004, pp. 296, 299.

30 DSU Art. 16.4 and 17.14.

31 See Judith Bello, "The WTO DSU: Less is More", 90 *American Journal of International Law* 416 (1996); John Jackson, "The WTO DSU: Misunderstandings on the Nature of Legal Obligation", 91 *American Journal of International Law* 60 (1997); Letters, 91 *American Journal of International Law* 89–90 (1997).

32 See the *Argentina-Chile Frontier Case*, 38 *International Law Reports* 10 (1966).
33 TN/DS/W/1, no. 1 (EC), and Attachment, no. 7.
34 Zimmermann, supra n.12, p. 133.
35 Ibid., p. 135.
36 A.H.A. Soons, ed., *International Arbitration: Past and Prospects*, Dordrecht: Nijhoff, 1990.
37 See Thomas Cottier, "The WTO Permanent Panel Body – A Bridge Too Far?", 6 *Journal of International Economic Law* 187 (2003).
38 DSU, Article 5(2), (3).
39 On the historical importance of secrecy as a diplomatic doctrine, see G.R. Berridge, *Diplomacy: Theory & Practice, 3rd edn*, London: Palgrave, 2005, p. 110.
40 *Idem*.
41 For a view on the resilience of the distinction between "legal" and "non-legal" disputes, see the discussion in M.C.W. Pinto, "The Prospects for International Arbitration: Inter-State Disputes", in Soons, supra n.36, pp. 93–95.
42 In having compulsory jurisdiction, automatic adoption of panel and Appellate Body reports, and automatic authorization of retaliation; in the Appellate Body's "rituals" such as the quasi-judicial principle of collegiality which it adopts, as well as the "swearing in ceremony" for Appellate Body members and the adversarial manner in which it conducts its proceedings; and in securing a fairly high degree of predictability in its decision-making, as well as a pious reliance on the Vienna Convention on the Law of Treaties in facing interpretative issues, and so on: Steger, supra n.29, pp. 300–305.
43 Jackson, supra n.31, p. 60. See further, DSU Articles 6.1, 16.4, 17.14 and 22.6.
44 See further, Keisuke Iida, *Legalization and Japan: The Politics of WTO Dispute Settlement*, London: Cameron May, 2006, p. 21 (the Appellate Body is legalistic, unlike the panels, and leaves political considerations to the DSB).
45 See further, C.L. Lim, "Law and Diplomacy in World Trade Disputes", 6 *Singapore Journal of International and Comparative Law* 436 (2002).
46 See, for example, the Nicaraguan complaint against the 1985 US embargo – GATT/C/M/188 (28 June 1985) – where Nicaragua itself blocked the adoption of the report on account of the fact that the panel was prevented from addressing the issues which Nicaragua wanted addressed (i.e. the legality of the US embargo under GATT Article XXI).
47 Cf. Steger, supra n.29, p. 300.
48 See, e.g. "Ruggiero Calls on Members Not to Talk About Cases Undergoing Dispute Settlement", *International Trade Reporter*, vol. 15, no. 8, 25 February 1998; "WTO Chief Floats Solutions to Problem of Leaked Reports", *International Trade Reporter*, vol. 15, no. 17, 29 April 1998. See also the further sources cited in Zimmermann, supra n.12, p. 167.
49 *Idem*.
50 Attributed to Jagdish Bhagwati, see Walter Goode, *Dictionary of Trade Policy Terms, 4th edn*, Cambridge: Cambridge University Press, 2003, p. 105.
51 James Bacchus, "Let the Sunshine In: One View of Dispute Settlement Understanding Review", in Julio Lacarte and Jaime Granados eds, *Inter-Governmental Trade Dispute Settlement*, London: Cameron May, 2004, p. 143.
52 Ibid., 143–144. For a survey of individual WTO Members' views, see C.L. Lim, "The *Amicus* Brief Issue at the WTO", 4 *Chinese Journal of International Law* 85 (2005).
53 TN/DS/W/13 (US).
54 WT/GC/W/98, 22 September 1998 (Submission by Canada); WT/GC/W/106, 13 October 1998 (Joint Submission by Canada and US).
55 TN/DS/W/1, Attachment, no. 32 (EC).
56 TN/DS/W/22 (Japan). For all these positions, see Zimmermann, supra n.12, pp. 169–170.

57 Ibid., p. 170.
58 See C.L. Lim, "The Asian WTO Members and the *Amicus* Brief Controversy: Arguments and Strategies", 1 *Asian Journal of WTO & International Health Law and Policy* 85 (2005).
59 Mercurio and LaForgia, supra n.12, p. 504.
60 TN/DS/M/1, para. 30.
61 TN/DS/M/4, para. 45. The Norwegian and Swiss objections are discussed in William J. Davey, "Reforming WTO Dispute Settlement", in Mitsuo Matsushita and Dukgeun Ahn, eds, *WTO and East Asia: New Perspectives*, London: Cameron May, 2004, p. 135, footnote 126.
62 Steve Charnovitz, "The WTO and Cosmopolitics", 7 *Journal of International Economic Law* 675 (2004), pp. 677–678.
63 *US and Canada – Continued Suspension of Obligations in the EC – Hormones Dispute*, supra n.13 (Communication from the Chairman of the Panels).
64 Ibid., p. 496.
65 Other potential parties include Japan, which announced its intention to join during the APEC Summit in Honolulu in November 2011 as well as Canada, Mexico and South Korea. The United States is also interested in Thailand and the Philippines joining the TPP.
66 See further, below.
67 WT/DS320/8, WT/DS321/8, see supra n.13.
68 Thomas Franck, "The Emerging Right to Democratic Governance", 86 *American Journal of International Law* 46 (1992); James Crawford, "Democracy and International Law", 64 *British Year Book of International Law* 113 (1994).
69 Ibid., pp. 125–126.
70 For writing in the popular arena, see, e.g. John R. MacArthur, *The Selling of "Free Trade": NAFTA, Washington and the Subversion of American Democracy*, New York: Hill and Wang, 2000.
71 See, e.g. "Memorandum to Ambassador Michael Kantor", Office of Legal Counsel, US Department of Justice, 22 November 1994 (concerning Professor Lawrence Tribe's testimony on the effect of the WTO DSM on States' rights); *Re the Uruguay Round Treaties*, Court of Justice of the European Communities (Opinion 1/94), 15 November 1994 (concerning the scope of the Commission's powers under Article 113 E.C.).
72 See, e.g. John H. Jackson, *Sovereignty, the WTO and Changing Fundamentals of International Law*, Cambridge: Cambridge University Press, 2006.
73 Housman, supra n.16, p. 701.
74 Ibid., p. 703. Housman's argument draws on Carole Pateman, *Participation and Democratic Theory*, Cambridge: Cambridge University Press, 1970, but see also Keohane and Nye who argue that democratic arguments are judged by their "inputs" where the main issues here are transparency and accountability. See Robert O. Keohane and Joseph S. Nye Jr., "The Club Model of Multilateral Cooperation and Problems of Democratic Legitimacy", in Porter et al. eds, supra n.11, pp. 281–282.
75 For this criticism, see Comment by Robert E. Hudec in Porter, supra n.11, p. 298; also discussed in Steger, supra n.29, p. 264.
76 See further, Raj Bhala, "Enter the Dragon: An Essay on China's WTO Accession Saga", 15 *American University International Law Review* 1469 (2000).
77 Zimmermann, supra n.12, p. 170 (citing Malaysia and Taiwan).
78 TN/DS/W/22 (Japan, on publicizing party submissions in WTO disputes).
79 Discussed below.
80 See further Bacchus, supra n.21, especially pp. 51–198 for an attempt to throw light on what the Appellate Body does, and to justify what the WTO is and what it does on the basis of liberty.
81 See Thomas M. Franck, *The Power of Legitimacy among Nations*, New York: Oxford University Press, 1990; also discussed in Steger, supra n.29, pp. 264–266. For its

application to NAFTA Chapter 11 (investor–state) arbitration, see Charles H. Brower II, "Structure, Legitimacy, and NAFTA's Investment Chapter", 36 *Vanderbilt Journal of Transnational Law* 37 (2003).

82 In the context of DSU reform, the majority of members, including the developing countries, have supported the US proposal for swifter circulation of panel reports: Davey, supra n.61, p. 135, footnote 125.

83 Charnovitz, supra n.62, pp. 677–678.

84 Ibid., p. 675.

85 See Raj Bhala, "New WTO Dumping Precedents (Part One: The Dumping Margin Determination)", 6 *Singapore Journal of International and Comparative Law* 335 (2002), p. 401; Steger, supra n.29, p. 288.

86 Robert E. Hudec, *Essays on the Nature of International Trade Law*, London: Cameron May, 1999, pp. 227, 236.

87 Contra ibid., pp. 227–250 (arguing against the incoherence of such a standard of fairness in the first place).

88 Schott, supra n.19, pp. 3, 5–8.

89 Joseph Stiglitz, *Globalization and its Discontents*, London: Penguin, 2002, pp. 3–4, 227–228.

90 Margaret Liang, "The *Realpolitik* of Multilateral Trade Negotiations from Uruguay to the Doha Round", 8 *Singapore Year Book of International Law* 149 (2004), p. 152.

91 Davey, supra n.61, p. 136.

92 *Idem.*

93 Ibid., p. 135, footnote 129, citing the Indian delegation's criticism in TN/DS/M/3, para. 59.

94 *Idem.*

95 Stiglitz, supra n.89, pp. 227–228.

96 See the Foreword to the Symposium on "The Boundaries of the WTO" by José E. Alvarez, 96 *American Journal of International Law* 1 (2002), and the various symposium papers published in that issue.

97 Mercurio and Laforgia, supra n.12, pp. 512–514.

98 Hong Kong, Japan, Philippines, Malaysia, Singapore, Thailand, India, Pakistan have also featured prominently in resisting unsolicited amicus briefs, with Singapore often speaking for ASEAN as a whole; see Lim, supra n.58.

99 *Case Concerning Sovereignty over Pulau Ligitan and Pulau Sipadan(Indonesia v. Malaysia) (Merits)* [2002] ICJ, available at http://www.icj-cij.org. See John Merrills, "*Sovereignty over Pulau Ligitan and Pulau Sipadan (Indonesia /Malaysia)*, Merits, Judgment of 17 December 2002", 52 *International and Comparative Law Quarterly* 797 (2003).

100 *Case Concerning Sovereignty over Pedra Branca/Pulau Batu Puteh, Middle Rocks and South Ledge (Malaysia/Singapore) (Merits)* [2008] ICJ, available at http://www.icj-cij.org.

101 *Case Concerning Land Reclamation by Singapore in and around the Straits of Johor (Malaysia v. Singapore) (Provisional Measures)*, [2003] ITLOS, available at http://www.itlos.org; *Case Concerning Land Reclamation by Singapore in and around the Straits of Johor (Malaysia v. Singapore) (Award)*, [2005] PCA, available at www.pca-cpa.org. See further, C.L. Lim, "The Uses of Pacific Settlement Techniques in Malaysia-Singapore Relations", 6 *Melbourne Journal of International Law* 313 (2005).

102 *Temple of Preah Vihear (Cambodia v. Thailand) (Merits)*, [1962] ICJ, available at http://www.icj-cij.org.

103 *Right of Passage over Indian Territory (Portugal v. India)*, [1960] ICJ, available at http://www.icj-cij.org.

104 *Aerial Incident of 10 August 1999 (Pakistan v. India) (Jurisdiction)*, [1999] ICJ; *Trial of Pakistani Prisoners of War (Pakistan v. India) (Removal)*, [1973] ICJ; *Appeal*

Relating to the Jurisdiction of the ICAO Council (India v. Pakistan) (Merits), [1972] ICJ, available at http://www.icj-cij.org.

105 The dispute was eventually settled. See *Malaysia – Prohibition of Polyethylene and Polypropylene*, WTO Doc WT/DS1/1 (1995) (Request for Consultations by Singapore).

106 See Iida, supra n.44; Ichiro Araki, "Beyond Aggressive Legalism: Japan and the GATT/WTO Dispute", in Mitsuo Matsushita and Dukgeun Ahn, *WTO and East Asia: New Perspectives* (London: Cameron May, 2004), 149; Saadia M. Pekkanen, "International Law, the WTO and the Japanese State: Assessment and Implications of the New Legalized System", (2001) 27 *Journal of Japanese Studies* 79.

107 See, e.g. Chulsu Kim, "East Asia in the WTO Dispute Settlement Mechanism", in Yasuhei Taniguchi et al. eds, *The WTO in the Twenty-First Century*, Cambridge: Cambridge University Press, 2007, p. 262.

108 Henry Gao, "Taming the Dragon; China's Experience in the WTO Dispute Settlement System", 34 *Legal Issues of Economic Integration* 369 (2007); Tina Wang, "China's Coming of Age in the WTO War", *Forbes*, 20 April 2009.

109 Kim, supra n.107, p. 261.

110 Ibid., 262.

111 Peter van den Bossche, *The Law and Policy of the World Trade Organization 2nd edn*. Cambridge: Cambridge University Press, 2008, p. 231.

112 See Tina Wang, supra n.108; Denise Tsang, "Beijing Hits Back at Trade Partners on Protectionism", *South China Morning Post* [Hong Kong], 25 June 2009; Denise Tsang, "Beijing Hits Out at US Duty on Steel Pipes", *South China Morning Post* [Hong Kong], 11 September 2009; Agence France-Presse and Associated Press, "Beijing Starts Dumping Probe after US Tyre Move", *South China Morning Post* [Hong Kong], 14 September 2009; "The Tyre Wars: Playing with Fire", *Economist*, 19 September 2009; "Chinese Import Restrictions on Publications and Entertainment Products Found to be WTO Inconsistent", *ASIL Insights*, Vol. 13, Issue 19, 27 October 2009; Brendan McGivern, "US-China Disputes Round-Up", *ICTSD China Programme*, Vol. 14, No. 1, 13 January 2010; "China Sets Anti-Dumping Penalties on US Poultry Imports", *Bridges Weekly*, Vol. 14, No. 5, 10 February 2010; "US Group Urges WTO Case to Bring Down Chinese Internet Firewall", *ICTSD China Programme*, Vol. 14, No. 3, 27 January 2010; "China Brings Anti-Dumping Case against EU in Shoe Dispute", *Bridges Weekly*, Vol. 14, No. 5, 10 February 2010.

113 Kim, supra n.107, p. 264.

114 Concerning the need to await the conclusion of non-compliance hearings before engaging in unilateral retaliation.

115 Kim, supra n.107, p. 264.

116 Dispute Settlement Body, Minutes of Meetings – Held in the Centre William Rappard on 6 November 1998, WT/DSB/M/50 (14 December 1998) (Hong Kong, Japan, Malaysia and Thailand); Dispute Settlement Body, Minutes of Meetings – Held in the Centre William Rappard on 7 June 2000, WT/DSB/M/83 (7 July 2000) (Hong Kong, Japan, Philippines, Malaysia and Thailand); WTO General Council, Minutes of Meeting, WT/GC/M/60 (23 January 2001) (Hong Kong, Singapore and ASEAN). See Lim, supra n.58; C. L. Lim, supra n.52.

117 There are often significant differences even when we compare the FTAs of a single East Asian nation. For example, China's FTA with ASEAN is currently not as comprehensive as its FTAs with Singapore, New Zealand and Chile. See Jiangyu Wang, "The Role of China and India in Asian Regionalism", in Muthucumaraswamy Sornarajah and Jiangyu Wang eds, *China, India and the International Economic Order*, Cambridge: Cambridge University Press, 2010, pp. 352–356. Another example would be Singapore's FTAs. Even when we compare Singapore's purely bilateral FTAs, there are significant differences in structure and design. Singapore's FTAs with Australia and the United States adopt a negative list approach in its services

commitments, while its FTAs with New Zealand and Japan do not. There is no "Singapore template" as such. See Ong Ye Kung, "An Intuitive Guide to the Services Chapter of the US-Singapore Free Trade Agreement", in C.L. Lim and Margaret Liang eds, *Economic Diplomacy: Essays and Reflections by Singapore's Negotiators*, Singapore: Institute of Policy Studies, 2010, p. 172.

118 As of June 2010, Singapore had concluded bilateral FTAs with Australia, China, the Hashemite Kingdom of Jordan, India, Korea, Japan, New Zealand, Panama, Peru, the United States and Costa Rica, in addition to its FTAs as an ASEAN Member, the Trans-Pacific Strategic Economic Partnership Agreement, (with Brunei, New Zealand and Chile) and FTAs with other regional trading areas such as the European Free Trade Area and the Gulf Cooperation Council. See Lim and Liang, supra n.117, Annex, pp. 293–295.

119 For the origins of this policy, see Noboru Hatakeyama, "A Short History of Japan's Movement to FTAs (Part 3)", 22 *Journal of Japanese Trade & Industry*, March/April 2003, p. 42.

120 Dukgeun Ahn, "Korea's FTA Policy", in *The New International Architecture in Trade & Investment*, Singapore: APEC, 2007, p. 49.

121 See further, Chin, "ASEAN's Journey towards Free Trade", in Lim and Liang, supra n.117, p. 209.

122 *Idem*.

123 For the reasons given earlier, divergences from the East Asian model in individual, bilateral FTAs are not as significant from a regional viewpoint. The significance of such bilaterals are further reduced where they proceed from an extra-regional "template", such as in the case of US FTAs. Thus, the US-Singapore FTA has uncharacteristic provisions which are the result of a US, as opposed to a Singapore, "FTA template". According to the dispute provisions of the US-Singapore FTA, public consultations follow a request for consultations made by either of the two parties. There is also provision for the submission of unsolicited amicus curiae briefs by NGOs in relation to disputes occurring under the US-Singapore FTA. Interestingly, Singapore's late counsel for the US-Singapore FTA negotiations had described these provisions in his recollections of the negotiations in functional, not cosmopolitan, terms: "The idea is to take into account the views of all those affected and draw upon a broad range of perspectives in arriving at a solution". See Sivakant Tiwari, "The Role of Legal Counsel and Dispute Settlement", in Tommy Koh and Chang Li Lin eds, *The United States–Singapore Free Trade Agreement: Highlights and Insights*, Singapore: Institute of Policy Studies, 2004, p. 157. This contrasts with the US Chief Negotiator's published recollections of the negotiations which highlights the importance given to "enhanced transparency" in the negotiations. See Ralph F. Ives, "The USSFTA: Personal Perspectives on the Process and Results", in ibid., p. 28. Transparency provisions will also likely be a negotiating issue in East Asian nations' bilateral FTAs with the EU as the latter begins to negotiate more FTAs with the East Asian nations. Until recently, the EU had been slow to engage East Asia in its FTA negotiations but, at the time of writing, this situation is swiftly changing as the EU competes with the US in the East Asian region.

124 Notwithstanding the provision for investor–state dispute settlement within AFTA (i.e. ASEAN's 1987 Agreement on the Promotion and Protection of Investment), the Korea-ASEAN FTA's Investment Agreement, and Chapter 11 of the AANZFTA, there is little which can usefully be said at the present time about confidentiality in the case of investor–state disputes under these treaty regimes. Unlike the corresponding provisions on inter-state trade dispute settlement, the investment treaties themselves are largely silent on the issue. Much will depend on the applicable arbitration rules, and it remains to be seen whether the decisions emanating from NAFTA supporting greater transparency in investor–state proceedings will be applied to East Asian and Australasian investor–state disputes. Taking the Korea-ASEAN FTA's Investment

Agreement as an example, the investor may choose from ICSID Arbitration (including arbitration under the ICSID Additional Facility Rules), arbitration under UNCITRAL arbitration rules or "any other arbitration or any other arbitration rules". The treaty is otherwise silent on the issue of confidentiality. See *Agreement on Investment under the Framework Agreement on Comprehensive Economic Cooperation Among the Governments of the Member Countries of ASEAN and the Republic of Korea* (entered into force June 2007), available online at http://www.fta.gov.sg/fta_akfta.asp?hl=3.

125 While discussing investor–state disputes in the context of internationalized contracts, some commentators have however suggested that a party may in such circumstances reveal its own case, or the existence of the dispute without the consent of the other party. See Nigel Rawding, "Protecting Investments under State Contracts: Some Legal and Ethical Issues", 11 *Arbitration International* 341 (1995), p. 343. In ICSID Arbitration under NAFTA Chapter 11, there have been tribunal pronouncements in favor of the freedom of the parties to make information regarding the arbitration publicly available, and also the suggestion that confidentiality would be undesirable; Cindy G. Buys, "The Tensions between Confidentiality and Transparency in International Arbitration", 14 *American Review of International Arbitration* 121 (2003), pp. 132–133; Jeffery Atik, "Legitimacy, Transparency and NGO Participation in the NAFTA Chapter 11 Process", in Todd Weiler ed., *NAFTA Investment Law and Arbitration*, New York: Transnational Publishers, 2004, p. 148, citing *Metalclad* v. *United Mexican States*, ICSID Case No. ARB(AF)/97/1, Award (2 Sept., 2000); *S.D. Myers, Inc.* v. *Canada*, UNCITRAL Decision (13 May 2000) (Procedural Order No. 16); *Loewen Group, Inc.* v. *United States*, ICSID Case No. ARB(AF)/98/3, Decision (28 September 1999). NAFTA parties have also confirmed that "[n]othing in NAFTA imposes a general duty of confidentiality"; Notes of Interpretation of Certain Chapter 11 Provisions, NAFTA Free Trade Commission, 31 July 2001, para. 1(a). Under the PCA's rules, which are based largely on the UNCITRAL Arbitration Rules, confidentiality is generally a matter for parties to agree upon. However, a presumption lies in favor of confidentiality: hearings are held in camera, unless the parties agree otherwise under Article 25(4), whereas under Article 32(5) the Award may only be made public with the parties' consent; PCA Optional Rules for Arbitrating Disputes between Two States.

126 ASEAN Protocol on Dispute Settlement Mechanism, done at Manila, 20 November 2006, in force 26 May 1998.

127 See Paul Davidson, "The ASEAN Way and the Role of Law in ASEAN Economic Cooperation", 8 *Singapore Year Book of International Law* 165 (2004), p. 173.

128 ASEAN Protocol on Enhanced Dispute Settlement Mechanism, done at Vientiane, 29 November 2004, in force 29 November 2004 ("2004 Protocol").

129 Ibid., see Arts 5(1), 9(1), 12(13) and 16(6).

130 Ibid., Art. 3.

131 Ibid., Art. 4.

132 2004 Protocol, Arts 8(5), 12(9) and Appendix II, Art. II(2).

133 See also, ibid., Appendix II, Sect. II, para. 3. The drafting language is unclear. What is the distinction between written submissions which must be disclosed to the other party but is otherwise *automatically* to be treated as confidential, and the rule that "Member States" shall treat as confidential "information submitted by another Member State" which has been *designated* as such? The better interpretation may be that a party should always mark its written submissions confidential.

134 Ibid., Appendix II, Sect. II, para. 11.

135 See Barry Desker, "In Defence of FTAs: From Purity to Pragmatism in East Asia", 17 *Pacific Review* 3 (2004).

136 "[W]hile affirming our commitments to the Bogor Goals and the successful conclusion of the WTO/DDA negotiations, we instructed Officials to undertake further studies on ways and means to promote regional economic integration, including a Free Trade

Area of the Asia-Pacific as a long-term prospect, and report to the 2007 APEC Economic Leaders' Meeting in Australia"; Ha Noi Declaration, 14th APEC Economic Leaders' Meeting, Vietnam, 18–19 November 2006.

137 "Rudd Pushes for Asia-Pacific Community", *The Age* (Melbourne), 4 June 2008; Hadi Soesastro, "Kevin Rudd's Architecture for the Asia-Pacific", *The Jakarta Post* (Jakarta), 6 November 2008; "Kevin Rudd Suggests Formation of Asia-Pacific Community", *The Hindu* (Chennai), 12 August 2008. See further, C.L. Lim "Australia's 'Rudd Proposal': Business as Usual", 14 *Asian Yearbook of International Law* 287 (2008).

138 See David Chin, "ASEAN's Journey Towards Free Trade" in Lim and Liang, supra n.117, p. 209.

139 Investor–state arbitration is also provided for under AFTA, the Korea-ASEAN FTA's Investment Agreement, and the AANZFTA. See further, Agreement Among the Governments of Brunei Darussalam, the Republic of Indonesia, Malaysia, the Republic of the Philippines, the Republic of Singapore and the Kingdom of Thailand for the Promotion and Protection of Investments (hereafter, "Agreement for the Promotion and Protection of Investment 1987"), done in Manila, 15 December 1987, Art. X; as amended subsequently by the Protocol Amending the Agreement for the Promotion and Protection of Investment 1987, done in Jakarta, 12 September 1996, Art. 5; Agreement on Investment under the Framework Agreement on Comprehensive Economic Cooperation Among the Governments of the Member Countries of ASEAN and the Republic of Korea, done at Jeju-do, 2 June 2009, Article 18; AANZFTA, Chapter 11, Art. 20. In the case of the Agreement for the Promotion and Protection of Investment 1987, the investor–state dispute settlement clause is infelicitously worded, but the intent seems clear enough. See further, M. Sornarajah and Rajenthran Arumugam, "An Overview of the Foreign Direct Investment Jurisprudence", in Denis Hew ed., *Brick by Brick: The Building of an ASEAN Economic Community*, Singapore: ISEAS, 2007, p. 144.

140 China-ASEAN DSA, Arts 9(1), (4); Korea-ASEAN DSA, Arts 10(3) and Annex Art. 21; the Japan-ASEAN FTA, Art. 68(8), (10), (11); AANZFTA, Arts 13(6), (10), Annex, para. 21.

141 Korea-ASEAN DSA, Annex Art. 11. The rule that what is already in the public domain cannot by definition be confidential or secret is self-explanatory. It can hardly be a secret that "the Sun rises in the East", for example. For similar provisions, see AANZFTA, Annex on Rules of Procedure for Arbitral Tribunal Proceedings, para. 11.

142 See Buys, supra n.125, p. 124, citing Art. 9 of the International Bar Association's Ethics for Arbitrators; Canon VI.B of the AAA/ABA Code of Ethics for Arbitrators in Commercial Disputes; Rule 6 of the ICSID Rules of Procedure for Arbitration Proceedings.

143 China-ASEAN DSA, Art. 19; Korea-ASEAN DSA, Art. 10(3); Japan-ASEAN FTA, Art. 68(8); AANZFTA, Ch. 17, Art. 13.

144 2004 Protocol, Appendix II, Sect. II, para. 2.

145 Japan-ASEAN FTA, Art. 68(9); Korea-ASEAN DSA, Annex, para. 16; AANZFTA, Art. 10.

146 *Idem.*

147 2004 Protocol, Art. 11(2) (third-parties "shall have an opportunity to be heard by the panel").

148 Ibid., Appendix II, Sect.II, para. 6; AANZFTA, Annex, para. 19.

149 2004 Protocol, Appendix II, Art. II(3).

150 In addition to a provision requiring their tribunals to meet in closed session; see China-ASEAN DSA, Art. 9(4), (6); Korea-ASEAN DSA, Annex, Art. 11; the Japan-ASEAN FTA Art. 68(10); AANZFTA, Annex, para. 11.

151 See, e.g. AANZFTA, Annex, para. 10.

152 See, e.g. ibid., para. 9.

153 See ibid., para. 11; Korea-ASEAN DSA, Annex Art. 11.

154 2004 Protocol, Art. 8(5); China-ASEAN DSA, Art. 9(6); Korea-ASEAN DSA, Annex, Art. 17; the Japan-ASEAN FTA, Art. 69(1).

155 China-ASEAN DSA, Art. 9(9); Korea-ASEAN DSA, Art. 12(3); the Japan-ASEAN FTA Art. 69(9).

156 AANZFTA, Art. 13(16). AANZFTA also contains a further express provision protecting all confidential information in the report.

157 The US-Singapore FTA mandates open proceedings under Art. 20.4(4)(d)(i) subject to the protection of confidential information, written responses to a request or questions from the panel to be made public under Art. 20.4(d)(iii), as well as a clause for amicus curiae briefs under Art. 20.4(d)(iv): "that the panel shall consider requests from nongovernmental entities in the Parties' territories to provide written views regarding the dispute that may assist the panel in evaluating the submissions and arguments of the Parties"; done at Washington, DC, 6 May 2003. For a comprehensive overview of the US-Singapore FTA, see the essays in Koh and Chang, supra n.123.

158 The US-Australia FTA mandates open proceedings under Art. 21.8(1)(a) and requires written party submissions, written versions of the parties' oral statements, and written responses to a request or questions from the panel to be made public under Art. 21.8(1)(d) subject to the protection of confidential information; done at Washington DC, 18 May 2004. For an overview of the US-Australia FTA, see Andrew D. Mitchell, "The Australia-United States Free Trade Agreement", in Ross Buckley, Vai Io Lo and Laurence Boulle eds, *Challenges to Multilateral Trade: The Impact of Bilateral, Preferential and Regional Agreements*, Hague: Kluwer, 2008, p. 115.

159 KORUS mandates open proceedings in Art. 22.10(1)(b) subject to the protection of confidential information; Korea-US Free Trade Agreement, done at Washington, DC, 30 June, 2007. For an overview of KORUS, see Yong-Shik Lee, "The Beginning of Economic Integration between East Asia and North America?", in Buckley et al., ibid., p. 125.

160 See, e.g. "USTR Ron Kirk Comments on Trans-Pacific Partnership Talks", USTR Press Release, 18 June 2010, available at www.ustr.gov.

161 Trans-Pacific Strategic Economic Partnership Agreement, Annex 15 B, para. 21.

162 Ibid., para. 27.

163 See Joel Lee and Teh Hwee Hwee eds, *An Asian Perspective on Mediation*, Singapore: Academy, 2009.

164 Qi Zhang, *Consultations within WTO Dispute Settlement: A Chinese Perspective*, Bern: Peter Lang, 2007. See further, Randall Peerenboom, *China's Long March toward Rule of Law*, Cambridge: Cambridge University Press, 2002, arguing that China is not transitioning towards a liberal democratic conception of the rule of law.

165 Jonathan R. Bauer and Daniel A. Bell eds, *The East Asian Challenge for Human Rights*, Cambridge: Cambridge University Press, 1999; Daniel A. Bell, *East Meets West: Human Rights and Democracy in East Asia*, Princeton: Princeton University Press, 2000.

166 This conclusion is reinforced by Asian comparative legal scholarship's distinction between the acceptance by some Asian nations of a "thin" (formalist), but not a "thick" (liberal) conception of the rule of law in their internal constitutional arrangements. See Randall Peerenboom ed., *Asian Discourses on Rule of Law: Theories and Implementation of Rule of Law in Twelve Asian Countries, France and the United States*, London: Routledge, 2004.

167 Recent scholarship on Chinese attitudes towards mediation in the People's Republic of China has avoided such a singular perspective, and has sought to explain attitudes in China along philosophical and historical-ideological lines (i.e. the influence of Communist ideology), in addition to the "cultural" explanation; see Gabrielle Kaufmann-Kohler and Fan Kun, "Integrating Mediation into Arbitration: Why it Works in China", 25 *Journal of International Arbitration* 479 (2008).

168 Zhang, supra n.164, pp. 9–13.
169 Iida, supra n.44; Araki, supra n.106; Pekkanen, supra n.106.
170 Gao, supra n.108.
171 "Are Jobs Being Created or Lost in AFTA?", *The Jakarta Post* (Jakarta), 31 May 2005.
172 *The ASEAN Free Trade Area: A Proposal* (Thai discussion paper, October 1991), cited in Rudolfo Severino, *Southeast Asia in Search of an ASEAN Community*, Singapore: ISEAS, 2006, p. 223.
173 Cf. David Mitrany, *A Working Peace System*, Chicago: Quadrangle Books, 1966, pp. 92–99; Ernst B. Haas, "The Uniting of Europe", in Mette Eilstrup-Sangiovanni ed. *Debates on European Integration*, New York: Palgrave Macmillan, 2006, p. 111.
174 Hans Kelsen, *Peace through Law*, Chapel Hill: University of North Carolina Press, 1944, p. 116; Hans Kelsen, *Law of the United Nations*, London: Stevens, 1951, p. 484.
175 Charnovitz, supra n.62, p. 678. See further Tesón, supra n.15.
176 For "realism" and "liberalism" in international relations theory, see Kenneth W. Abbott, "International Relations Theory, International Law, and the Regime Governing Atrocities in Internal Conflicts", Symposium on Methods in International Law, 93 *American Journal of International Law* 361 (1999).
177 Frederick M. Abbott, "A New Dominant Trade Species Emerges", in William J. Davey and John Jackson, *The Future of International Economic Law*, Oxford: Oxford University Press, 2008, p. 133.
178 See Trans-Pacific Strategic Partnership Agreement, Art. 20.6 para. 1 which invites the participation of APEC economies and other states.
179 G. Evelyn Hutchinson, "Concluding Remarks", 22 *Cold Spring Harbor Symposia on Quantitative Biology* 415 (1957), p. 417.
180 See Simon S.C. Tay, *Asia Alone*, Singapore: Wiley, 2010.
181 For the, now, classic work on the systemic causes of trade friction during the Cold War era, see Sylvia Ostry, *The Post-Cold War Trading System*, Chicago: University of Chicago Press, 1997.
182 The Lisbon Treaty obliges the Member States of the European Union to work together for a "highly competitive social market economy, aiming at full employment and social progress"; Treaty of Lisbon, 13 December 2007, OJ 2007/C 306/01, Art. 2(3).
183 See Randall Peerenboom, *China Modernizes: Threat to the West or Model for the Rest?*, Oxford: Oxford University Press, 2007.
184 Adam Smith, *An Inquiry into the Nature and Causes of the Wealth of Nations*, New York: Modern Library, 1994.
185 James Bacchus, supra n.21, p. 155.
186 *Whitney* v. *California*, 274 U.S. 357 (1927).
187 *Virginia State Board of Pharmacy* v. *Virginia Citizens Consumer Council, Inc.*, 425 U.S. 748 (1976).

5 Webcasting

A tool to increase transparency in judicial proceedings

Sofia Plagakis[1]

Introduction

In May 2010, the International Centre for Settlement of Investment Disputes (ICSID), for the first time, webcast its hearing in real-time to the public in the *Pac Rim Cayman LLC* v. *Republic of El Salvador* case. This case involves a dispute on halting harmful metals mining in El Salvador, and webcasting the proceedings allowed people in El Salvador and elsewhere greater access to information affecting their health and environment. ICSID followed this precedent by webcasting proceedings in two additional investor–State disputes: the *Commerce Group* v. *Republic of El Salvador* case and the *Railroad Development Corporation* v. *Republic of Guatemala* case. By webcasting these three cases, did ICSID introduce a new standard of transparency in international economic dispute settlement proceedings?

Webcasting is the method of broadcasting live audio and video in real-time to audiences all over the world via the Internet. Webcasting is used extensively in the commercial sector, e.g. for investor presentations, seminars, and other communications activities. Webcasting should not be confused with web-conferencing or webinars, which are designed for person-to-person interaction. Although webcasting has been in existence for twenty years, it was initially slow to gain acceptance for several reasons: poor video quality, obtrusive equipment, network bottlenecks, and high cost. But technological and other improvements have led to better quality, lower costs, and increased accessibility, making webcasting an excellent tool for expanding public access to judicial proceedings.

International non-economic and domestic judicial bodies began webcasting their proceedings over fifteen years ago, and the debate over webcasting courts has moved to international economic dispute settlement bodies. ICSID's decision to webcast the proceedings in the three cases was a major step towards increasing transparency in international arbitrations. International economic dispute bodies, which have long been criticized for their lack of transparency (especially given that disputes affect the daily life of citizens) have been reluctant to webcast their oral proceedings. International economic dispute settlement bodies have taken steps to make hearings more publically accessible in its dispute settlement proceedings (e.g. physical access to the room where the hearing is taking place and live one-way video streaming to a specific room); yet, they have fallen short of webcasting their proceedings, despite having the equipment and capability to do so. For instance, the World Trade Organization (WTO) and World Bank provide webcasting of events and conferences for training and educational purposes.

This chapter analyzes the extent to which webcasting international economic dispute settlement proceedings can be a tool for expanding public access to information that affects public health, safety and environment (ultimately concluding that webcasting has excellent potential in this respect). Hence, this chapter is focused on those disputes where the State is a party. International non-economic and domestic judicial bodies, which have made considerable strides by webcasting their oral arguments, provide a useful starting ground in examining the advantages and concerns that webcasting may bring to international economic dispute settlement bodies. The webcasting experiences of international non-economic courts, including the European Court of Human Rights (ECHR), the International Court of Justice (ICJ), and the Permanent Court of Arbitration (PCA), and domestic judiciaries in Brazil, Canada and even China, for example, are illustrative. Further, ICSID's own experience webcasting proceedings in its first three investor–State disputes serves as a model by which international economic dispute bodies can follow.

This chapter proceeds in four parts. First, it provides a brief overview of the history of using cameras in courts. Second, the chapter explains the context in which international economic dispute settlement bodies have increased public access to information in their procedures, and the efforts and challenges this poses regarding webcasting proceedings. Third, it examines the strides made by domestic and international judicial bodies in webcasting their proceedings, highlighting the advantages and concerns of webcasting proceedings. Fourth, it looks more closely at ICSID's first two experiences webcasting investor–State disputes.

From television to Internet: history of cameras in courts

The ability of the public and the press to watch judicial proceedings is a significant component of what makes governments transparent, accessible, and accountable. This principle, referred to as open justice, has long been formally recognized in constitutional and human rights texts. It has become enshrined domestically, for example, in the Sixth Amendment to the US Constitution and in international human rights instruments, such as Article 14 of the International Covenant on Civil and Political Rights (ICCPR), and Article 6 of the European Convention for the Protection of Human Rights.[2] In both the ICCPR and the European Convention, the right entitles everyone to a fair and public hearing by an independent and impartial tribunal established by law.

Traditionally, open public proceedings limited access to those members of the public who could physically attend judicial proceedings. Although the advancement of audio-visual technology – photographic equipment and television cameras – provided broader public access to open proceedings, the ability to see judicial proceedings in action before the twenty-first century still remained fairly limited. Bans and restrictions on allowing cameras to record proceedings were initially imposed in countries, such as the United States and United Kingdom, in response to the disruption of judicial proceedings caused by excessive media coverage and the use of distracting and intrusive cameras and photographic equipment during judicial proceedings (Strickland, 1994). However, as cameras and photographic equipment became smaller and less intrusive, judiciaries began permitting cameras to record their proceedings. Although judiciaries do not always permit cameras, or have granted camera use only with special permission, camera access to proceedings has been allowed in numerous countries, including Australia, Canada, China, France, Israel, Italy, the Netherlands, New Zealand, Norway, Russia, Singapore, and Spain, to name a few. The greatest experience of cameras in the court is in the United States, where television coverage of court cases has been massive, and thousands of cases are televised each year locally, regionally and nationally.

The continued advancements of audio-visual technology – less obtrusive camera equipment, and more recently, the Internet – have moved us towards a broadened concept of open justice, expanding the audience of judicial proceedings. In this context, the principle of open justice has often interacted with the principles of freedom of speech and of the press, which have been at the forefront of many judicial decisions and discussions.

Webcasting judicial proceedings raises important issues regarding how to provide public access to judicial proceedings, especially since judicial rules regarding coverage of trials were written prior to the advent of the Internet, and were written with media and television cameras in mind. There has been much scholarly literature as well as judicial consideration on allowing television cameras in courts (e.g. Lassiter, 1996; Cohn and Dow, 1998; and Nashiri, 2002). The primary argument in support of allowing television cameras in the courtroom, advocated largely by the media, is that the public, and particularly the media, has a right to see and report what goes on in judicial proceedings. This argument coincides with the principle of open justice, inherent in many domestic and international human rights laws, as well as the long recognized view that the media acts as surrogates for the public through its presence in judicial proceedings.[3] The arguments against cameras in court include the following: television cameras, and hence the media, sensationalize proceedings; jurors are distracted; a parties' right to privacy is invaded; witnesses are intimidated; and lawyers and judges, particularly elected judges, grand stand. In sum, these arguments often are variants on the theme that allowing cameras in courts would deprive parties of their right to a fair trial. Although many courts remain opposed to televising court proceedings, new technology and changed attitudes have begun to tip the scales in this longstanding debate and judiciaries have begun using Internet technology to promote and facilitate public access to their proceedings by webcasting.

Technological advances have ensured that audio-visual recording of judicial proceedings need not distract or disrupt proceedings. Many judiciaries have installed their own recording equipment, no longer relying on media cameras to record proceedings, which makes camera coverage less daunting for parties, witnesses, juries, and judges, and hence, more acceptable to the public. Further, many studies and experiments have shown that the presence of television cameras in court does not inherently deprive a parties' right to a fair trial.[4] However, other studies have been inconclusive regarding the effect of televising proceedings (Stepniak, 2004). In some cases, this perceived inconclusiveness of evidence, coupled with judges' traditional mistrust of media reporting and cameras in courts have led judges to continue to deny camera access. In other cases, it led judiciaries, such as the Supreme Court in Canada and the International Criminal Tribunal for the former Yugoslavia, to apply regulations and controls with respect to televising and webcasting proceedings to reduce any possibility of detrimental effects.

There has not been much scholarly work addressing the advantages and concerns of webcasting. However, judicial decisions, press releases, interviews, newspaper and brief articles reveal that decisions to webcast have been prompted by judicial bodies and the public demanding more direct public access, awareness and transparency in judicial proceedings. The webcasting literature differs from the cameras-in-court literature in that it focuses more on describing the experiences of the judicial bodies providing webcasting, the specific technology available, the quality of that technology, and the financial costs associated with providing webcasting. It does not focus on similar concerns arising with televising judicial proceedings, as judiciaries control the installation of cameras and distribution of content, not the media. Additionally, the webcasting literature focuses largely on the experiences in local US judiciaries, and does not address the developments in other domestic judiciaries, including Canada, Australia, Brazil and China, or in international judicial or international economic dispute settlement bodies. This chapter addresses these gaps by addressing developments and efforts in webcasting domestic judiciaries, international judicial and international economic dispute settlement bodies.

International economic dispute settlement: setting the context for webcasting

The tradition of secrecy

International investment arbitration, both under treaties and contracts, remain the fastest-growing form of dispute resolution, and also one of the fastest-developing areas of international law. The growth of international investment since the 1990s has led to over 2500 bilateral investment treaties between foreign states, in addition to multilateral treaties and other forms of contracts or agreements. Disputes are often resolved in, and or in accordance with the rules, of several institutions, such as ICSID and the United Nations Commission on International Trade Law (UNCITRAL) for investment disputes, and the WTO for trade disputes.

However, unlike many judicial processes, international economic dispute settlement is marked by secrecy and has long been criticized for its lack of transparency. International economic dispute proceedings are often held in a confidential manner; for example, in some instances, knowing that dispute settlement proceedings have been initiated, learning what the issues and arguments are in the dispute, and viewing the awards granted in these disputes are not permitted (Bernasconi-Osterwalder, 2006). Although the principle of open justice is embodied in constitutional and international human rights laws, international economic dispute settlement processes are based on an entirely secretive model. For example, it is often impossible to even know whether an arbitration has been initiated or what the outcome is – even in cases involving large potential or actual monetary liability for public treasuries. This secrecy results in an unacceptable deficit in those values commonly reflected in modern democracies. Further, the secrecy thwarts both domestic freedom of information laws and States' ability to respect the human right to access to information.

Part of this secrecy is because international economic dispute settlement bodies, in particular, investment dispute bodies, find their origin in private commercial arbitration. The other part is, quite simply, States often prefer secrecy over transparency. Although trade and investment disputes involving States implicate public interest issues, they are decided in processes designed to address private and commercial issues, without regard to the transparency and participation values of democratic governance.

The public interest element: shifting from secrecy to transparency

The public interest character of proceedings involving States or State entities has shifted the focus of international economic arbitration disputes from secrecy to transparency. This shift occurred largely because of the considerable efforts made by civil society organizations, advocating that international economic dispute settlement involving a State can not be treated as private arbitration, and that the public has a right to watch its proceedings (Center for International Environmental Law, 2007).

WTO and investor–State disputes involve issues of public interest not only in the substantive and financial outcome of the arbitration, but also in the arguments and factual assertions exchanged during the process (Magraw et al., 2008). The subject matter of many international economic disputes affects the daily life of citizens, and many cases impact the cost and availability of public services, such as water, waste management, electricity, and the management of important natural resources, such as oil, minerals, forests, fisheries and water. Examples of public policy measures contested under international investment rules include: a Mexican town's refusal to grant a permit for a waste-disposal facility; Argentina's response to its fiscal crisis (over 35 cases were filed with ICSID, claiming several billions of dollars); and Cochabamba, Bolivia's and Dar es Salam, Tanzania's regulation of their drinking water system. These cases penetrate deeply into domestic policy-making, and affect policies that protect public health, safety and the environment. Additionally, trade and investment arbitrations raise public policy concerns based on the amount of money involved (Delaney and Magraw, 2008). That is, arbitrations often involve large potential monetary liability for public treasuries, and any award of compensation would greatly affect a State's budget. For example, many recent claims are "for US$500 million or even US$1 billion, significant amounts for any investor and just as importantly, for any respondent State, many of which would struggle to pay even one award of US$500 million" (Center for International Environmental Law, 2007).

Some States and international dispute settlement bodies have begun recognizing the public interest element and the need for transparency, taking steps to increase transparency in dispute settlement procedures. This shift is visible, for example, in disputes under the North American Free Trade Agreement's (NAFTA) Chapter 11;[5] ICSID's revised rules; the process to revise UNCITRAL arbitration rules; and in open hearings at the WTO.

NAFTA tribunals began emphasizing the public interest element inherent in disputes involving a state in *Methanex Corp* v. *United States*. This case was significant in advancing transparency for several reasons: the tribunal ruled that it had authority to accept and consider amicus curiae briefs; the disputing parties agreed to conduct public hearings (except for one procedural hearing that was privately held at Methanex's request); and the parties agreed to make public all the major procedural documents in the case (McRae, 2006: 374). The NAFTA Tribunal hearing the case emphasized the importance of transparency in public interest arbitrations in the following statement:

> There is undoubtedly public interest in this arbitration. The substantive issues extend far beyond those raised by the usual transnational arbitration between commercial parties. This is not merely because one of the Disputing Parties is a State . . . The public interest in this arbitration arises from its subject-matter, as powerfully suggested in the Petitions. There is also a broader argument, as suggested by the Respondent and Canada: the Chapter 11 arbitral process could benefit from being perceived as more open or transparent; or conversely be harmed if seen as unduly secretive.[6]

In general, NAFTA is silent on the issue of public access to arbitration hearings; however, hearings have been open to the public only with the consent of both disputing parties.[7] In addition to the *Methanex* case, NAFTA tribunals have allowed public hearings in the *UPS* and *Canfor* cases. According to NAFTA's Free Trade Commission, NAFTA itself contains no express duty of confidentiality, and subject to Article 1137(4), parties in NAFTA disputes are not prohibited from releasing to the public the documents exchanged during the arbitration. In October 2003, Canada and the United States publicly stated their intent to consent to open hearings for investor–State disputes in every case. Mexico joined this consensus in July 2004.[8] In each country's statement, each country recommends that "tribunals determine the appropriate logistical arrangements for open hearings in consultation with disputing parties. These arrangements may include, for example, use of closed-circuit television systems, Internet webcasting, or other forms of access."[9]

The NAFTA Tribunal experimented with using technology to increase public access in the *Cases Regarding the Border Closure due to BSE Concerns*, or BSE case. This case allowed a one-way transmission to the University of Calgary in Canada, which is where a lawyer representing the claimants taught. Though the one-way transmission increased access to the claimants, civil society organizations, including the Center for International Environmental Law (CIEL), suggested the hearing be open to physical public presence and webcast, arguing that the one-way video transmission of the hearing to a room at the University of Calgary in Canada is insufficient to fulfill the US public's interest in this case.[10] The experiences in the NAFTA cases proved that allowing public access to investment arbitral hearings and providing video transmission was possible at low cost and without interfering with the hearing or causing any other problems.

On the issue of public access to hearings, rule 32 of the 2003 ICSID Arbitration Rules authorizes tribunals to allow non-parties to attend ICSID arbitration hearings, but only with the consent of the parties. During the drafting process of the 2003 amendments, it was proposed that the tribunal be given the right to open the hearings over the objection of the parties, with only consultation of the parties being required. Instead a compromise was reached and rule 32 of the ICSID Arbitration Rules provides that "[u]nless either party objects" the tribunal, after consultation with ICSID's Secretary-General, may allow non-parties to attend or observe all or part of the arbitration hearings. While explicit consent of the parties is no longer necessary, each party retains a veto right by way of objection to non-parties being allowed to attend.

The shift to transparency can also be seen in the process to revise UNCITRAL Arbitration Rules. These rules are the most widely used in private commercial disputes, and are also used for arbitrations by foreign investors against host states. However, the true number of UNCITRAL investor–State arbitrations is unknown, as the rules do not require such proceedings to be made public. Existing UNCITRAL rules do not adequately reflect transparency and public participation concerns as they apply to State arbitrations. This deficiency is not surprising, because the existing rules were drafted primarily, if not exclusively, with commercial arbitrations in mind. In addition, the rules were adopted before the influx of bilateral investment treaties, which have been used to enable private investors to initiate numerous disputes against host states in the past ten years.

UNCITRAL embarked on a process of revising its arbitration rules in 2006. Since 2006 public interest organizations, particularly CIEL and the International Institute for Sustainable Development, have been urging members of UNCITRAL's Working Group II (the group mandated to revise the arbitration rules) to get the issue of transparency onto the agenda, recommending that hearings are open and webcast to the public. At UNCITRAL's Commission meeting in June 2008, UNCITRAL's main body reached consensus that the UNCITRAL arbitration rules should provide for transparency in arbitrations brought by investors against states. It mandated Working Group II to begin discussions on transparency immediately after it finished its work revising the generic arbitration rules. The Working Group completed its work on the generic arbitration rules in 2010, and at the time of this writing is engaged in meeting the challenge to ensure transparency in its rules regarding treaty-based investment disputes.

With respect to the WTO, oral proceedings are kept confidential under the Dispute Settlement Understanding (DSU).[11] However, there have been proposals to make the disputes more transparent, contending that open hearings, including webcasting hearings, would increase transparency, accessibility and confidence (including that of WTO Members). Both the United States and Canada[12] submitted proposals, calling for all substantive meetings of the panels, Appellate Body and all arbitrations to be open to the public; and for all submissions to panels, the Appellate Body and arbitrators to be public, except those portions dealing with confidential information. However, the proposals remain controversial among many government delegations. In particular, there was much opposition to the US proposal, as many developing county Members, such as Brazil, Chile, India, Indonesia, Mexico, Malaysia, the Philippines and Uruguay, rejected the proposal, which they said would undermine the intergovernmental character of the WTO (International Centre for Trade and Sustainable Development, 2002).

Despite the controversy of its previous proposal, the United States, submitted another proposal in July 2005 on improving transparency in the WTO dispute settlement rules.[13] This proposal suggested that the WTO broadcast its proceedings, recommending that: the WTO Secretariat control any electronic broadcast; the WTO explore various options to ensure that the broadcast be as unobtrusive as possible, including a voice-activated camera to focus on and track only those who are speaking; and the WTO discuss the possibility of allowing the hearings to be broadcasted, as that would provide greater flexibility concerning viewing times, although it would raise questions about who would have rights to re-broadcast. As the proposals to increase transparency, including webcasting, remain controversial, they have not, as of yet, been included in the *Proposed Amendments to the WTO's Dispute Settlement Understanding*. Although there has been support and progress in improving transparency in the WTO's Dispute Settlement, only time will tell whether open hearings or webcasting become an amendment to the DSU (Sutherland, 2004).

Despite the failure to allow open hearings in the WTO's dispute settlement rules, certain WTO Member States, as consenting disputing parties, have taken measures to provide open hearings in dispute's involving them (Orellana, 2009). In 2005, the three disputing parties in the *US – Hormones (Continued Suspension)* case[14] – the European Commission, the United States and Canada – requested that the proceedings with the parties and scientific experts be open to the public, which enabled the WTO panel to allow closed-circuit television cameras into the courtroom. The *Beef Hormones* case set a precedent in cases where all parties agreed to make hearings accessible to the public.

Soon after, other hearings were open to the public (Ehring, 2008: 1023),[15] and in July 2008, the first ever public viewing of the WTO's Appellate Body procedures occurred, as the three disputing parties in the *Beef Hormones* case continued the call for open hearings by requesting the WTO's Appellate Body proceedings in the *Beef Hormones* case be open to the public, again via closed-circuit broadcasting in Geneva. Although the parties hailed the Appellate Body hearing as an "improved evolution" for increasing transparency in WTO's dispute settlement, some Members participating in the case as third parties, particularly China and Brazil, were opposed to open hearings.[16] Hence, to reflect the dissension among Members, the broadcast of the public hearing was cut whenever China and Brazil intervened, as they had not given their permission for an open hearing. As open processes have not been formalized in the WTO, there has been inconsistency in supporting open hearings and in the method to which hearings are open (i.e. hearings have been open only where all parties in the dispute, as well as the dispute settlement panel agree, and only certain cases have been opened) (Orellana, 2009).

Civil society organizations have called for WTO Members to formalize open proceedings, including webcasting. For example, CIEL wrote letters to the European Commission, the office of the US Trade Representative, and Canada's Minister of International Trade requesting their governments make open hearings and webcasting their official policy in all WTO disputes.[17] Moreover, since open processes have not been formalized in the WTO, civil society has also intervened by requesting that hearings are open and webcast is available in specific cases.

Despite the increased number of public hearings within the WTO dispute settlement process, panel and Appellate Body hearings remain closed to the public in general, with a very few exceptions being recognized. Perhaps the WTO's open hearings will contribute to a more informed discussion of possible institutional changes to the system, including webcasting of its dispute proceedings.

Hence, a general consensus exists that the public has a legitimate and substantial interest in disputes involving states. People affected by decisions have a right to know what decisions are being made and what the arguments are. Similarly, in order to voice their opinion with respect to judicial decisions, people need to know what those decisions are and the reasoning involved in making them. As international economic dispute settlement bodies wrestle with the idea of increasing transparency by webcasting their proceedings, debates over technology in formerly technology-free venues are becoming more common, especially as the number of domestic and international courts that webcast their hearings continues to grow. The next section highlights the domestic and international courts that have paved the way to webcast their judicial proceedings, highlighting the advantages and concerns that webcasting proceeding will bring to international economic dispute settlement bodies and to the public.

Webcasting international non-economic and domestic courts: advantages and concerns

With the advancement of technology over the past decade, webcasting judicial proceedings has become more common, driven by improvements in the quality, speed and reliability of the Internet to distribute content, and increasingly accepted by international non-economic and domestic court systems for the advantages that it brings.

This section examines the international non-economic and domestic judicial bodies that have decided to webcast theirs proceedings, along with the different ways in which they provided webcasting services. In doing so, it assesses: (1) the main advantages to webcasting court proceedings, highlighting those bodies that either currently allow or have, at one time, allowed their judicial hearings to be webcast (see Tables 5.1 and 5.2 for a list (as of publication date) of the international and domestic courts that have webcast their proceedings); (2) additional benefits of webcasting; and (3) concerns associated with webcasting.

Advantages of webcasting

The main advantages to webcasting court proceedings are that it increases transparency, awareness, and accessibility. Although these issues overlap, they will be discussed separately in this section.

Table 5.1 International and multinational courts and tribunals

Court Name	*Live (L) or Archived (A) Webcast*	*Access*
Cambodia War Crimes Tribunal	A	Partial recordings made available to public at http://www.cambodiatribunal.org/
European Court of Human Rights	L/A	http://www.echr.coe.int/ECHR/EN/Header/Press/Multimedia/Webcasts+of+public+hearings/
International Court of Justice	L/A (temporary)	Webcasts of select court decisions are available on a temporary "Video Archive" link on the ICJ website http://www.icj-cij.org/homepage/index.php
International Criminal Court	L (30 min. delay)	Public hearings are screened online with 30 minutes delay. http://www.icc-cpi.int/Menus/ICC/Press+and+Media/Audiovisual+Gallery/
International Criminal Tribunal for the Former Yugoslavia	L	http://www.icty.org/
International Criminal Tribunal for Rwanda	L	Live coverage via free satellite service. Instructions on use available at: http://www.unictr.org/Portals/0/English/News/Satellite/ictr_by_Satellite.pdf
International Tribunal for the Law of the Sea	L/A	http://www.itlos.org/start2_en.html
Permanent Court of Arbitration	A	http://www.pca-cpa.org/showpage.asp?pag_id=1318
International Centre for Settlement of Investment Disputes	L/A	Select cases. http://worldbank.org/icsid

Table 5.2 Domestic (non-US) courts and tribunals

Court Name	*Live (L) or Archived (A) Webcast*	*Access*
Federal Constitutional Court of Germany	A	http://www.bundesverfassungsgericht.de/rss/entscheidungen/
Supreme Court of Western Australia	A	Selected hearings and webcasts only, through Supreme Court Webcasting Project http://www.law.uwa.edu.au/courses/webcasting_project
Supreme Court of Canada	L/A	http://www.scc-csc.gc.ca/case-dossier/cms-sgd/webcasts-webdiffusions-eng.aspx
Supreme Federal Court of Brazil	L/A	Via "TV Justica" http://www.tvjustica.jus.br/
China – District and County Court Webcasts	L	http://bjfyzb.chinacourt.org
Supreme Court of the United Kingdom	L	http://news.sky.com/skynews/Supreme-Court

Improving transparency and awareness

The main advantage of, and reason for, webcasting oral proceedings is that it acts as an additional mechanism to increase transparency, making public hearings truly public. Webcasting can provide immediate access to information with live footage with which viewers can associate, and it can also improve awareness by directly reaching out to the public and educate them about the operation of the judicial branch. The literature provides several important advantages that may be associated with increased transparency in relation to arbitration proceedings. Daniel Magraw and Niranjali Amerasinghe (2009) describe several advantages, which fall into nine categories: higher quality decision-making; democratic values and realization of human rights; protection of interests; consistency; legitimacy; accountability; implementation; systemic reform; and demonstration. Scholars and practitioners have also shown that secrecy in governmental affairs may harbor corruption, but that increased information technology (including webcasting), which is closely linked to the goal of transparency, is critical in combating corruption (Salbu, 2001: 10; Florini, 1998). Space constraints prevent a full examination of these.

Though improving transparency and awareness were seen as the primary advantages and reasons for webcasting, each court differs as to how it provides webcasting services. For instance, some proceedings are only available live; others are only offered archived; and others are available only by special court permission. In addition, several courts have decided to provide webcasting in all of their court proceedings, where others have decided to webcast select cases based on the level of public interest involved. In the realm of international criminal law, webcasting was seen as a necessary tool to promote transparency and accountability. The International Criminal Tribunal for the former Yugoslavia (ICTY), Cambodia War Crimes Tribunal and International Criminal Court decided to webcast their proceedings to ensure that they were as open and accessible as possible.

The ICTY set precedent in 1995 by being the first judicial body to webcast its proceedings. The ICTY represents the first attempt by an international community to enforce international humanitarian law in armed conflict since the International Military Tribunal at Nuremberg after the Second World War (O'Brien, 1993). Its mandate was to prosecute those persons responsible for serious violations of international humanitarian law committed in the former Yugoslavia since 1991. Judges in the ICTY decided that the proceedings should be recorded and made available to the public for the following reasons: "to make sure that justice would be seen to be done, to dispel any misunderstandings that might otherwise arise as to the role and the nature of the Tribunal proceedings and to fulfill the educational task of the Tribunal" (Mason, 2000). In a report on the impact of webcasting the ICTY's proceedings, Dr. Paul Mason found that cameras contribute to a proper administration of justice (2000).

In 2005, the court began covering all three courtrooms in relevant languages. ICTY proceedings are available in English, French, as well as Bosnian, Croatian and Serbian. In cases pertaining to Kosovo or the Former Yugoslav Republic of Macedonia, proceedings are also available in Albanian and/or Macedonian. Webcasting services were set up and operated by an outside provider on a voluntary basis with no direct involvement of the Tribunal's technical services. Each courtroom is equipped with six remote-controlled and silent cameras that record the proceedings both for archiving and media purposes. Following strict instructions intended to ensure a full, balanced, fair and accurate account of the public hearings, the Tribunal's audio-visual staff selects pictures from the six cameras on a full and live basis. Though judgments and initial appearances – when the accused faces the court for the first time – are broadcast live, all other sessions are broadcast with a 30-minute delay to protect any confidential information that any party may accidentally provide the court.

The Cambodia War Crimes Tribunal, formally known as the Extraordinary Chambers in the Courts of Cambodia for the Prosecution of Crimes Committed during the Period of Democratic Kampuchea, is a special Cambodian court that functions in partnership with the United Nations to prosecute "senior leaders" of the Khmer Rouge and those "most responsible" for atrocities committed between 1974 and 1979. It is composed of Cambodian and international judges, prosecutors, and court staff.

Though conceived in 1997, the Cambodia War Crimes Tribunal did not indict its first suspect until 2007. There were no original plans designated to webcast the proceedings until Illinois State Senator Jeff Schoenberg, who visited Cambodia in 2006 on a fact-finding mission, secured funding to create a website that would provide information about the trials, including webcasting them. According to Schoenberg:

> I asked the representatives of the United Nations who were leading the tour if they were going to be showing the Khmer Rouge leadership tribunal on the Internet. I just assumed that they were going to. And I found out that there were no plans whatsoever, largely out of budgetary constraints . . . And it immediately sparked my thinking that this is a very powerful story that needs to be told . . . not just within Cambodia, but throughout the world. We had all witnessed a genocide where people needed to be held accountable for their actions. (Quaraishi, 2010)

The Cambodia Tribunal Monitor was launched in September 2007 by a consortium of academic, philanthropic and non-profit organizations committed to providing public access to the tribunal and open discussion throughout the judicial process.[18] The website provides daily tape delayed video of the court proceedings, as well as video of interviews with Cambodian citizens documenting their reaction to the events. A private company created the website for the Tribunal, developing and managing the design and content for the website,[19] and operates the website on behalf of Northwestern University School of Law Center for International Human Rights and the Documentation Center of Cambodia. Although the Tribunal has allowed webcasting of the trials, a trial chamber may order that the press and public be excluded from all or part of the proceeding for reasons of 'public order or morality,' safety and security, non-disclosure of the identity of a victim or witness, and the protection of the interests of justice.[20]

Other international non-economic courts webcast only those proceedings they consider to be of exceptional public interest. The International Court of Justice, the principal judicial organ of the United Nations, first announced in February 2004 that it would provide webcasting in cases of exceptional public interest in oral proceedings and the delivery of Court decisions.[21] The ICJ webcast its public hearing live and in its entirety in the case concerning the *Legal Consequences of the Construction of a Wall in the Occupied Palestinian Territory* (request for advisory opinion), commonly referred to as the *Israeli Wall* case. The Court's decision was made in response to the interest shown by the general public, civil society and the media worldwide, and to better accommodate the public and the media due to very limited seating space at the Peace Palace in The Hague.[22] Although the ICJ's press release claims that it "intends to provide such webcasting in the future for cases of a similar nature", it is unclear what the criteria would be for providing future webcasts. How much of a public interest is needed for proceedings to be webcast? What constitutes 'exceptional public interest'?

Although those questions remain unanswered, in an email communication from the Court's Registry, dated 29 June 2007, an ICJ Information Officer expressed the Court's interest in utilizing Internet broadcast technology with greater frequency and regularity in the future, while admitting that the ICJ is currently unable to do so due to financial constraints.[23] As of January 2011, the ICJ has webcast, at least some portion (e.g. advisory opinion, reading of the court's judgment, or the public hearings) of four cases.[24] In each of the four cases, the ICJ provided webcasting in real-time on the Court's website in the Court's two official languages, French and English. The Court provides archived videos of the webcast, but for only three months after the proceeding. Having such a short timeframe for viewing the archived videos makes it difficult for lawyers, scholars, students and the general public to research the case at hand.

In domestic courts that do not have rules requiring court proceedings to be webcast, the decision to webcast is usually the judges' decision and usually in cases that involve exceptional public interest. For instance, Canada's first judicial proceeding to allow webcasting occurred in 2001 in the Supreme Court of British Columbia, which was an ad hoc decision by its Chief Justice.[25] The Supreme Court of British Columbia allowed a petition by the Independent Media Center to webcast live the entire proceeding in *United Mexican States* v. *Metalclad Corporation*, which involved a challenge to an international arbitral tribunal's award under the NAFTA. The presiding judge ruled that Independent Media could record the proceeding and webcast it on the Internet on condition that the hearings were covered in their entirety. As a result, ten days of hearings were recorded and some 40 hours of video together with background documents and interviews were made publicly available on Independent Media's webpage.

In 2011, the Philippines Supreme Court allowed a live webcast through its website of the trial of the Maguindanao Massacre (the country's worst political violence, involving a political clan accused in the massacre of 57 people) for the first time. A court statement says that through webcasting the trial will be accessible to viewers worldwide without interruption. The Court had also granted media groups requesting live coverage to broadcast the proceedings live on their networks. Though media groups welcomed the Court's decision, it also caused some conflict due to the very strict conditions that the court imposed upon them in order to webcast the proceedings, including continuous broadcast without commercials and a commitment to air all the hearings, without exception, until the trial's end. Sonny Fernandez, director of the National Union of Journalists of the Philippines said: "They want a continuous coverage so that the public will be able to watch the full trial without biases, we understand that. But the reality in broadcast is we have commercial breaks, because we have contracts and commitment with our sponsors" (Ong, 2011). The decisions of both the Supreme Court of British Columbia and the Philippines Supreme Court also exemplify the advantage that webcasting has versus traditional media, i.e. televising court proceedings, which will be discussed in further detail later.

In certain international non-economic courts, webcasting is only permitted when both parties in the arbitration consent. For instance, in 2009, the Permanent Court of Arbitration (PCA), an intergovernmental organization with over one hundred member States, featured a complete webcast of the proceedings in the Abyei case, which was the arbitration between Sudan and the SPLM/A over the Abyei region (Crook, 2009). This was the first webcast of arbitration between a State and a non-State actor. The complete webcast took place over five and a half days of proceedings at The Hague in April 2009, which are divided into 90-minute clips following the issues as argued by the parties.[26]

Transparency varies from dispute to dispute in the PCA, which was established in 1899 to facilitate arbitration and other forms of dispute resolution between States and State entities, intergovernmental organizations, and private parties. The reason for this variation is because under the PCA rules the decision whether to webcast depends on the parties to each dispute, not to the PCA secretariat or to PCA Member States as a whole. As the PCA is not a "court" in the traditional sense and depends upon party consent to ensure transparency, the Abyei case was webcast because both parties – the SPLM/A and the Sudanese government – committed to the "maximum transparency throughout the proceedings", including opening the oral proceedings to the public. In a press release, the SPLM/A emphasized its belief "that unrestricted access to public information is central to good governance and justice as per the provisions of our National Constitution."[27]

Like international non-economic courts, domestic courts have also begun webcasting to improve transparency, awareness and accessibility. But, unlike international courts, there are more challenges in webcasting domestic courts because of the different levels of government (e.g. federal or local), and therefore, court systems. For example, some states, such as Brazil, the United Kingdom and Canada, allow their supreme courts, but not their local courts to webcast their proceedings. For instance, Brazil's Supreme Federal Court, the Supremo Tribunal Federal, is the country's highest Constitutional Court. It operates a television channel called TV Justica (Justice Television), which can also be watched via the Internet from its website. TV Justica aims to raise awareness among citizens about their constitutional rights, and inform them about the activities and decisions from the Constitutional Court. TV Justica shows the hearings from the Plenary of the Supreme Federal Court, as well as different programs including interviews with scholars, justices, and citizens. Not only does Brazil's Supreme Federal Court embrace webcasting technology, but also some of the hearings are archived and available via YouTube. Individuals can also sign-up and receive messages from the Supreme Tribunal Federal on Twitter, a social networking and blogging service that enables its users to send and read messages known as tweets.[28]

The United Kingdom, which has long banned photographs and cameras in courtrooms in England, Wales and Northern Ireland, has also begun allowing its Supreme Court to webcast its proceedings in real-time, but not its lower courts. The Supreme Court of the United Kingdom, which replaced the Law Lords as the highest court in the United Kingdom in October 2009, is the final court of appeal in the United Kingdom for all civil and criminal cases from England, Wales and Northern Ireland, but not Scotland. The Supreme Court's objective is "to transform the public's awareness of justice at the highest level, with the aim of being as transparent as possible in its judgments and proceedings" (Supreme Court of the United Kingdom, 2009). In May 2011, the Court began allowing Sky News, a media company in the United Kingdom, to webcast its court hearings and judgments in real-time via the media company's website. To enable webcasting, there are four cameras installed in each of the three court rooms. The website also contains direct links to the Supreme Court's own summaries of each case, to enable viewers to read some background material.

The United Kingdom's decision was a welcomed step in advancing transparency and accessibility. Previously, the newly established Court had a more restrictive policy by only allowing the media to access recordings of its oral hearings, which had generally been limited to news coverage of the judgments (Supreme Court of the United Kingdom, 2009). According to the Court, "the move means that legal professionals, students and members of the public interested in the work of the Supreme Court do not have to travel to London to see proceedings" (Supreme Court of the United Kingdom, 2011). However, cameras have been largely kept out of Scottish courts, with some exception, most notably the hearing and decision of the Lockerbie bombers' appeal. The appeal process, which was conducted in the Netherlands but under Scottish law, were broadcast live by BBC television and streamed live in English and Arabic on the BBC's website and via a number of overseas websites.

In Canada's Ontario Court of Appeal, cameras in the courtroom are generally prohibited under Ontario law; however, they are permitted for educational or instructional purposes – i.e. for increasing awareness – with approval from the presiding judge and consent from the parties and witnesses to the proceeding. The Ontario Court of Appeal began a pilot project to webcast some of its proceedings in September 2007.[29] As part of a two-month pilot project, called the *Cameras in the Court of Appeal Pilot Project*, certain proceedings were recorded and streamed live on the Ontario Court of Appeal's website. DVD copies of recorded proceedings were distributed to accredited media twice per day on request, and available for use by journalism and law schools and other organizations for educational and training purposes. In addition, recorded proceedings were archived on the Court's website for 90 days to ensure continuous public access. The final report of the pilot project was given to the Ministry of the Attorney General for review; however, there are no plans to release the report to the public.[30] And as of December 2010, there were no plans by the Ontario Court of Appeal to resume webcasting.[31]

The Supreme Court of Canada began webcasting its proceedings in February 2009 to increase awareness and transparency,[32] becoming the first Supreme Court to webcast its hearings (though not accessible to the public in real-time). The Court features on its website a list of the webcast of the hearings,[33] and individuals can use the Court's website to search for webcast proceedings by year and section (fall, winter, spring or all).[34] However, the Court requires permission to use a webcast or obtain a video recording for commercial or educational use, requiring interested individuals to fill out and submit an on-line form to the Court.[35]

Unlike the states discussed previously, the United States is unique in that numerous state supreme or appellate courts have made considerable strides in webcasting. However, federal courts, including the Supreme Court, fall behind. This is surprising given that the United States became the first country to webcast judicial proceedings in 1997, when the Florida Supreme Court put live audio and video of its oral arguments on the Internet. In 1996, the Florida Supreme Court conducted a survey, which revealed that Floridians were unhappy and lacked public trust and confidence in their judiciary because of a lack of access to the courts and court-related information. The survey also pointed out that most

Floridians lacked basic knowledge about the courts, i.e. how the courts worked and the role of judges (Waters, 2001). Responding to this survey, the Florida Supreme Court, in 1997, pioneered the use of the Internet for increasing public awareness and accessibility and became the first domestic court to put live audio and video of its oral arguments on the Internet (Waters, 2001). Many US states, mostly in state supreme courts and appellate courts, began to follow suit. The number of US states that use the Internet to provide live and archived webcasts of their oral arguments and other judicial proceedings continues to grow. Live and/or archived proceedings are available on the Internet from at least 27 US state judiciaries, including at least four district and county courts. Tables 5.3 and 5.4, respectively, provide lists of the US state and local courts that provide some form of webcasting services.

Table 5.3 US courts and tribunals: US appellate courts

Court Name	*Live (L) or Archived (A) Webcast?*	*Access*
Alaska Supreme Court	L/A	http://www.ktoo.org/gavel/court.cfm
Arizona Supreme Court		http://www.azcourts.gov/AZSupremeCourt/LiveArchivedVideo.aspx
Arkansas Supreme Court	L/A	http://arkansas-sc.granicus.com/ViewPublisher.php?view_id=2
California Supreme Court		http://www.courtinfo.ca.gov/courts/supreme/audio-arch.htm The Supreme Court of California webcasts oral arguments from selected cases.
Florida Supreme Court	L/A	http://www.wfsu.org/gavel2gavel/index.php
Illinois Supreme Court	A	http://www.state.il.us/court/Media/On_Demand.asp (pilot project)
Indiana Supreme Court	L/A	http://www.in.gov/judiciary/webcast/
Kentucky Supreme Court	L	http://courts.ky.gov/
Louisiana Supreme Court	L	http://www.lasc.org/
Maryland Court of Appeals	L/A	http://www.courts.state.md.us/coappeals/webcast.html
Massachusetts Supreme Judicial Court	L/A	http://www.suffolk.edu/sjc/
Minnesota Supreme Court	A	http://www.tpt.org/courts/
Mississippi Court of Appeals	L/A	http://www.mssc.state.ms.us/appellate_courts/sc/scoralarguments.html
Missouri Supreme Court	L/A	Live: http://www.courts.mo.gov/page.jsp?id=1977 Archived: http://supremecourt.missourinet.com/audio_archive/
Montana Supreme Court	L/A	http://courts.mt.gov/oral_cal.mcpx Began webcasting selected hearings in January 2012.

Nebraska Appellate Courts	L/A	http://www.supremecourt.ne.gov/oral-arguments/livevideo.shtml
Supreme Court of Nevada	L	http://www.nevadajudiciary.us/index.php/webcast-of-oral-arguments/113-webcast-of-oral-arguments
New Hampshire Supreme Court	L/A	http://www.courts.nh.gov/cstream/index.asp
New Jersey Supreme Court	L/A	http://www.judiciary.state.nj.us/webcast/
New York Court of Appeals	L/A	http://www.courts.state.ny.us/CTAPPS/index.htm
North Dakota Supreme Court	L/A	http://www.ndcourts.com/court/webcasts.htm
Ohio Supreme Court	L/A	http://www.sconet.state.oh.us/video stream/default.asp
Oregon Supreme Court	L/A	http://oregoncourts.mediasite.com
South Dakota Supreme Court	L/A	Live: http://www.sdjudicial.com/sc/liveaudiosessions.aspx# Archived: http://www.sdjudicial.com/sc/archivedevents.aspx
Supreme Court of Texas	L/A	http://www.stmarytx.edu/law/index.php?site=supremeCourtWebcasts or http://www.supreme.courts.state.tx.us/sc-podcasts.asp
Washington Supreme Court	L/A	http://tvw.org/index.cfm?bhcp=1
Supreme Court of Appeals of West Virginia	L	http://www.state.wv.us/wvsca/Webcast.htm

Like state courts, federal US courts have also begun experimenting with webcasting to increase awareness. The First Circuit Judicial Council had experimented with video recordings of civil proceedings within the First Circuit through a pilot program; however, the program was canceled, and video recordings were again prohibited. In December 2009, the Ninth Circuit Court of Appeals, which includes 15 federal district courts, allowed its courts to experiment with video

Table 5.4 US courts and tribunals: US trial courts

Court Name	*Live (L) or Archived (A) Webcast*	*Access*
Ninth Judicial Circuit of Florida (Orlando)	L	http://www.ninthcircuit.org/news/live_broadcast.shtml
Delaware County Ohio Municipal Court	L	http://www.delawareohio.net/MunicipalCourt/CourtHome/default.aspx
Quincy District Court (Massachusetts)	L/A	
Wise County Virginia	L	http://www.courtbar.org/

coverage in civil, non-jury matters. As part of this pilot project, a district court judge in the Northern District of California approved a plan to webcast live video and audio of the *Perry* v. *Schwarzenegger* trial, which questioned the validity of the California Marriage Protection Act, or Proposition 8, to an overflow courtroom in the same courthouse, as well as to several other federal courthouses throughout the country.

Although US state and federal judiciaries are increasingly webcasting (or experimenting with webcasting) their proceedings, they are doing so against the grain of long-standing negative views in federal judiciaries on the issue of live coverage. These negative views have deep roots in US Supreme Court rulings, such as *Sheppard* v. *Maxwell* in 1966, in which the Court found that press presence in the courtroom in the sensational murder trial of Dr. Sam Sheppard was a factor in depriving him of his right to a fair trial. In more recent years, for example, the US Supreme Court issued a stay in the Northern District of California district court judge's decision to webcast *Perry* v. *Schwarzenegger* in 2010. In *Hollingsworth* v. *Perry*, the Supreme Court issued a stay based on two grounds: (1) the process that led to the approval of the pilot project to webcast the trial was flawed; and (2) irreparable harm to defense witnesses would result.[36]

In 2009, the First Circuit Court of Appeals overturned a decision by a Massachusetts' judge to allow webcasting of civil proceedings in the *Sony BMG Music Entertainment et al.* v. *Tenenbaum*,[37] copyright infringement case. Although existing Court of Appeals and local District Court rules prohibited broadcasting, a Massachusetts' District Court Judge concluded that she had the discretion to approve webcasting in individual cases. Rejecting arguments that the potential jury pool for the impending trial would be prejudiced by webcasting, Judge Gertner concluded: "the public benefit of offering a more complete view of these proceedings is plain, especially via a medium so carefully attuned to the Internet Generation captivated by these file sharing lawsuits."[38] In its ruling, the First Circuit Court of Appeals concluded that Judge Gertner had misinterpreted the District Court's local rule, and that there was no "discretionary catch-all" exception to the general prohibition against broadcasting civil proceedings. The appeals court also rejected the defendant's argument that the blanket prohibition in the local rule violated his right to a public trial.

From the court's ruling and individual judge's dissensions, it is evident that disagreement exists over whether courts should webcast their proceedings. For example, on the emergence of new technologies for providing access to trials, the Court commented: "While the new technology characteristic of the Information Age may call for the [change] of some boundaries, the venerable right of members of the public to attend federal court proceedings is far removed from an imagined entitlement to view court proceedings remotely on a computer screen."[39] However, in Circuit Judge Lipez's dissension, he argued that there were "no sound policy reasons" not to allow the broadcasting plan, arguing that, "Since [the adoption of the District Court rule], dramatic advances in communications technology have had a profound effect on our society . . . These new technological capabilities provide an unprecedented opportunity to increase public access to the judicial system in appropriate circumstances. They have also created expectations that judges will respond sensibly to these opportunities."[40] Accordingly, Judge Lipez called for an immediate re-examination of the blanket prohibition in the local rule. Proposals for webcasting or televising oral arguments before the US Supreme Court have been advanced numerous times by various Congress members, media and the public, but have been defeated by individual justices. Former Justice David Souter once said, "the day you see a camera come into our courtroom it's going to roll over my dead body."[41]

Even in domestic judiciaries that practice a more restrictive policy of webcasting, increasing transparency is a reason for webcasting. China, a country where the Internet is highly regulated by the government and closed judicial hearings occur quite frequently, launched its first website broadcasting Beijing's court trials in September 2009.[42] On the day of the website launch, reporters watched the live broadcast of four cases being heard at Dongcheng District Court, Fengtai District Court, Mijyun County Court and Mengtougou District Court. The website includes the live broadcast page, "on which the debate between the prosecutor and the defendant is transcribed," and updated every second. There are also photos of the court scene on the left of the transcription, as well as real-time releases of broadcast forecasts and processes, broadcast reviews and other columns on the website's home page. Trials, interviews and court scenes are broadcasted separately for easier selection and viewing.[43] In discussing China's decision to webcast Beijing's court trials, Zhai Jingmin, Vice President of Higher People's Court of Beijing, noted that: "the establishment of the live broadcast website not only plays an active role in strengthening open trials, promoting justice, improving efficiency and enhancing judges' trial level, but also makes it more convenient for the public to supervise the people's courts."[44] He further noted that: "courts in Beijing will continue to develop a live online broadcast video system, so that the public's wish to watch court trials at home can be satisfied."[45]

Rather than allowing live webcasting of judicial proceedings, the judiciary of Western Australia embarked on a project with the University of Western Australia to create edited packages of civil and criminal trials to be screened on the university's and the court's websites. For this project, the court routinely records selected hearings/extracts of its hearings, making the footage available to the Faculty of Law for editing by Law and Communication Studies students into videos that provide voiceovers and explanations of legal arguments and procedures. The length of the video will vary depending on the legal issue being examined, but it could, for example, entail turning a 10-day trial into a 30-minute video. The object of the collaborative project is to make court proceedings and decisions more accessible and understandable to the public, media, courtroom participants, and students by producing materials designed to enhance the teaching of law related topics to students (from primary school to law school). University of Western Australia law professor Daniel Stepniak advocates this project, noting that real time webcasts is "actually quite boring," adding that "by condensing the footage we're making it more likely that people will want to watch it."[46] This project has received considerable criticism. University of Ottawa law professor Teresa Scassa was concerned about the serious risks to editing court proceedings, especially to the viewer's contextual understanding of the footage. Her main criticisms include: editing court proceedings brings personal biases into play, especially regarding what is left out; it fails to advance open court principles; and the judicial role is not to create highlight videos, but to ensure that justice is done.[47]

In sum, these examples illustrate that improving transparency and awareness are main advantages and reasons for webcasting judicial proceedings; however, improving transparency by webcasting is more effectively achieved when court rules require webcasting in all proceedings, as opposed to requiring webcasting at either the disputants' request or ad hoc by a judge or court or publishes only edited excerpts.

Increased accessibility

Webcasting is the most efficient way of making hearings more publicly accessible. Webcasting holds accessibility advantages over traditional media, particularly in regards to its direct accessibility, potential for in-depth coverage, and global distribution. Webcasting has no geographic boundaries, unlike more traditional media sources, such as newspaper, radio or television stations, which are centralized within a limited geographical area. Through the use of webcasting, the public is able to access content wherever and whenever they want, depending on whether the hearings are available via 'live' or archived format.

Human rights bodies, including the Inter-American Commission of Human Rights (IACHR) and European Court of Human Rights (ECHR), have started webcasting their proceedings not only to advance transparency, but to increase accessibility as well. Beginning in March 2007, the IACHR webcast its thematic hearings "to deepen the transparency of its processes and broaden access to the information it generates."[48] The proceedings of the European Court of Human Rights (ECHR), established by the 1950 European Convention for the Protection of Human Rights and Fundamental Freedoms (the European Convention) with the task of supervising the observance of the rights and freedoms listed in the Convention, are open to the public, unless the Court in exceptional circumstances decides otherwise.[49] In June 2007, the ECHR began webcasting its public hearings, which was financed by the Irish government. The European Court of Human Right's President Jean-Paul Costa described webcasting as "a significant step forward in making the Court's activities more visible and accessible" (European Court of Human Rights, 2007). He further described some of the benefits of webcasting:

> Lawyers, academics, journalists and ordinary citizens, many of whom would never have been able to come to Strasbourg to attend a hearing, will be able to follow the proceedings from their homes and offices. They will be able to

> see and hear for themselves the arguments advanced for and against a finding of a human rights violation in respect of some of the most sensitive issues of the day. This will bring the Convention closer to the ordinary citizens whom it is intended to serve and protect. (European Court of Human Rights, 2007)

In its 2004 budget report requesting funding for webcasting, the ECHR discussed three main advantages and reasons for webcasting: first, the public nature of court hearings is a fundamental component of the fair trial guarantee; second, webcasting increases the visibility of the Convention system and the court; and third, webcasting serves as an educational tool in increasing human rights awareness and preventing human rights abuse (European Court of Human Rights, 2003).

As a result of increased accessibility, webcasting reduces discrimination against the poor, especially those in the Global South. International economic dispute settlement bodies, such as the WTO, have recently begun to open their dispute hearings to public observation via closed-circuit television broadcast. However, many interested citizens and government officials, especially from developing countries, are unable to spend the time and money to travel, e.g. to Geneva for WTO hearings or to Washington, DC for ICSID hearings, to watch the proceedings in person.

Most citizens and groups around the world have access to the Internet, which would eliminate the access limitations inherent in the current practice. As with closed-circuit televising of WTO panel hearings, webcasting would neither delay the panel process nor interfere with it in any other way. Moreover, webcasting would be more efficient than using closed-circuit television in several respects: it would not require to such an extent the WTO to undertake the pre-hearing clearance process it now conducts before individuals are allowed into the WTO premises to watch the proceedings; and it would not require as many WTO security personnel to clear people for entrance on the day of the proceeding. Because the WTO and the World Bank already provide webcasting of major events and for training purposes, it is clear that the WTO and ICSID possess the technical capacity to webcast proceedings – the question remains as to whether it will display the same willingness to enable citizens of the world to participate in proceedings via the Internet. Although not everyone has access to the Internet, webcasting reaches a vastly wider audience than does making the hearing available only via closed-circuit television. For this reason, among others, the use of the Internet would greatly facilitate access to citizens and government officials around the world. Webcasting is a logical way to resolve this dilemma and to further increase the transparency and credibility of the international economic dispute settlement process.

In addition, webcasting enables the viewer to see the hearings directly rather than through a third party, such as a reporter or editor, and allows proceedings to be covered in their entirety, which is often not possible for the media because of a lack of media resources, an inconvenient forum and limited interest in a case. The media's interests in judicial proceedings do not always coincide with the interests of the administration of justice. This was evidenced in *United Mexican States* v.

Metalclad Corporation[50] when the Supreme Court of British Columbia allowed a petition by the Independent Media Center to webcast live the entire proceeding on the Internet on condition that the hearings were covered in their entirety, as well as in the Philippines' Supreme Court webcast of the Maguindanao massacre trial.

Additional benefits of webcasting

In addition to creating a judiciary that is both more transparent and accessible to the public, as well as a public that is more aware of judicial proceedings, the use of webcast technology leads to additional benefits including: time and cost savings associated with increased accessibility; more accurate reporting; and content review, self-evaluation and insights.

Time and cost savings

Webcasting allows the potential for time and cost savings by the public, including media, lawyers, and government officials. For instance, individuals do not always have to attend hearings, and they can continue to work at their desks during a meeting, rather than waiting for a hearing to be called. In addition, individuals can view proceedings via webcast and clarify decisions made and issues raised. If they do not need to attend the hearing, they do not need to travel, thus saving on travel costs. For example, in October 2002, a newspaper reporter in Gary, Indiana saved himself a 240-mile roundtrip drive by accessing an oral argument via webcasting provided by the Indiana Supreme Court website (Osborn, 2005). In addition, there can be a reduction in the need to brief members of staff on what went on in a meeting, as staff would have the opportunity to watch for themselves. Finally, people inquiring about particular points in a hearing, or certain decisions can be directed to the webcast.

More accurate reporting

Webcasting has led not only to increased media coverage of the courts, but to more positive and accurate reporting. For example, the ECHR noted in its 2004 budget report requesting funding for webcasting that "it is undeniable that webcasting the Court's most important hearings would facilitate media coverage of the proceedings thereby raising the overall visibility of the Court, of the Convention system and therefore of the Council of Europe in general. In this connection and in terms of potential audience, it is worth recalling that the Court's Internet site received some 27 million visits in 2002" (Osborn, 2005). News media – especially reporters from smaller organizations that cannot afford to travel – no longer have to rely on secondhand reports of court cases, as they can now watch them on the Internet. Also, reporters who are able to attend the proceedings are able to use the archived webcasts to check the accuracy of their quotations.

Content review: self-evaluation and insights into judicial thinking

Webcasting benefits many groups. According to a staffer at Maryland's Court of Information Office, many lawyers use the archived videos of the webcast in order to see how they performed in court that day.[51] Lawyers and even clients can watch a webcast of an oral argument on a similar topic to provide significant insights into a tribunal's thinking to prepare for an argument.

Concerns regarding webcasting

Although research indicates that most judiciaries that have webcast their arguments have had positive experiences, several concerns remain. Concerns associated with webcasting involve financial costs, quality concerns, personal identification and privacy, and content manipulation.

Financial cost

Like any system, webcasting technology comes at a financial cost. These costs vary depending on how the courts and governments concerned want to use the system. Operating the system comes with the cost of staff time, in terms of running a proceeding. That is, courts need to take into account the amount of staff and other resources needed to operate the system effectively. For most courts providing webcasting, they have the choice of whether they want to webcast live, archived or both, and the equipment they need to do this (in terms of cameras, decoders, etc.).

The price to purchase and install the technology needed to begin webcasting could be expensive. In terms of its initial outlay, for example, the ECHR, in its 2004 budget request for webcasting, asked for a sum of 600,000 Euros as a one-off investment and 120,000 Euros for annual costs to webcast its public hearings – 30 to 40 public hearings a year. The ECHR noted in its request that "although the costs involved may be regarded as high, it should be recalled that 600,000 is a one-off investment" (Council of Europe, 2003). The Arkansas Supreme Court, which meets weekly to hear oral arguments, estimated in 2010 that costs for webcasting software and cameras were less than $100,000. The court expects to spend around $20,000 annually for on-going upkeep (Bleed, 2010).

Unlike most judicial proceedings, the costs for webcasting international economic dispute settlement cases do not usually include purchasing new equipment or training personnel, as many international institutions that house international disputes, such as the World Bank, the United Nations, and the WTO, already have the equipment and capability to webcast, and even use that capability to webcast other types of activities. The costs for webcasting proceedings at ICSID will be discussed in the next section.

Judiciaries have also partnered with universities to defray the costs. For example, in the United States, the Supreme Court of Texas partnered with St. Mary's University in 2007 to webcast its oral arguments live and archived, with the university providing the design, construction, and equipment costs for the webcasting project (Hermes, 2007). To ensure the court's right to the material, the Texas Office of Court Administration, in its contract with the university, required that any intellectual property produced as part of an oral argument webcast is the property of the state, including any value added provided by the law school, such as titling on the video. The Supreme Court of Texas formed the partnership with the university, beginning in 2005, after the Texas Legislature rejected the Court's request for legislative funding to provide webcasting services of its court proceedings. The Court was interested in creating the webcasting project to raise awareness of the judiciary, while the law school was interested in the joint project because it would, among other reasons, provide an educational opportunity for its students and the general public. Similar situations exist with Suffolk University Law School, in cooperation with the Supreme Judicial Court of Massachusetts, and the University of Kentucky's School of Law, working with the Kentucky Supreme Court (Day, 2007). Universities abroad have followed suit. For example, the courts of Western Australia embarked on a project with the University of Western Australia to create edited packages of civil and criminal trials to be screened on the university's and the court's websites.

Quality concerns

As with using any type of technology, there are quality concerns that need to be considered in webcasting. This refers to the quality of the image and audio transferred from the servers of the distributor to the home screen on a user, also referred to as stream quality. Higher quality video requires higher bandwidth and faster connection speeds. If there are too many viewers attempting to access the webcast for the available bandwidths, the result can be server overloads. For example, in December 2007, the ICTY's provider experienced technical difficulties, which caused serious disruption to broadcasts of all on-going ICTY trials. Both the ICTY Registry and the outside provider looked for ways to ensure that the system became operational again and worked on a transitional project to solve the malfunction and subsequently to transfer the responsibility for the operation of the Internet broadcast to the ICTY technical services.

To ensure that the webcast hearings reached the widest possible audience, the ICJ decided to provide for two streaming options that would be suitable for different types of Internet connection: audio and video streaming for fast broadband connections; and audio and video streaming for slower ordinary telephone connections.[52] Although there still may be temporary pauses in the live video coverage due to high traffic on the ICJ's website, the same footage is made available via the archive link. Thus, if someone misses the live hearings because of website congestion or of the time difference in someone's country, the hearings are available on the "Video Archive", which is where the webcast hearings will be archived after every half-day session.

Protecting personal identification and privacy

In deciding whether or how to webcast, courts and the public are especially concerned with how to balance transparency with protecting confidential and personal information in the digital age. Though disclosing such personal information may be in the public interest, courts are concerned that doing so without restriction, as can easily happen on the Internet, compromises the fair balance between transparency in court procedures and the right to privacy provided in many court rules. Making personal information public may increase the risk of identity theft, stalking, fraudulent use of clustering or data mining software and discriminatory practices; it may also act as an obstacle to justice if persons are fearful of having their personal information permanently available to the public via the Internet. In the cases discussed above, both international non-economic and domestic courts have found methods to webcast their proceedings without compromising their objectives of transparency and accountability with those of protecting confidential and personal information.

Content manipulation

There has been fear among some judges and webcasting opponents that once judicial proceedings are webcast the content could be edited and manipulated by those who are tech-savvy. For example, in *R. v. Pilarinos and Clark*, heard in the Supreme Court of British Columbia in 2002, the media requested to bring one camera into the courtroom, pooling to other media outlets and to webcast the trial, showing the trial on a Court television station. In her judgment, Madam Justice Bennett upheld the trial court's ruling, affirming that although webcasting would present more thorough coverage than television, "if the trial were webcast on the Internet, it would provide millions of people with uncontrolled access to the proceedings. The ability to manipulate images on the Internet is well-known and would seriously affect not only the privacy of all those whose images are captured and broadcast, but also the dignity and decorum of the courtroom."[53] Despite the concern for content manipulation, many judiciaries, such as Canada, Australia and the United Kingdom, have created mechanisms that enable the judiciary to control who sees the content and how they view it.

In sum, this section illustrated the advantages and concerns of webcasting judicial proceedings. It also demonstrated that international non-economic and domestic judicial bodies have increasingly accepted and successfully employed webcasting as a tool to increase transparency, awareness, and accessibility. It also described the various methods in which courts may provide webcasting services to show that courts have found ways to mitigate their concerns with webcasting.

Webcasting international economic dispute settlement

International economic dispute settlement bodies and rules play an increasingly important role, yet often lack transparency, opportunities for public participation, and accountability. Given the clear presence of important public interest in these cases, it is essential that these institutions and their respective processes be as transparent and accessible as possible, rather than being far-removed from, and closed to, the people they ultimately affect.

ICSID's experience webcasting oral proceedings in the *Pac Rim*, *Commerce Group* and *Railroad Development Corporation* cases were favorably received by many, including El Salvadorans, Guatemalans, civil society organizations, and the media. ICSID's decision to webcast the hearings occurred after many years of advocacy. As discussed previously, civil society organizations, including CIEL and the International Institute for Sustainable Development (IISD), have long advocated for more transparent mechanisms for dispute settlement generally, including webcasting the proceedings at ICSID and the WTO.

ICSID's webcasting experience confirms that international economic dispute settlement bodies can successfully webcast public interest proceedings, without delay or disruption, serving as a model for future international economic dispute settlement bodies. ICSID's webcasting experience also has the potential to change the dynamics of the webcasting debate in future international dispute settlement proceedings.

ICSID's experience in webcasting

In a landmark decision, ICSID made its hearing on preliminary objections in the *Pac Rim Cayman LLC* v. *Republic of El Salvador*[54] available to the public via webcast in real-time in May and June 2010. ICSID followed this precedent by webcasting additional proceedings including: the preliminary objections in the *Commerce Group* case in November 2010; a hearing on the objections to jurisdiction in the *Pac Rim* case in May 2011; and a hearing on the merits in the *Railroad Development Corporation* case in December 2011, which concerns a railroad concession contract in Guatemala.

ICSID based its decision in all three cases on Article 10.21.2 of the Dominican Republic-Central America-United States Free Trade Agreement (DR-CAFTA), which requires hearings to be 'open to the public.' As DR-CAFTA does not specify the method by which hearings are to be open to the public, the decision to webcast was agreed to by both parties in each dispute (El Salvador and Pac Rim Cayman LLC in the *Pac Rim* case; El Salvador and Commerce Group Corporation in the *Commerce Group* case; and the Railroad Development Corporation and Guatemala in the *Railroad Development Corporation* case), as well as the particular ICSID Tribunal hearing each case.

The decision to provide webcasting was a major step towards increasing transparency in international economic dispute settlement, as it meant that the public around the world had the opportunity to access the hearings. Importantly, the proceedings in each of the three cases were webcast in both English and Spanish, informing persons in the affected country, and elsewhere. For instance, in the *Pac Rim* case, persons in El Salvador were informed of the efforts to halt harmful metals mining in their country and the private sector's response to those efforts in their own language. ICSID reported that, on the first day of the hearing on 31 May 2010, there were 150 hits during the live webcast. Out of the 150 hits, 120 of them viewed the hearings in English, and 30 in Spanish.[55] The hearings have since been archived on ICSID's website for further viewing.

Though the exact costs of webcasting the three cases have not been made public, in comments submitted to UNCITRAL's Working Group II, ICSID prepared estimates of the costs related to holding open hearings using broadcast facilities: webcasting and closed circuit broadcasting (i.e. side room open to the public where the hearing is broadcast live). As the World Bank already owns webcasting equipment, there was no need to purchase additional equipment. Based on conservative estimates, ICSID reported a cost of $4750 to webcast for one weekday (at 8-hours a day) or $15,750 for five weekdays within the World Bank's headquarters in Washington, DC. The estimated costs for closed circuit broadcasting are not much different than webcasting: $4550 to provide closed circuit broadcasting for one weekday and $14,250 for five weekdays.[56] In closed circuit broadcasting, there are logistical costs and challenges involved to ensure the safety of the participants and order of the proceedings, which webcasting removes. Further, webcasting enables a greater number of individuals to access the proceedings than with closed circuit broadcasting. In each of the webcast proceedings, DR-CAFTA's requirement for open hearings was used as the basis for a decision to webcast (as opposed to specific ICSID arbitration rules requiring webcasting) to justify the webcast; and each webcast occurred because both parties agreed to it.

Recommendations and future outlook

ICSID's experience webcasting each of the proceedings exemplifies how access to public hearings in international economic arbitration should work: oral proceedings were webcast in real-time in the languages of the affected communities and archived on the dispute settlement body's website for later viewing. To protect confidentiality, webcasts were interrupted whenever confidential information was discussed. However, these cases were webcast only because both parties involved in the dispute agreed to the webcast.

To improve upon this model, provisions should be added to international economic dispute settlement rules requiring webcasting in all public interest cases involving a state. More specifically, a rule should be adopted that would make webcasting oral hearings the norm in state arbitrations (with exceptions to protect confidential business information, and information which is privileged or otherwise protected from disclosure under that party's domestic law). Thus, transparency in international economic dispute settlement can be increased by establishing webcasting as a rule, no longer dependent upon the disputing parties' request (while ensuring protection for confidentiality as disputes demand). Further, to prevent states and investors from overusing confidentiality claims, arbitration rules should include conditions for confidentiality, where the party invoking confidentiality must demonstrate the reasons for protecting the information and the adverse risk if the information is made public during the hearing (Alvarez-Jiménez, 2010). That is, the burden of proof should lie on the party denying access to the confidential information.

The decision to allow webcasting could possibly serve as precedence, a creation of a new standard with regard to transparency in international economic disputes – one that others may decide to adopt in future disputes. In fact, webcasting the cases at ICSID is of particular relevance to the operation of rules used in trade and investment dispute settlement. As previously discussed, UNCITRAL embarked on a process of revising its arbitration rules, which is a unique opportunity to create a template for more transparent and participatory investment dispute settlement, including webcasting. ICSID has already begun sharing its webcasting experiences, providing UNCITRAL's Working Group II with a description on the potential costs of holding open hearings.

ICSID's experience in webcasting its proceedings has only occurred in three separate cases, using DR-CAFTA as a basis (as opposed to specific ICSID arbitration rules requiring webcasting), and only because both parties agreed to webcast the hearings. As this was the case, the question remains as to whether webcasting will become a 'trend' in international dispute settlement proceedings. If the usage of webcasting technology becomes an accepted 'trend', receives positive feedback from the public and governments, and can be easily implemented, states and international economic dispute settlement bodies, such as ICSID, UNCITRAL and the WTO, may choose to include similar requirements in their future rules on dispute settlement procedures, especially as both the World Bank, which houses ICSID, and the WTO have the equipment and capability to webcast.

Concluding remarks

Webcasting enables judicial proceedings to be readily accessible to the general public, wherever it may be. It expands the audience of judicial proceedings, enabling people around the world to access them, oftentimes from the comfort of their home, office, library or Internet café. It is perhaps the only means through which many peoples, especially those in developing countries, will have to see international economic dispute settlement proceedings that affect their health and environment. Local, federal and international judiciaries increasingly began webcasting their hearings, while international economic dispute bodies have been reluctant to webcast theirs.

The main advantages to webcasting dispute proceedings include increased transparency, awareness and accessibility. Additional benefits involve: more accurate reporting; time and cost savings; and content review, self-evaluation and insights. The concerns of webcasting relate to the financial costs, quality concerns, protecting confidential and personal information, and content manipulation brought by its technology. However, to minimize those disadvantages many courts have used partnerships with universities to control costs, and created mechanisms to enable the judiciary to control the content and who sees the content, thereby reducing, if not eliminating, any potential for content manipulation and protection of confidential information.

ICSID's precedent-setting decision to webcast the *Pac Rim, Commerce Group* and *Railroad Development Corporation* cases occurred after many years of advocacy, and carries profound implications for the conduct of international economic dispute settlement. Civil society organizations, including the Center for International Environmental Law (CIEL) and the International Institute for Sustainable Development (IISD), and some governments have long advocated for webcasting in dispute settlement generally, including in proceedings at (or conducted using the rules of) the International Centre for Settlement of Investment Disputes (ICSID), the United Nations Commission on International Trade Law (UNCITRAL), the North American Free Trade Agreement (NAFTA), and the World Trade Organization (WTO). In addition, ICSID's decision carries profound implications for the conduct of international economic dispute settlement, especially as UNCITRAL revises its arbitration rules.

ICSID's webcasting experience confirms that webcasting international economic disputes can be done effectively and without disruption or delay. However, for webcasting to become an effective tool to increase transparency in international dispute settlement proceedings, international dispute settlement bodies must pass rules that require all hearings to be webcast, with appropriate safeguards to protect confidential business information or state secrets that needs to be protected.

Notes

1 Sofia Plagakis is a Policy Analyst at OMB Watch in Washington, DC. Prior to that, she worked as Program Associate for the Center for International Environmental Law (CIEL). This chapter is based on work by CIEL. The author would like to thank Daniel B. Magraw for his insightful comments and peer review. Valuable research was provided by Ana Paula Parente and Kristie Disney.

2 See International Covenant on Civil and Political Rights, 16 December 1966, S. Treaty Doc. No. 95–20, 6 *International Legal Materials* 368 (1967), 999 U.N.T.S. 171; and European Convention for the Protection of Human Rights and Fundamental Freedoms, 4 November 1950, ETS 5; 213 U.N.T.S. 221.

3 According to Stanley R. Tiner, chairman of the Freedom of Information Committee of the American Society of Newspaper Editors, "ASNE embraces the long American tradition of open courts and open trials . . . The press serves as a surrogate to the public. The American public can't be crammed into a trial room . . .". See American Society of Newspaper Editors, "On the Move", *The American Editor*, 1997. Available at http://asne.org/kiosk/editor/97.mar-may/move4.htm (accessed 25 January 2012).

4 *Chandler* v. *Florida*, 449 U.S. 560 (1981) evaluated the constitutionality of revised Canon 3A (7) of the Florida Code of Judicial Conduct, which permits electronic media coverage of judicial courts.

5 North American Free Trade Agreement, *32 International Legal Materials* 289 and 605 (1993). Chapter Eleven of NAFTA focuses on investment and provides for arbitration before an impartial tribunal to resolve disputes between investors and NAFTA Parties. Investors and Parties have recourse to one of the following arbitral mechanisms: ICSID; ICSID's Additional Facility Rules; UNCITRAL; or alternative mechanisms, including domestic courts.

6 *Methanex Corp. v. United States of America*. UNCITRAL (NAFTA), Decision of the Tribunal on Petitions from Third Persons to Intervene as "*Amici Curiae*", para. 49 (15 January 2001).

7 See e.g. *Methanex*, Decision of the Tribunal on Petitions from Third Persons to Intervene as "*Amici Curiae*", at paras 41–42.

8 Mexico announced its support for open hearings in investor–State disputes following the 2004 NAFTA Commission Meeting. See NAFTA, Free Trade Commission Joint Statement, *Decade of Achievement* (16 July 2004). Available at http://www.dfait-maeci.gc.ca/nafta-alena/JS-SanAntonio-en.asp (accessed 25 January 2012).

9 The United States and Canada announced their intention to consent to open public hearings at all NAFTA Chapter Eleven arbitrations to which either is a party following the 2003 NAFTA Commission Meeting. See Department of Foreign Affairs and International Trade News Release No. 152, *NAFTA Commission Joint Statement*, (7 October 2003). Available at http://w01.international.gc.ca/minpub/Publication.asp?publication_id=380398&Language=E (accessed 25 January 2012).

10 In a letter sent to Andrea J. Menaker, Chief, NAFTA Arbitration Division, US Department of State on 5 October 2007, CIEL argued that the *BSE case* raised a number of highly relevant environment and health issues. Generally, the U.S. border was closed to the import of live Canadian cattle after an outbreak of "mad cow" disease was detected in Canada. Canadian cattle-ranchers affected by this measure brought a claim under the investment chapter of the NAFTA. CIEL asserted that it is important for both the Canadian and the U.S. public to know and understand what exactly is at stake in this dispute and others like it.

11 Understanding on Rules and Procedures Governing the Settlement of Disputes, 15 April 1994. Available at http://www.wto.org/English/docs_e/legal_e/28-dsu.pdf (accessed 25 January 2012), Article 18.2 (no. 3).

12 See Dispute Settlement Body, *Contribution of the United States to the Improvement of the Dispute Settlement of Understanding of the WTO related to Transparency*, Communication of the United States, TN/DS/W/13 (22 August 2002); Special Session of the Dispute Settlement Body, *Further Contribution of the United States to the Improvement of the Dispute Settlement Body*, Communication from the United States, TN/DS/W/46 (11 February 2003); Dispute Settlement Body, *Transparency and Derestriction–Communication by Canada*, WT/GC/W/98 (22 September 1998); and Dispute Settlement Body, *Transparency in WTO Work – Procedures for the Circulation and Derestriction of WTO Documents – Revised Proposals by the United States and Canada*, WT/GC/W/106 (13 October 1998).

13 Special Session of the Dispute Settlement Body, *Contribution of the United States on some practical considerations in improving the dispute settlement understanding of the WTO related to Transparency and open meeting*, TN/DS/W/79 (13 July 2005).

14 *US – Continued suspension of obligations in the EC – Hormones dispute*, DS320; and *Canada – Continued suspension of obligations in the EC – Hormones dispute*, DS321.

15 In November 2007, at the request of the parties, the WTO dispute panel opened to the public the hearings of the meeting on compliance in the *EC – Bananas III* case: See *European Communities – Regime for the Importation, Sale, and Distribution of Bananas: Recourse to Article 21.5 of the DSB by the United States*, WT/ DS27 (2007).

16 Center for International Environmental Law, "CIEL attends first open WTO Appellate Body hearing in the famous Hormones dispute". Available at http://www.ciel.org/Tae/WTO_Hormones_30Jul08.html (accessed on 28 January 2012).

17 In October 2006, the Center for International Environmental Law sent letters requesting open hearings to the European Commissioner, Ambassador of the Office of US Trade, and Canada's Minister of International Trade. See "Open dispute settlement hearings in the WTO", Letter to European Commissioner, 4 October 2006, available at http://www.ciel.org/Publications/WTODispute_EC_Oct06.pdf; Center for International

Environmental Law; Letter to Ambassador Schwab at USTR, 10 October Available at http://www.ciel.org/Publications/WTODispute_USTR_Oct06.pdf; Letter to Canada's Minister of International Trade , 10 October, available at http://www.ciel.org/Publications/WTODispute_Canada_Oct06.pdf; Letters were also sent regarding *Brazil-Measures Affecting Imports of Retreaded Tyres, Request for Public Hearing* (20 June 2006). Available at http://www.ciel.org/Tae/WTO_DisputeSettlement_11Oct06.html (accessed 25 January 2012).

18 The consortium includes: Northwestern University School of Law Center for International Human Rights; the Documentation Center of Cambodia; Illinois Holocaust Museum and Education Center; and the J.B. and M.K. Pritzker Family Foundation.

19 For information on the company, Jasculca Terman and Associates, Inc. (JT), see http://www.jtpr.com/index.php?option=com_content&view=article&id=33:cambodia-tribunal-monitor-&catid=18:case-studies&Itemid=61.

20 Blaškić (IT-95-14-T), Decision of Trial Chamber I on the Protective Measure for General Philippe Morillon, Witness of the Trial Chamber, 12 May 1999.

21 In an email communication from the ICJ's Registry, dated 29 June 2007, an ICJ Information Officer indicated that the ICJ is interested in utilizing Internet broadcast technology with greater frequency and regularity in the future, however is currently unable to do so due to financial constraints.

22 Press Release 2004/26: Live Internet video coverage of the reading of the Court's Advisory Opinion on Friday 9 July 2004, from 3 p.m. (25 June 2004). Available at http://www.icj-cij.org/docket/index.php?pr=5&p1=3&p2=1&case=131&p3=6&search=%22webcast%22 (accessed 20 January 2012).

23 Email communication from the Court's Registry, 29 June 2007.

24 In addition to the *Israeli Wall* case, the ICJ has webcast the following cases: (1) Advisory Opinion on the question of the Accordance with International Law of the Unilateral Declaration of Independence by the Provisional Institutions of Self-Government of Kosovo, (22 July 2010); Reading of the Court's Judgment, Pulp Mills on the River Uruguay (Argentina v. Uruguay) (20 April 2010); and the public hearings in the Jurisdictional Immunities of the State (Germany v. Italy: Greece intervening) (12–16 September 2011).

25 In the 2001 appeal of *Metaclad* v. *Mexico*, the Supreme Court of British Columbia allowed a petition by the Independent Media Center to webcast live the entire proceeding. In the British Columbia Supreme Court hearing, the presiding judge ruled that Independent Media could record the proceedings and streamline it on the Internet on condition that the hearings were covered in their entirety.

26 The documents can be found at the PCA website. Available at http://www.pca-cpa.org/showpage.asp?pag_id=1306 (accessed 20 January 2012).

27 Republic of South Sudan, "Abyei Arbitration Oral Pleadings Open to Public Media", SPLM Press Release No. 1, 14 April 2009. Available at http://www.gossmission.org/goss/index.php?option=com_content&task=view&id=835&Itemid=193 (accessed 24 January 2012).

28 The website for TV Justica is http://www.tvjustica.jus.br/. The YouTube page for the STF is http://www.youtube.com/stf; and the Twitter page for the STF is http://twitter.com/stf_oficial.

29 See Ministry of the Attorney General, "Webcasting of Court Proceedings begins Today", 7 September 2007. Available at http://www.attorneygeneral.jus.gov.on.ca/english/news/2007/20070907-cam-nr.asp.

30 Email from Counsel, Court of Appeal for Ontario, 16 December 2009.

31 *Idem.*

32 Phone interview with Catherine Laforce, Director, Information Management and Technology, Information Management and Technology, Supreme Court of Canada, 4 March 2010.

33 Since then, the Canadian Broadcasting Corporation has taped a few trials in courts in Ontario, Alberta and the Northwest Territories.
34 See Supreme Court of Canada, http://www.scc-csc.gc.ca/case-dossier/cms-sgd/webcasts-webdiffusions-eng.aspx.
35 See Supreme Court of Canada, http://www.scc-csc.gc.ca/contact/photo-video-eng.asp.
36 *Dennis Hollingsworth et al.* v. *Kristen M. Perry et al.* on application for stay (13 January 2010) 558 U.S., Per Curiam Supreme Court of the United States, No. 09A648. Available at http://www.supremecourt.gov/opinions/09pdf/09a648.pdf (accessed 22 January 2012).
37 *Sony BMG Music Entertainment et al.* v. *Tenenbaum*, No. 07cv11446-NG (D. Mass. 9 July 2010).
38 *Idem.*
39 *Idem.*
40 *Idem.*
41 Associate Press, "On Cameras in Supreme Court, Souter Says, 'Over My Dead Body'", *New York Times*, 3 March 1996. Available at http://www.nytimes.com/1996/03/30/us/on-cameras-in-supreme-court-souter-says-over-my-dead-body.html (accessed 19 January 2012).
42 To access the court trials, go to: http://bjfyzb.chinacourt.org. "China's first website broadcasting live court trials launched in Beijing", (18 September 2009), http://www.cctv.com/english/special/news/20090918/104130.shtml.
43 CCTV, "China's first website broadcasting live court trials launched in Beijing", 18 September 2009. http://www.cctv.com/english/special/news/20090918/104130.shtml (accessed 18 January 2012).
44 *Idem.*
45 *Idem.*
46 "New Spin on Court TV", *Globe and Mail*, 1 October 2009. Available at http://www.theglobeandmail.com/news/technology/new-spin-on-court-tv/article1307279/ (accessed 25 January 2012).
47 *Idem.*
48 Inter-American Commission of Human Rights, "IACHR Announces Webcast of Public Hearings of the 127th Regular Period of Sessions", 26 February 2007. Available at http://www.cidh.org/Comunicados/English/2007/8.07eng.htm (accessed 20 January 2012).
49 The press and the public may not have access to oral proceeding in those cases when all or part of a hearing in the interests of morals, public order or national security in a democratic society, where the interests of juveniles or the protection of the private life of the parties so require, or to the extent strictly necessary in the opinion of the Chamber in special circumstances where publicity would prejudice the interests of justice.
50 BCSC 664, 2001. In the 2001 appeal of *Metaclad* v. *Mexico*, the Supreme Court of British Columbia allowed a petition by the Independent Media Center to webcast live the entire proceeding. In the British Columbia Supreme Court hearing, the presiding judge ruled that Independent Media could record the proceedings and streamline it on the Internet on condition that the hearings were covered in their entirety.
51 Interview, Staffer at Maryland's Court of Information Office, 10 January 2008.
52 International Court of Justice, "Legal Consequences of the Construction of a Wall in the Occupied Palestinian Territory (Request for advisory opinion)", *Press Release*, International Court of Justice, 1 October 2009. Available at http://www.icj-cij.org/docket/index.php?pr=157&code=mwp&p1=3&p2=1&p3=6&case=131&k=5a (accessed 24 January 2012).
53 *R.* v. *Pilarinos* (2001) B.C.J. No. 1936 (B.C.S.C.), para. 203.
54 *Pac Rim Cayman LLC* v. *Republic of El Salvador*, ICSID Case No. ARB/09/12, registered 15 June 2009.
55 Interview with ICSID Legal Counsel, 7 December 2010.

56 Broken down, the estimated costs for webcasting include: a one-time standard room set up fee of $2000; video recording fee of $900; audio recording of $250; streaming weekday fee of $1200; and a recording fee of $400. The estimated costs for closed circuit broadcasting include: one-time standard set up fee of $2000; video recording fee of $900; technician for the overflow room for $500; audio recording for $250; video conferencing services for $500; and security costs for $300. These costs only involve broadcasting a hearing in one language, without any interpretation. See UNCITRAL, A/CN.9/WG.II/WP.170/Add.1, 13 December 2011. Available at http://daccess-dds-ny.un.org/doc/UNDOC/LTD/V11/880/28/PDF/V1188028.pdf?OpenElement (accessed 25 January 2012).

References

Bernasconi-Osterwalder, B. (2006), *Democratizing International Dispute Settlement: The Case of Trade and Investment Disputes*, Doha: 6th International Conference of New or Restored Democracies. Online. Available HTTP: http://www.ciel.org/Publications/ICNRD6_30Oct06.pdf> (accessed 14 January 2012).

Center for International Environmental Law and the International Institute for Sustainable Development (2007), *Revising the UNCITRAL Arbitration Rules to Address Investor-State Arbitrations*. Online. Available HTTP: <http://ciel.org/Publications/CIEL_IISD_RevisingUNCITRAL_Dec07.pdf> (accessed 14 January 2012).

Cohn, M. and Dow, D. (2002), *Cameras in the Courtroom: Television and the Pursuit of Justice*, Lanham, MD: Rowman & Littlefield Publishers.

Council of Europe, Rapporteur Group on Administrative and Budgetary Questions (2003), "European Court of Human Rights – Budget requests for 2004", (10 Nov.) Online. Available HTTP: <https://wcd.coe.int/ViewDoc.jsp?id=84745&BackColorInternet=9999CC&BackColorIntranet=& BackColorLogged=FDC864> (accessed 14 January 2012).

Crook, J. R. (2009), "Abyei Arbitration – Final Award," *ASIL Insights* 13, no. 15 (September 16, 2009), http://www.asil.org/insights090916.cfm.

Day, R. (2007), "Webcast to air Kentucky Supreme Court's oral arguments," (25 Oct.) Online. Available HTTP: <http://theprincipal.blogspot.com/2007/10/webcast-to-air-kentucky-supreme-courts.html> (accessed 14 January 2012).

Delaney, J. and Magraw, D. B. (2008), "Procedural Transparency," eds. Peter Muchlinski, et. al. in *The Oxford Handbook of International Investment Law*, Oxford: Oxford University Press.

Ehring, L. (2008), "Public Access to Dispute Settlement Hearings in the World Trade Organization," 11 *Journal of International Economic Law*, 1021–34.

European Court of Human Rights, Press release, Registrar, *Launch of webcasting and new information about pending Court cases* (June 25, 2007), http://cmiskp.echr.coe.int/tkp197/view.asp?action=html&documentId=819328&portal=hbkm&source=externalbydocnumber&table=F69A27FD8FB86142BF01C1166DEA398649.

Florini, A. (1998), "The End of Secrecy," 111 *Foreign Policy*, 50–63.

Hermes, B. (2007), "Webcasting in the Supreme Court of Texas," *Technology Experience Bulletin TEB: 2007–03*, Court Information Technology Officers Consortium (21 June) Online. Available HTTP: <http://www.citoc.org/docs/teb-webcast.pdf> (accessed 14 January 2012).

International Centre for Trade and Sustainable Development (ICTSD). *DSU Review: Developing Countries Reject US Proposal on Transparency, Suggest Other Options*,

Bridges Weekly Main Page, V. 6, No. 31 (Sept 18, 2002), http://www.ictsd.org/weekly/02–09–18/story2.htm.

Lassiter, C. (1996), "TV or not TV – that is the question," 86 *The Journal of Criminal Law & Criminology*, 928–59.

Magraw, D.B., and Amerasinghe, N.M. (2009), "Transparency and public participation in investor-state arbitration," 15 *Journal of International & Comparative Law*, 337–60.

Magraw, D., Plagakis, S. and Schifano, S. (2008), "Ways and Means of Citizens" Participation in Trade and Investment Dispute Settlement Procedures', *Society of International Economic Law Inaugural Conference*, Social Science Electronic Publishing, Inc. Online. Available HTTP: http://papers.ssrn.com/solu3/papers.cfm?abstract_id=1159770 (accessed 14 January 2012).

Mason, P. (2000), "A Report on the Audiovisual Coverage of the ICTY's Proceedings Finds that Cameras Contribute to a Proper Administration of Justice," The Hague (Apr 19, 2000), http://www.icty.org/sid/7869.

Nashiri, H. (2002), *Crime and Justice in the Age of Court TV*, New York: LFB Scholarly Publisher.

O'Brien, J.C. (1993), "The International Tribunal for Violations of International Humanitarian Law in the Former Yugoslavia," *The American Journal of International Law*, 87: 639–659.

Orellana, Marcos (2009), WTO and Civil Society, in Daniel Bethlehem et al. eds., *The Oxford Handbook of International Trade Law*.

Osborn, E.R. (2005), "Webcasting: It's not just about oral arguments anymore," Future Trends in State Courts, National Center for State Courts. Online. Available HTTP: <http://www.ncsconline.org/WC/Publications/Trends/2005/AppCtsWebcastTrends2005.pdf> (accessed 15 January 2012).

Quraishi, A. (2010), "Remembering the Killing Fields of Cambodia," WTTW Chicago Tonight, Online. Available HTTP: http://blogs.wttw.com/moreonthestory/2010/07/26/remembering-the-killings-fields-of-cambodia/.

Salbu, S.R. (2001), "Information Technology in the War against International Bribery and Corruption: The Next Frontier of Institutional Reform," 38 *Harvard Journal on Legislation*, 67–102.

Stepniak, D. (2004), "Technology and Public Access to Audio-Visual Coverage and Recordings of Court Proceedings: Implications for Common Law Jurisdictions," 12(3) *William and Mary Bill of Rights Journal*, 791–823.

Strickland, R.A. and Moore, R.H. (1994), "Cameras in State Courts: A Historical Perspective," 78 *Judicature*, 128–135.

Supreme Court of the United Kingdom, Customer Service and Education Assistant of the Supreme Court of the United Kingdom (2009), "Webcasting Inquiry". E-mail (13 October 2009).

Sutherland, P. (2004), "*The Future of the WTO: Addressing Institutional Challenges in the New Millennium*," Report by the Consultative Board to the Director-General Supachai Panitchpakdi. Online. Available HTTP: http://www.wto.org/english/thewto_e/10anniv_e/future_wto_e.pdf.

Waters, R.C. (2001), "Netcasting Court Arguments," National Center for State Courts Available HTTP: <http://contentdm.ncsconline.org/cgi-bin/showfile.exe?CISOROOT=/tech&CISOPTR=538> (accessed 14 January 2012).

6 Transparency of investment awards

External and internal dimensions

Federico Ortino[1]

The aim of the present contribution is to address the issue of transparency of investment decisions looking at both external and internal dimensions. In particular, this chapter analyzes, first, the extent to which investment decisions are and should be made publicly available. This is the "external" dimension of the issue of transparency of investment decisions. Second, this chapter examines the rationales for, and failures in, providing a high level of clarity in investment tribunals' reasoning. This is the "internal" dimension of transparency of investment decisions.

The chapter's underlying thesis is that given the public nature of the issues at stake in international investment arbitration (particularly the fact that investment arbitration always involves a State as one of the disputing parties and revolves around the compatibility of a State conduct with international law), there is a growing consensus on the need both to favour making investment decisions publicly available and to impose on investment tribunals a high level of clarity in their reasoning.

Part I: External transparency of investment awards

The issue of external transparency in investor–State arbitration usually focuses on three main aspects: (1) knowledge of the existence of, and basic information on, the dispute, (2) access by non-disputing parties to the arbitral proceedings (including documents submitted to the arbitral tribunal or attendance of hearings); and (3) publicity of decisions (including the final award) of the arbitral tribunal. The focus of this chapter is on the latter aspect, only. In other words, it deals with the 'external' transparency of investment decisions.

In order to describe the three main approaches to the issue of the publicity of investment arbitration awards, the chapter employs the following three concepts: 'duty of confidentiality', 'right to transparency' and 'duty of transparency'. Duty of confidentiality means that the award shall remain confidential. Duty of transparency means that the award shall be publicly available. Right to transparency means that there is neither an express duty of confidentiality nor an express duty of transparency, the issue being thus left to the discretion of each individual participant in the arbitral process. Depending on their exact scope, these duties and rights may also be described as 'absolute' or 'partial'. Moreover, any of the three approaches to the issue of the publicity of arbitration decisions is often (but not always) subject to change through agreement between the disputing parties.

Moreover, there are at least three sets of participants in the arbitral process that may be subject to confidentiality or transparency requirements. These are: (a) the arbitral tribunal, (b) the arbitral institution, and (c) the disputing parties.

In addressing the issue of whether decisions rendered in investor–State arbitration are and/or should be made publicly available, Part I is divided in the following three sections: an examination of the arbitration rules provided for by the major arbitration institutions as well as those found in international investment treaties with regard to the transparency of arbitral decisions; an empirical analysis of the investment decisions rendered in the last five years which are publicly and not publicly available; and an examination of the arguments in favour of confidentiality and in favour of transparency of investment decisions.

Arbitration rules

The ICSID Convention and Arbitration Rules (as well as the ICSID Additional Facility rules) provide for a set of rules exclusively applicable to investor–State arbitration (also referred to as 'investment arbitration').[2] Investment arbitration may also be conducted on the basis of a predetermined set of arbitration rules drafted by a multiplicity of national or international institutions (which are applicable to international arbitration in general). These include the ICC Rules of Arbitration,[3] the UNCITRAL Arbitration Rules,[4] the LCIA Arbitration Rules,[5] and the SCC Arbitration Rules.[6] Furthermore, while the majority of international investment treaties providing for investor–State arbitration generally refer to such sets of rules, a few of these treaties provide for more or less detailed arbitration rules. The following sections examine some of these rules with regard to the external transparency of investment awards.

ICSID convention, regulations and arbitration rules

The ICSID Convention, Regulation and Arbitration Rules (hereinafter "ICSID rules") expressly regulate the publication of the arbitral awards by the Centre and the arbitrators only. As explained below, while arbitrators have an 'absolute' duty of confidentiality with regard to the contents of any arbitral decisions, the Centre's traditional 'partial' duty of confidentiality has recently been revised to a 'partial' duty of transparency.

With regard to the *arbitral institution*, Article 48(5) ICSID Convention provides that "The Centre shall not publish the award without the consent of the parties." Such prohibition is reiterated in Rule 48(4) of the ICSID Arbitration Rules (first sentence).

In the case the parties grant their consent, Regulation 22 of the ICSID Administrative and Financial Regulations requires the Secretary-General to arrange for the publication of the arbitral awards "in an appropriate form with a view to furthering the development of international law in relation to investments".

In 1984, Rule 48(4) of the ICSID Arbitration Rules was revised to include, next to the prohibition on the Centre to publish the award without the consent of the parties, the Centre's discretion to publish "excerpts of the legal rules applied by the Tribunal" (ICSID 1984: Rule 48.4).[7] As explained by Professor Schreuer, the idea was to permit the Secretariat to identify certain aspects of the practice under the Convention in order to shed light on its application (Schreuer 2001: 820). Following a further revision in 2006, the added sentence in Rule 48(4) was modified to *require* the Centre to publish "excerpts of the legal reasoning of the Tribunal" (ICSID 1984: 48.4).[8]

While Article 48 and Rule 48 only refer to the 'award' (which includes the final decision of an arbitral tribunal as well as the decision of an ad hoc annulment committee), for purposes of their publication, the Centre has treated other decisions of the tribunal such as recommendations of provisional measures, preliminary decisions on jurisdiction or procedural orders in the same way as awards (Schreuer 2001: 823).

With regard to the *arbitral tribunal*, Rule 6(2) requires an arbitrator to sign a declaration that provides in part that he or she keeps "confidential [. . .] the contents of any award made by the Tribunal".

It is generally recognized that the *disputing parties* are free from releasing any arbitral decision to the public (except in the case they have agreed to keep the decision confidential) (Schreuer 2001: 822; Egonu 2007: 484; Delaney and Magraw in Muchlinski et al. 2008). It is not surprising that most of ICSID decisions find their way into the public domain, and rather sooner than later appear on one of the specialized, freely accessible websites on the Internet.[9] This practice may be encouraged by the fact that the registry of ICSID arbitrations is publicly available as the ICSID Secretary-General is under an obligation to publish information about requests of arbitration (Article 22.1 Administrative and Financial Regulations).

ICSID jurisprudence seems to confirm the absence of any general per se rule either imposing a duty of confidentiality or a duty of transparency in ICSID arbitration. Seized with the decision regarding the issue of confidentiality of its proceedings, the ICSID tribunal in *Biwater Gauff* noted as follows:

> In the absence of any agreement between the parties on this issue, there is no provision imposing a general duty of confidentiality in ICSID arbitration, whether in the ICSID Convention, any of the applicable Rules or otherwise. Equally, however, there is no provision imposing a general rule of transparency or non-confidentiality in any of these sources.
>
> (*Biwater Gauff* v. *Tanzania* 2006: para. 121)[10]

It is interesting to note that, while the Tribunal in *Biwater* imposed certain confidentiality restrictions on the parties in order to safeguard the procedural integrity of the arbitration and avoid aggravating the dispute, the Tribunal emphasized the limited temporal scope of such restrictions. The Tribunal noted that:

> Once the arbitration has finally concluded, most restrictions would not normally continue to apply. While the proceedings remain pending, however, there is an obvious tension between the interests in transparency and in procedural integrity.
>
> (*Biwater Gauff* v. *Tanzania* 2006: para. 140)

Accordingly, it is likely that such confidentiality restrictions would not be imposed by the Tribunal with regard to the final award.

Arbitration rules by national and international institutions

ICC Rules of Arbitration

The ICC Rules of Arbitration only expressly regulate the publication of the arbitral awards by the *arbitral institution*. Article 28(2) prohibits the ICC Secretariat to make available a certified copy of an award to any third party to the arbitration.[11] Equally, Article 1(3) of the Internal Rules of the International Court of Arbitration (which organizes and supervises an ICC arbitration) requires confidentiality with regard to any documents submitted to the Court (including arbitral tribunals' awards).[12] Interestingly, Article 1(4) of the Court of Arbitration Rules allows the Chairman or Secretary General of the Court to "authorize researchers undertaking work of a scientific nature on international trade law to acquaint themselves with Awards".[13] Despite these confidentiality requirements, the ICC publishes extracts from a number of ICC arbitral awards. However, these extracts have been redacted in order to ensure that the parties remain anonymous and in compliance with the duty of confidentiality under which the ICC Secretariat and Court of Arbitration operate. It may thus be concluded that the ICC operates under a regime of 'partial' confidentiality with regard to arbitral decisions.

Despite confidentiality being one of the perceived advantages of ICC arbitration, nothing in the ICC Rules of Arbitration binds the *disputing parties* to keep the award (as well as other information relating to the arbitration) confidential. While the tribunal under the ICC may take measures for protecting trade secrets and confidential information,[14] the ICC Rules of Arbitration have no general provision for confidentiality applicable to the parties.[15] However, the parties may agree otherwise. Accordingly, in an ICC arbitration the parties enjoy a 'right to transparency' with regard to the publication of arbitral decisions. This general approach is confirmed expressly by the ICC Secretariat on its website. Among the advantages of ICC arbitration, the Secretariat includes confidentiality, which is explained as follows:

> In contrast with ordinary courtroom proceedings under public and media gaze, ICC does not divulge details of an arbitration case and keeps the

> identities of the parties completely confidential. So your business remains nobody else's business. Sometimes, of course, parties will publicize an award – but ICC's lips are always sealed. If you wish, you may also enter into a confidentiality agreement with the opposing party as an additional safeguard.[16]

However, the degree of confidentiality (including of arbitral awards) may also depend on the applicable arbitral rules and the procedural law of the seat of arbitration. Whilst some national courts, such as the English courts and the French courts have confirmed the principles of confidentiality and privacy in arbitration proceedings, other courts such as the US, Australian and Swedish courts, do not recognize these principles, or at least the principle of confidentiality. Accordingly, there may be cases where an award will be made public without the consent of the parties for example in challenge or enforcement proceedings (Delaney and Magraw in Muchlinski et al. 2008 citing *Hassneh Insurance Co* v. *Stewart J. Mew* and *Esso*: 755).[17]

UNCITRAL Arbitration Rules

UNCITRAL Arbitration Rules, adopted in December 1976, are premised on the recognition of the value of arbitration as a method of settling disputes arising in the context of international commercial relations.[18] These rules include a 'duty of confidentiality' with regard to the publication of the arbitral award. Article 34(5) of the UNCITRAL Arbitration Rules, as revised in 2010, provides that "An award may be made public with the consent of all parties or where and to the extent disclosure is required of a party by legal duty, to protect or pursue a legal right or in relation to legal proceedings before a court or other competent authority." Accordingly, it appears that such duty of confidentiality applies to the *arbitral tribunal* and the *parties to the arbitration*. In other words, publication of the award is generally permitted only with the parties' consent or where required by a legal duty or to protect a legal right.

Furthermore, it should be noted that, during its recently concluded revision process, transparency of treaty-based arbitration proceedings and the resulting award received at least in principle wide support from delegations. However, in order to avoid any work on treaty arbitration delaying the completion of the revision of the UNCITRAL Arbitration Rules in their generic form, at its 41st session the UNCITRAL Commission gave the Working Group on Conciliation and Arbitration a mandate to consider the issue of transparency in investor–State arbitrations as its next priority, after the adoption of the revised Rules.[19]

UNCITRAL has no secretariat to oversee or administer arbitrations conducted according to its Arbitration Rules. However, since the parties may choose an established institution (such as ICSID or the Permanent Court of Arbitration, PCA) to run such arbitration, in the case that they do, the *arbitration institution* will also be bound by the confidentiality requirement in Article 34(5).

SCC and LCIA Arbitration Rules

The Arbitration Rules of the Arbitration Institute of the Stockholm Chamber of Commerce (SCC Arbitration Rules)[20] impose a 'duty of confidentiality' with regard to the arbitral award on the *arbitral institution* (the SCC Institute) and *arbitral tribunal*. Article 46 provides that "Unless otherwise agreed by the parties, the SCC Institute and the Arbitral Tribunal shall maintain the confidentiality of the arbitration and the award." Article 9 of the Organization of the SCC Institute reiterates this obligation.[21] It would seem that *disputing parties*, on the other hand, are at liberty to disclose the arbitral award, if they so wish (right to transparency).

On the contrary, the Arbitration Rules of the LCIA expressly provide for a 'duty of confidentiality' of all arbitral awards on the *disputing parties*.[22] Article 30.1 provides that "Unless the parties expressly agree in writing to the contrary, the parties undertake as a general principle to keep confidential all awards in their arbitration".[23] This duty extends also to the *arbitral tribunal*, as Article 30.2 provides that a tribunal's deliberations are confidential to its members. Moreover, a duty of confidentiality with regard to the award or any part thereof is imposed on the *arbitral institution*. Article 30.3 prohibits the LCIA Court to "publish any award or any part of an award without the prior written consent of all parties and the Arbitral Tribunal."

Ad hoc arbitration rules in investment treaties

While the vast majority of international investment treaties refer back to a set of predetermined arbitration rules (such as ICSID, UNCITRAL and ICC rules), some investment treaties (often investment chapters in free trade agreements) do provide for additional (and at times extensive) rules regulating investment arbitration. Given the fact that most investment arbitrations find their jurisdictional basis in such treaties, it seems that, as a general rule, any specific arbitration rules in such treaties will take precedence over any conflicting institutional arbitration rules.

NAFTA Chapter 11

The investment chapter of the North-American Free Trade Agreement (NAFTA), for example, includes an extensive section on investor–State dispute settlement (Chapter 11, Section B). With regard to the publication of arbitral awards, the Annex to Article 1137(4) NAFTA allows for the publication of the award by either party when Canada or the United States are the disputing host state parties (right to transparency). Where Mexico is the disputing party, the applicable arbitration rules apply to the publication of an award. In an official statement in July 2001, the parties to the NAFTA have agreed that:

> Nothing in NAFTA imposes a general duty of confidentiality on the disputing parties to a Chapter Eleven arbitration, and, subject to the application of

> Article 1137(4), nothing in the NAFTA precludes the Parties from providing public access to documents submitted to, or issued by, a Chapter Eleven tribunal.

Despite the different regime depending on the host State party to the dispute, all arbitral awards rendered under NAFTA, including those involving Mexico, are public (even the award in *Gami Investments* v. *Mexico*, rendered in an UNCITRAL arbitration).[24]

Algiers Accord and Iran-US Claims Tribunal

In establishing the Iran-US Claims Tribunal, the Algiers Accord of 19 January 1981 provided that the Tribunal conduct its business in accordance with UNCITRAL Arbitration Rules "except to the extent modified by the parties or by the Tribunal to ensure that this agreement can be carried out" (Article III.2). Article 32(5) of the UNCITRAL Arbitration Rules was modified to provide for a broad duty of transparency. The modified paragraph reads as follows:

> All awards and other decisions shall be made available to the public, except that upon the request of one or more arbitrating parties, the arbitral tribunal may determine that it will not make the entire award or other decision public, but will make public only portions thereof from which the identity of the parties, other identifying facts and trade or military secrets have been deleted. (Iran–US Claims Tribunal, Rules of Procedure 1983)[25]

The Iran–US Claims Tribunal's awards and decisions are published in their entirety in the Iran–United States Claims Tribunal Reports, published by Cambridge University Press (Grotius Publications).

Recent international investment instruments

While most recent international investment instruments (particularly BITs) remain silent on the issue of procedural transparency in general and transparency of the arbitral award in particular,[26] there are a growing number of investment instruments that take an expressly pro-transparency stance with regard to investment arbitration decisions.

The 2004 CAFTA-DR contains extensive transparency provisions applicable to its investor–State dispute settlement mechanism. Article 10.21 addressing transparency of investor–State arbitration proceedings provides that the respondent shall make inter alia "orders, awards and decisions of the tribunal" available to the public (paragraph 1).[27] The tribunal shall however, make "appropriate arrangements to protect the information from disclosure" (paragraph 2).[28] This language is mirrored in Article 29 of the 2004 United States model BIT.

Article 38 on "Public Access to Hearings and Documents" of the 2004 Canada's model Foreign Investment Promotion and Protection Agreement (FIPA) provides that "any Tribunal award under this Section [on investor–State dispute settlement] shall be publicly available, subject to the deletion of confidential information" (Article 38.4).[29] Interestingly, this duty of transparency may not be derogated by the parties' agreement (in other words, it is an 'absolute' duty of transparency).[30]

The draft model BIT released by Norway in 2007 also includes broad transparency requirements. Article 17.1 provides that "All awards and substantive decisions of the Tribunal shall be made publicly available" and Article 19 provides that "All documents submitted to, or issued by, the Tribunal shall immediately be made publicly available by the Tribunal."[31] Accordingly, it would appear that the Norwegian draft model BIT takes an approach based on an 'absolute' duty of transparency.

These recent examples emphasize the move to more pro-transparency approaches to the issue of publication of investment decisions within certain governments. Compare for example the approach taken by the US and Canada in NAFTA (right to transparency) with those taken in the 2004 US model BIT and 2004 Canada model FIPA (duty of transparency).

Equally interesting is also the evolution of the approach to transparency of awards by the Mexican government. From a pro-confidentiality approach (evidenced in NAFTA and in the 1998 BIT between Mexico and the Netherlands),[32] Mexico seems to have moved more recently towards an increasingly pro-transparency approach. Among the rules on the settlement of investor–State disputes, the 2004 Mexico–Japan Agreement for the Strengthening of the Economic Partnership (EPA) establishes a right to transparency for the parties with regard to the arbitral award (subject to certain limitations to protect inter alia confidential business information). Article 94.4 provides that "Either disputing party may make available to the public in a timely manner all documents, including an award, submitted to, or issued by, a Tribunal established under this Section". Accordingly, an approach based on the duty of confidentiality adopted in NAFTA and the Mexico–Venezuela BIT, the more recent Mexico–Japan EPA has endorsed an approach based on the right to transparency.

Preliminary remarks

Looking at the five arbitration rules examines above (UNCITRAL, ICC, SCC, ICSID and LCIA), the general stance seems to be one favouring confidentiality of arbitral awards or at least one that does not include any strong transparency requirements. This is certainly true for UNCITRAL and LCIA rules, which provide for a duty of confidentiality on all the three main participants in the arbitral process.[33] ICC and SCC rules also provide for a duty of confidentiality on the arbitral tribunal and on the arbitral institution but are silent with regard to the disputing parties. Thus, the parties enjoy, within an ICC and SCC arbitration, a right to transparency, if they wish to disclose the decision of the arbitral tribunal. ICSID rules take a similar approach with the exception that the Centre, following the 2006 changes, is now under an obligation to publish excerpts of the legal reasoning of the Tribunal (i.e. the arbitral institution is under a 'partial' duty of transparency). This is summarized in Table 6.1.

Table 6.1 Confidentiality/transparency of arbitral awards (Institutional Arbitration Rules)

	Arbitral Tribunal	*Arbitral Institution*	*Disputing Parties*
UNCITRAL (1976)	duty of confidentiality	NA	duty of confidentiality
ICC (1998)	(implied) duty of confidentiality	(partial) duty of confidentiality	right to transparency
SCC (1998)	duty of confidentiality	duty of confidentiality	right to transparency
ICSID (2006)	(absolute) duty of confidentiality	(partial) duty of transparency	right to transparency
LCIA (2007)	duty of confidentiality	duty of confidentiality	duty of confidentiality

This general stance may be easily explained by the fact that only ICSID rules are currently envisaged for purposes of investor–State arbitration, while all the other arbitration rules examined are aimed more generally at international arbitration (thus including principally international commercial arbitration or arbitration between commercial parties not based on an international treaty). Accordingly, the recent changes of the ICSID rules go in the direction of a stronger approach to transparency, including now a (partial) duty of transparency on the Centre itself. On the other hand, within the context of the review of the UNCITRAL Rules, there seems to be a consensus at least on the issue of keeping the rules for commercial arbitration separate from those concerning investment arbitration.

With regard to the additional rules regulating investment arbitration in international investment treaties, two remarks may be made here. First, most of these treaties (especially the bilateral investment ones) do not provide for any meaningful, additional rules regulating arbitration. However, as mentioned above, any specific arbitration rules in such treaties will take precedence over any conflicting institutional arbitration rules. Second, there are a limited but growing number of international investment treaties that are taking stronger approaches with regard to the external transparency of arbitral decisions. This is clearly shown by examining and comparing some of the treaties concluded by the US, Canada, Mexico and Norway in the last ten years (see Table 6.2).

Some empirical data

2003–2007 data

The number and percentage of publicly available key decisions (on jurisdiction, on the merits and on annulment requests) rendered in known investment arbitration is very high.[34] Taking into account the last five years (2003–2007), of the 109 key decisions rendered in known investment arbitrations, 98 are publicly available (90

Table 6.2 Confidentiality/transparency of arbitral awards (International Investment Instruments)

	Arbitral Tribunal	*Arbitral Institution*	*Disputing Parties*
Iran–US Claims Tribunal (1983)	duty of transparency	duty of transparency	duty of transparency
NAFTA Ch 11 (1994)		NA	right to transparency (Can & US. only)
Mexico–Netherlands BIT (1998)	duty of confidentiality	duty of confidentiality	duty of confidentiality
Mexico–Japan EPA (2004)	NA	NA	right to transparency
CAFTA-DR (2004)		NA	(absolute) duty of transparency
Canada model FIPA (2004)		NA	(absolute) duty of transparency
Norway draft model BIT (2007)	duty of transparency	NA	(absolute) duty of transparency

per cent) while 11 are still not public (10 per cent). See Figure 6.1. It should be emphasized that, since the only arbitration facility to maintain a public registry of claims is ICSID, the total number of actual investment decisions not publicly available is very much likely to be higher. Looking at the disaggregated data for the five years 2003–2007, in 2007 there appears to be a marked increase in decisions not publicly available. See Figure 6.2.

In 2007, there were at least 28 decisions (on jurisdiction, on the merits and on annulment requests) rendered in known investment arbitrations: 22 are publicly available,[35] while six remain not public. Of the 22 decisions available to the public, 17 were rendered in an arbitration conducted according to ICSID (or ICSID Additional Facility) Arbitration Rules, three according to SCC Arbitration Rules and two according to UNCITRAL Arbitration Rules. Of the six decisions still not available to the public, four were rendered within ICSID arbitration and two within UNCITRAL arbitration.

In 2006, there were at least 27 decisions (on jurisdiction, on the merits and on annulment requests) rendered in known investment arbitrations, all of which, except one, are publicly available. Of the 26 decisions available to the public, 19 were rendered in an arbitration conducted according to ICSID (or ICSID AF) arbitration rules, six according to UNCITRAL and one according to SCC. The one decision still not public was rendered in an ICSID arbitration.

In 2005, there were at least 19 decisions (on jurisdiction, on the merits and on annulment requests) rendered in known investment arbitrations, all of which, except one, are publicly available. Of the 18 decisions available to the public, 14 were rendered in an arbitration conducted according to ICSID, two according to SCC, one according to UNCITRAL, and one where the arbitration rules remain

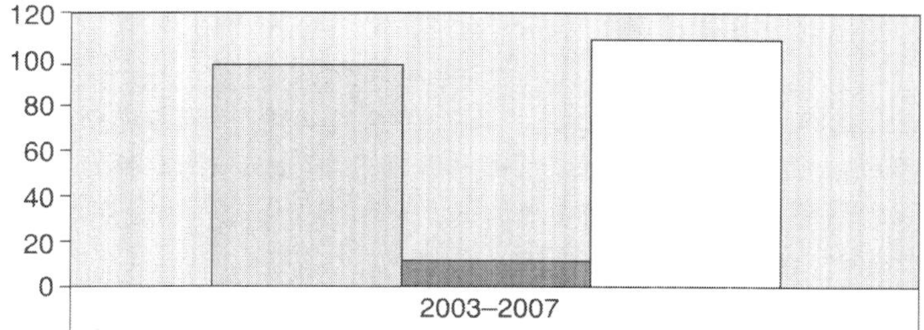

	2003–2007
public	98
not public	11
total	109

Figure 6.1 Cumulative public/not public decisions in known investment arbitrations (2003–2007)

unknown. The one decision still not public was rendered in an UNCITRAL arbitration.

In 2004, there were at least 19 decisions (on jurisdiction, on the merits and on annulment requests) rendered in known investment arbitrations, all of which except two, are publicly available. Of the 17 decisions available to the public, 13 were rendered in an arbitration conducted according to ICSID, two according to LCIA and two according to UNCITRAL. The two decisions, which are still not public, were rendered in an UNCITRAL arbitration and in a SCC arbitration.

In 2003, there were at least 16 decisions (on jurisdiction, on the merits and on annulment requests) rendered in known investment arbitrations, all of which except one, are publicly available. Of the 15 decisions available to the public, 11 were rendered in an arbitration conducted according to ICSID, two according to the SCC arbitration rules, one according to UNCITRAL and one according to

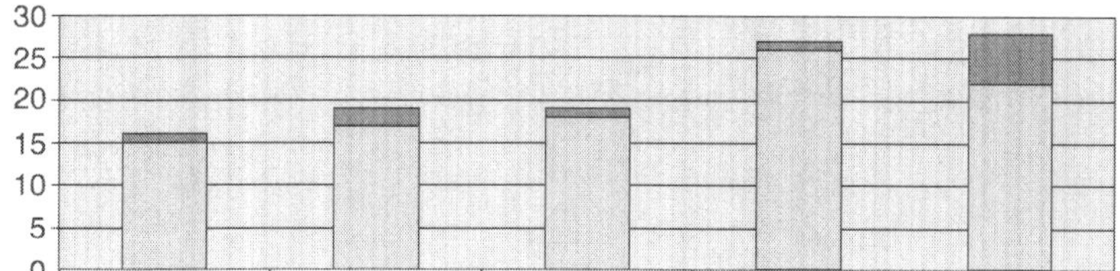

	2003	2004	2005	2006	2007
not public	1	2	1	1	6
public	15	17	18	26	22

Figure 6.2 Public/not public decisions in known investment arbitrations (year)

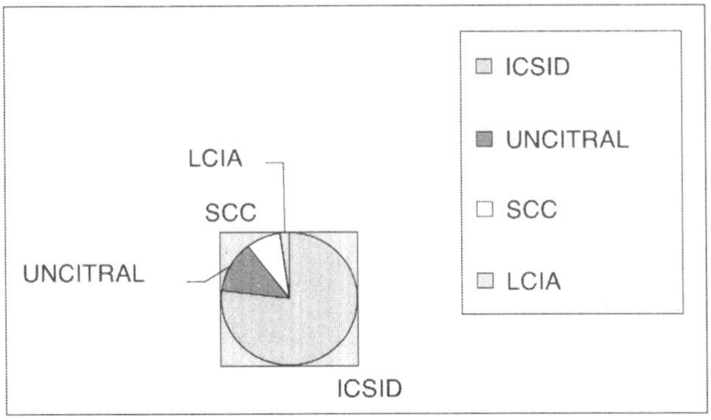

Figure 6.3 Publicly available decisions by arbitration rules (percentage)

ASEAN arbitration rules. The one decision still not public was rendered in an ICSID arbitration.

The vast majority of all publicly available decisions rendered between 2003–2007 stem out of ICSID arbitrations (74 or 77 per cent). 12 decisions were rendered in UNCITRAL arbitrations (13 per cent), eight decisions in SCC arbitrations (8 per cent) and two in LCIA arbitrations (2 per cent). See Figure 6.3.

With regard to all not publicly available decisions rendered between 2003–2007 in known investment arbitrations (11), six decisions stem out of ICSID arbitrations (55 per cent), four decisions out of UNCITRAL arbitrations (36 per cent) and one decision out of an SCC arbitration (9 per cent). See Figure 6.4. Accordingly, looking at the relative percentages of publicly and not publicly available decisions in known investment arbitrations, it may be noted that decisions rendered on the basis of UNCITRAL arbitration rules are more likely not to be publicly available compared to decisions in both ICSID and SCC arbitrations. A quarter (25 per cent) of all known decisions stemming out of UNCITRAL arbitrations remain unavailable to the public, while only 5 per cent of all ICSID decisions are not publicly available.

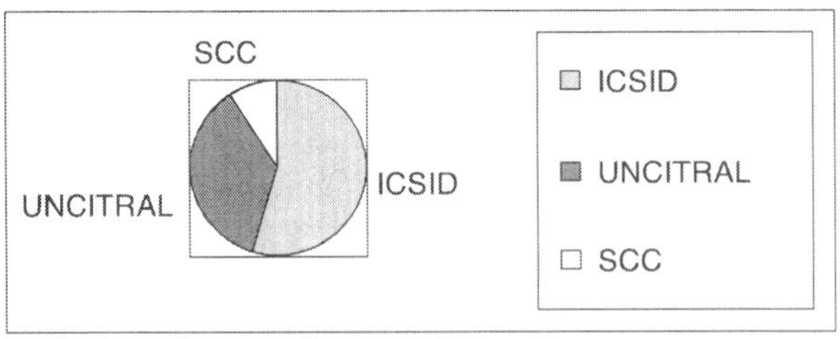

Figure 6.4 Not publicly available decisions by arbitration rules (percentage)

An update

At the time of finalizing this contribution (August 2010), a few additional findings may be put forward. First, the general conclusion that most key decisions rendered in known investment arbitrations are publicly available still stands.[36] Taking into account the seven years 2003–2009, of the 176 key decisions rendered in known investment arbitrations, 157 are publicly available (89 per cent) while 19 are still not public (11 per cent). See Figure 6.5. Equally, the recent trend of more confidential decisions appears also to be confirmed. If one focuses only on the three years 2007–2009, there is a slightly higher percentage (18 per cent) of key decisions not publicly available (of the 93 key decisions, 16 are still not public). There are several possible explanations for this. First, with time, decisions previously not publicly available become public. This is the 'time lag' issue: as there is no general duty to make arbitral decisions public, transparency takes time. Comparing the data for 2003–2007 as it stood in July 2008 with the data for the same period as it stands two years later (August 2010), one may find that some of the decisions that were publicly unavailable in 2008 are in the public domain today (only seven of the 11 publicly unavailable decisions in 2008 remain so in 2010). More investment arbitrations (as well as related decisions, whether publicly available or not) are surfacing for several factors (e.g. specialized reporting services (IAReporter) and generally greater interest from several stakeholders about investment arbitration). And claimants may willingly choose arbitration rules that provide for greater confidentiality (increase use of UNCITRAL rules) as well as both disputing parties agreeing to confidentiality requirements.

Second, combining the data from the entire period (2003–2009), decisions rendered in UNCITRAL arbitration are clearly more likely not to be publicly available compared to decisions in both ICSID and SCC arbitrations. Despite the fact that the great majority of known investment arbitrations are ICSID ones, of 19 key decisions rendered between 2003 and 2009 in known investment arbitration, ten stem from UNCITRAL arbitrations (more than 50 per cent), while seven stem from ICSID arbitrations, one from an ICC arbitration and one from an SCC arbitration.

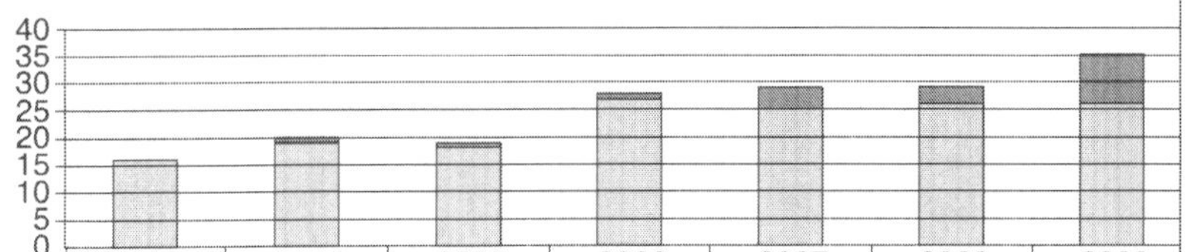

	2003	2004	2005	2006	2007	2008	2009
not public	0	1	1	1	4	3	9
public	16	19	18	27	25	26	26

Figure 6.5 Public/not public decisions in known investment arbitrations (year) (as of August 2010)

Third, one particular element that emerges is the high number of arbitral decisions in investment arbitrations involving the Czech Republic which remain not publicly available. The decisions relating to five out of 11 investment arbitrations involving the Czech Republic remain not publicly available. Most of the eleven arbitrations have been conducted on the basis of the UNCITRAL rules (including all those involving the publicly unavailable decisions).[37]

Confidentiality versus transparency: some policy considerations

Focusing on the issue of the publicity of arbitral decisions, it may be useful to set out some of the policy justifications supporting confidentiality, on the one hand, and transparency, on the other. It should be emphasized that many of the justifications set out below may well be applicable to the issue of confidentiality/transparency of the arbitration proceedings as a whole. Making arbitral decisions available to the public will, to a certain extent, shed light on many aspects of the arbitration proceedings.

In favour of confidentiality

It may be useful to distinguish between arguments in favour of confidentiality of arbitral decisions to protect certain specific interests of the disputing parties (whether investors or host governments) and arguments in favour of confidentiality to preserve arbitration as a pure dispute settlement mechanism.

Confidentiality of arbitral decisions may be said to protect the interests of the parties to investment arbitration as it prevents any matter related to the proceedings from being exposed to the wider public. These would include, for example, (1) past and current conducts of the investor or the host government, which would be at issue in the arbitration; (2) offensive and defensive allegations made by either party within the arbitration proceedings, and (3) the findings of fact and law by the tribunal in reaching its decision. Accordingly, from the perspective of the disputing parties, the rationale for keeping these matters confidential may include the following:

- to avoid embarrassment of government or company officials;
- to avoid alarming other foreign investors, who may be thinking of investing in the host State, as well as current or potential shareholders (especially minority ones) in the company instituting the arbitration;
- to reduce the possibility of other investors bringing similar claims against the host government;
- to reduce direct and indirect external influences on the proceedings and thus increase flexibility in parties' arbitration strategies (including greater potential for amicable resolution);
- to protect confidential or sensitive business or government information (Buys 2003: 123, 137; Schreuer 2001: 826; Delaney and Magraw in Muchlinski et al. 2008: 762–63).

Confidentiality of arbitral decisions may also be seen as necessary to preserve the pure dispute settlement nature of investment arbitration. First, publicity of awards may impose on the arbitral tribunal the responsibility for establishing a coherent body of law, instead of simply resolving the dispute at hand. Confidentiality would, in other words, prevent the introduction in investment arbitration of the tension between the need for justice in the specific case and the need for certainty and coherence in the law more broadly (Blackaby 2002: 5). Second, given the lack of any extensive review mechanism over investment decisions, wrong decisions may become public and influence subsequent arbitration. Third, if publication is done on a discretionary basis, selective circulation of awards may give a distorted view of investment law and arbitration as only certain views or philosophies may be disclosed and reflected in those awards made public.

In favour of transparency

It is useful to distinguish between arguments in favour of transparency of arbitral decisions to strengthen the system of international investment law and arbitration in the interest of its principal users (investors and host governments) and those arguments in favour of transparency to further broader policy objectives.

There exist several arguments supporting confidentiality of decisions in investor–State arbitration in order to strengthen the system of international investment law and arbitration in the general interest of investors and host governments. First, transparency of arbitral decisions improves the clarity, certainty and predictability of investment law. This in turn, increases participation and confidence in the system particularly of the less knowledgeable investors and host States; it facilitates parties' adopting conduct complying with investment law; it assists parties in avoiding arbitration as it may encourage other less contentious forms of dispute settlement (negotiation, mediation, etc.); and it increases pressure on parties to implement awards (Delaney and Magraw in Muchlinski et al. 2008: 761–62).

Second, transparency of arbitral decisions leads to the development of (and eventually consistency in) international investment law. By making all decisions publicly available, the quality of decisions is increased and case-law becomes more rational as tribunals and parties build on the experience and wisdom of past decisions (Schreuer 2001: 828; OECD 2005; Blackaby 2002: 7; Buys 2003: 136–37; Egonu 2007: 488; IISD 2007: 4; Delaney and Magraw in Muchlinski et al. 2008: 761–62.).

Third, transparency of decisions allows future arbitrating parties to assess who are the good arbitrators (Schreuer 2001: 827; Buys 2003: 136), and States to carry out any necessary modification of the substantive and procedural rules (OECD 2005; Delaney and Magraw in Muchlinski et al. 2008: 762).

Equally, there are arguments in favour of transparency of arbitral decisions in order to further broader policy objectives. First, transparency increases the understanding, confidence and legitimacy of the investment system beyond the traditional participants in the investment relationship to include civil society in general. Secrecy surrounding the outcome of arbitration is likely to arouse suspicion rather than instil confidence in the host government as well as in the investor (Schreuer 2001: 827). Thus, transparency attenuates fears and demands from civil society due to the public relevance of investment arbitration decisions (Buys 2003: 136).

Second, publication of arbitral decisions promotes good governance as it allows the broader public to observe and evaluate the conduct of the host government with regard to the exercise of its public functions. This applies equally to the conduct of the investor as its corporate governance is subject to increasing scrutiny (Blackaby 2002; Egonu 2007: 488; Delaney and Magraw in Muchlinski et al. 2008: 761–62).

Private interests versus public interests

It is argued that, despite the variety of the arguments advanced either in favour of confidentiality or transparency of investment decisions, the crucial difference between the two camps centres on the nature of the interests protected by confidentiality, on the one hand, and transparency, on the other. In other words, a regime of confidentiality of investment decisions gives priority to the specific interests of the two parties at dispute ('private interests' rationale), while a regime of transparency of investment decisions gives priority to the broader interests of the several stakeholders in international investment law and arbitration ('public interest' rationale). This is inherent in the very notions of confidentiality (accessible only to a limited number of authorized persons) and transparency (available to the general public).

For example, as noted above keeping awards confidential will avoid embarrassment of government or company officials whose conduct is at issue in the arbitration or will increase flexibility in the arbitration strategies of the parties. In this sense, confidentiality aims to protect very specific interests of the parties at dispute. From a different perspective, confidentiality of awards emphasizes the strictly pure dispute settlement nature of investment arbitration, the aim simply being that of resolving the dispute between the two parties.

On the other hand, making awards publicly available will improve the certainty and predictability of investment law in the general interest of all the participants in the investment relationship and will increase the understanding, confidence and legitimacy of the investment system beyond the traditional participants to include civil society in general. In this sense, transparency aims to protect broader interests of several stakeholders in the regulation of foreign investment rather than simply the two disputing parties. From the perspective of the nature of investment arbitration, transparency of awards emphasizes the need to establish a coherent, rational system of law rather than simply resolving the dispute between the specific foreign investor and host government.

At the normative level, there seems to be a growing consensus on the need to favour transparency over confidentiality of decisions in investor–State arbitration. This is principally premised on the public nature of the issues at stake in investment law and arbitration (Blackaby 2002: 1–2; Van Harten 2007). Contrary to commercial arbitration between two private parties, investment arbitration always involves a State as one of the disputing parties and revolves around the compatibility of a State conduct with international law. It is not difficult to see how investment awards may have a direct and significant impact on the State's future conduct as well as on its national budget.

Summary of findings

First, looking at the five arbitration rules examines above (UNCITRAL, ICC, SCC, ICSID and LCIA), the general stance seems to be one favouring confidentiality of arbitral awards (or at least one that does not include any strong transparency requirements). This is certainly true for UNCITRAL and LCIA rules, which provide for a duty of confidentiality on all the three main participants in the arbitral process. ICC and SCC rules also provide for a duty of confidentiality on the arbitral tribunal and on the arbitral institution but are silent with regard to the disputing parties. Thus, the parties enjoy, within an ICC and SCC arbitration, a right to transparency, if they wish to disclose the decision of the arbitral tribunal. ICSID rules take a similar approach with the exception that the Centre, following the 2006 changes, is now under an obligation to publish excerpts of the legal reasoning of the Tribunal (i.e. the arbitral institution is under a 'partial' duty of transparency). As noted above, this general stance may be easily explained by the fact that only ICSID rules are envisaged for purposes of investor–State arbitration, while all the other arbitration rules examined are aimed more generally at international arbitration (thus including principally international commercial arbitration or arbitration between commercial parties).

Second, there are a limited but growing number of international investment treaties that are taking stronger approaches with regard to the external transparency of arbitral decisions. This is clearly shown by examining and comparing some of the treaties (including model treaties) concluded by the US, Canada, Mexico and Norway in the last ten years. As arbitration rules contained in such treaties will, in general, take precedence over any conflicting institutional arbitration rules, including stronger transparency requirements, in future treaties may represent a valid option for those States willing to push for more transparency of arbitral decisions.

Third, the number and percentage of publicly available key decisions (on jurisdiction, on the merits and on annulment requests) rendered in known investment arbitration is very high. Taking into account the seven years 2003–2009, of the 176 key decisions rendered in known investment arbitrations, 157 are publicly available (89 per cent) while 19 are still not public (11 per cent). However, looking at the disaggregated data for the same period, in the last three years there appears to be a marked increase in decisions not publicly available. Sixteen decisions are not publicly available, while in the previous four years a total of three decisions remain not publicly available.

Fourth, combining the data from the entire period (2003–2009), decisions rendered in UNCITRAL arbitration are clearly more likely not to be publicly available compared to decisions in both ICSID and SCC arbitrations. Despite the fact that the great majority of known investment arbitrations are ICSID arbitrations, of the 19 key decisions rendered between 2003 and 2009 in known investment arbitration, ten stem from UNCITRAL arbitrations (more than 50 per cent), while seven stem from ICSID arbitrations, one from an ICC arbitration and one from an SCC arbitration.

Fifth, despite the variety of the arguments advanced either in favour of confidentiality or in favour of transparency of investment decisions, the crucial difference between the two camps seems to centre on the nature of the interests protected by confidentiality, on the one hand, and transparency, on the other. A regime of confidentiality of investment decisions gives priority to the specific interests of the two parties at dispute ('private interests' rationale), while a regime of transparency of investment decisions gives priority to the broader interests of the several stakeholders in international investment law and arbitration ('public interest' rationale).

Sixth, the choice between confidentiality and transparency of arbitral awards has also broader implications on the underlying nature of investor–State dispute settlement. Confidentiality of awards emphasizes the strictly pure dispute settlement nature of investment arbitration focused on resolving the dispute between the specific foreign investor and host government, while transparency of awards emphasizes the need to establish a coherent, rational system of law.

Seventh, given the public nature of the issues at stake in investment law and arbitration (particularly the fact that investment arbitration always involves a State as one of the disputing parties and revolves around the compatibility of a State conduct with international law), there seems to be a growing consensus on the need to favour transparency over confidentiality of (at least) decisions in investor–State arbitration.

Part II: Internal transparency of investment awards

The issue of internal transparency of investment awards addresses the extent to which decisions by investor–State arbitral tribunals are intelligible to any reader (whether one of the parties to the arbitration itself or somebody interested in the decision). In principle, the issue of internal transparency of an arbitral award may address several aspects of the award itself. These may include (1) the language in which the decision has been redacted,[38] (2) the inclusion in the written decision of a detailed table of contents,[39] (3) the extent to which the decision records the uncontroversial factual circumstances of the case, (4) the existence of (a summary of) the parties' arguments presented to the tribunal, (5) a record of the arbitral procedure leading up to the final decision, and (6) the tribunal's decision in the strict sense including the underlying reasoning. This part of the chapter addresses the latter aspect only: it focuses on the issue of whether the legal reasoning underlying investment decisions is transparent or comprehensible.

The next section examines the arbitration rules provided for by the major arbitration institutions as well as those found in international investment treaties with regard to the legal reasoning of arbitral decisions. Next, the importance of investment decisions' internal transparency is explained, followed by an analysis of some of the instances where the legal reasoning of investment decisions lacks clarity focusing on Tribunals' interpretation and application of the underlying treaty provisions. The methodology of this latter section is case-law based and selective: the analysis will focus on a few awards (*CMS*, *Metalclad*, *Vivendi*, *Enron*, *LG&E*, and *Continental*) dealing with a small selection of treaty provisions (expropriation, emergency exception).

The requirement to state reasons

It is today an undisputed principle that international arbitral awards (including awards rendered by investment treaty tribunals) must set forth the reasons for the tribunal's decision (Born: 2009: 2450–51).

Article 48(3) of the ICSID Convention provides that "The award shall [. . .] state the reasons upon which it is based." Article 48(4) ICSID adds that "Any member of the Tribunal may attach his individual opinion to the award, whether he dissents from the majority or not, or a statement of his dissent." The importance of providing reasons within the ICSID Convention is confirmed by the inclusion of the 'failure to state the reasons' on which the award is based as one of the few grounds for annulment of the award (ICSID 1965: Article 52(1)(e)).

At least in the ICSID context, the question remains, however, regarding the content of the requirement to state reasons, particularly as it relates to annulment proceedings. If the problem of total absence of reasons is at best an exceptional one, it is unclear whether, and the extent to which, a duty to state reasons also encompasses a duty to provide *clear coherent*, *accurate* and/or *cogent* reasons. The issue is one of quality rather than quantity (Schreuer 2001: 802).

Although the ICSID annulment practice is limited, there seems to be an emerging consensus of limiting the annulment avenue in order to keep it as "an unusual remedy for unusual situations" (Schreuer in Gaillard and Banifatemi 2004: 4). While it may be difficult to establish a definitive test for determining whether or not a tribunal has complied with the obligation to state reasons, a relevant criterion suggested by one notable commentator is the following: "The award must be supported by a consistent and logical line of reasoning sufficient to enable an informed reader, in particular the parties, to understand the tribunal's motives" (Schreuer 2001: 806). 'Logical', 'coherent' and 'clear' reasoning seem to suggest a minimal level of substantive review, excluding a more demanding review about the 'accuracy' or 'cogency' of the reasons given by the arbitral tribunal.

Looking at recent annulment practice, while it is undisputed that failure to state reasons cannot justify a review of the merits, there is still a certain level of uncertainty with regard to the extent of the minimal level of substantive review. Some ICSID annulment committees have emphasized the lack of clarity in the reasoning as the key benchmark for an annulment on the basis of failure to state reasons. As noted by the annulment committee in *Vivendi* v. *Argentina*:

> [I]t is well accepted both in the cases and the literature that Article 52(1)(e) concerns a failure to state any reasons with respect to all or part of an award, not the failure to state correct or convincing reasons. . . . Provided that the reasons given by a tribunal can be followed and relate to the issues that were before the tribunal, their correctness is beside the point in terms of Article 52(1)(e). Moreover, reasons may be stated succinctly or at length, and different legal traditions differ in their modes of expressing reasons. Tribunals must be allowed a degree of discretion as to the way in which they express their reasoning.
>
> (*Vivendi* v. *Argentina* 2002: para. 64)[40]

On the other hand, there are other annulment committees that seem to have included more demanding benchmarks such as 'coherence' of the reasoning. The annulment committee in *Mitchell* v. *Democratic Republic of Congo* stated as follows:

> the ad hoc Committee is of the opinion that a failure to state reasons exists whenever reasons are purely and simply not given, or are so inadequate that the coherence of the reasoning is seriously affected.
>
> (*Patrick Mitchell* v. *Democratic Republic of Congo* 2006: para. 21)[41]

In practice, however, there may not be such a fundamental difference in the two approaches as incoherent reasoning may be characterized as unclear, too.[42] What is important, for purposes of our analysis, is that the lack of clarity in the reasoning of an ICSID tribunal constitutes a ground to annul that tribunal's decision.

Most other international arbitration rules, which regulate non-ICSID investment arbitrations, also include a general duty on the arbitral tribunals to state the reasons of their decisions. Article 32(3) of the UNCITRAL Arbitration Rules states that "The arbitral tribunal shall state the reasons upon which the award is based, unless the parties have agreed that no reasons are to be given." Similarly, Article 25(2) of the ICC Rules of Arbitration states that "The Award shall state the reasons upon which it is based."[43]

Rationales for clarity in the legal reasoning of investment decisions

Commentators have highlighted several rationales for requiring arbitral tribunals to give reasons for their decisions (Bingham 1988: 142; Carbonneau 1984–85; Born 2009: 2453–54). Most of these can be equally employed to require a high level of *clarity* in the reasoning of arbitral decisions (including investment awards).

It is useful here to distinguish between arguments in favour of a high level of clarity in the reasoning of investment decisions to strengthen the internal functioning of the system of international investment law and arbitration and those arguments in order to strengthen the legitimacy of the system vis-à-vis external stakeholders. As noted by Kingsbury and Schill:

> the reasoning should nonetheless be transparent and accessible not only from the point of view of the parties to the proceeding, but to the tribunals' wider audience, including non-participating States, the investment community at large and those groups that may be impacted by specific decisions in the context of foreign investment activities. This is particularly true because of the precedential effect investment awards have in practice.
>
> (Kingsbury and Schill 2009: 45)

There are at least three main arguments in favour of clarity in the reasoning of investment awards in order to strengthen the internal functioning of the system of investment law and arbitration. First, requiring clarity in the reasoning constitutes a guarantee against a decision not based on the law. It is a principle entrenched in most modern legal systems that, aside from very narrow instances where the dispute is to be decided *ex aequo et bono*, any adjudicative body (whether a court or arbitral tribunal) must decide disputes by the rational application of principle and authority, and not his or her own personal view of the justice of the case (Landau 2009). Moreover, requiring clarity in the reasoning of investment awards will also represent in itself "a valuable intellectual discipline for the decision maker" (Bingham 1988: 142).[44]

Second, disputing parties expect to be told and, crucially, to understand why they have won or lost the case. This is particularly important for the correct functioning of the system as it would improve the enforceability of the award against the losing party, and would allow the possibility for another tribunal (whether a domestic court or an ICSID annulment committee) to subject the award itself to review.

Third, a clearly-reasoned investment award will contribute to the development of a coherent and effective body of law. Subsequent investment tribunals would be in a better position to interpret and apply the law in light of previous case-law thus facilitating the development of a more coherent jurisprudence. Equally, clearly-reasoned decisions will improve the effectiveness of this particular branch of international law as foreign investors and host States will be able to structure their conduct according to the relevant standards being enunciated by investment tribunals (Landau 2009).[45]

There are equally strong rationales for imposing a high level of clarity in the reasoning of investment decisions in order to strengthen the overall legitimacy of the system of international investment law and arbitration, particularly taking into consideration external interests and stakeholders. Landau has correctly highlighted several elements characterizing investment treaty arbitration, which strongly justify imposing on investment tribunals a duty to give reasons (and implicitly to give 'clear' reasons). I will only recall here what I believe are the main three. First, investment treaty disputes are essentially a form of public law adjudication. Investment tribunals are thus mandated to review the manner in which States exercise their sovereign discretion, raising broad policy issues that may well interact with the lives of ordinary people and the way they are governed (Landau 2009: 195–97).

Second, investment tribunals review State conduct (whether of a judicial, administrative or legislative nature) by applying extremely broad, open-textured, standards, as prescribed in investment treaties (these include, for example, restrictions on "expropriation", guarantees of "fair and equitable treatment" and requirements of "non-discrimination"). The result is a "delegation by States to private arbitrators of a vast discretion in the application of substantive standards to the particular facts of a dispute – a discretion that far exceeds that available to most national court judges who may be empowered to review sovereign conduct" (Landau 2009: 195–97).

Third, investment tribunals exercise their powers of review of any State conduct in a procedural regime that lacks any system of substantive appeal; is often insulated from, or susceptible of only limited, procedural review by national court judges; and leads in many cases to compulsory international recognition and enforcement (whether under the Washington Convention 1965, or the New York Convention 1958) (Landau 2009: 195–97).

In light of these key features, investment tribunals should be required to provide a high level of clarity in their reasoning.

Three failures

Given its infancy, it should come as no surprise that there have been instances where investment tribunals have indeed failed to provide a high level of clarity in their reasoning. In this section, I will explore three types of failures committed by investment tribunals in providing reasons for their decisions: (1) abuse of precedents, (2) lack of internal consistency and (3) minimalism.

Abuse of precedents

It is well established that a doctrine of precedent, at least in the sense of binding precedent (or *stare decisis*), does not apply in international adjudication, including in the field of investor–State dispute settlement (Schreuer and Weiniger in Muchlinski et al. 2008: 1189). However, it is also well established that investment tribunals (as well as disputing parties) do rely on previous decisions for purposes of adjudicating investment disputes. In this sense, while tribunals in investment arbitrations are not bound by previous decisions of other arbitral tribunals, previous decisions are indeed considered as a matter of comparison or inspiration particularly in the interpretation of the underlying investment treaty provisions (Newcombe and Paradell 2009: 102–103). More fundamentally, it has correctly been argued that relying on the experience of previous decisions plays an important role in securing uniformity and predictability of the law, which in turn will strengthen the authority and legitimacy of the underlying system of investment protection (Schreuer and Weiniger in Muchlinski et al. 2008: 1189).

Recent studies have shown that in the last decade the frequency of citation to previous investment decisions has increased exponentially (Commission 2007: 149). Commentators have also pointed out that in some instances investment tribunals have misused precedents either by incorrectly characterizing the legal findings of previous decisions or by altogether avoiding discussing the legal findings of previous decisions and taking an inconsistent approach to the same (or very similar) legal question (Commission 2007: 156; Landau 2009; Douglas 2006: 28). Both types of abuse of precedent have a negative impact on the clarity of investment decisions' legal reasoning. In this section, I will analyze a few instances of the former type of abuse of precedent (i.e. the misunderstanding of previous decisions) focusing on the controversial issue of the definition of 'indirect expropriation'.

As most investment treaties require that indirect expropriations (or 'measures having equivalent effect to expropriation') be compensated,[46] the definition of indirect expropriation is unsurprisingly one of the hotly debated issues in international investment law. What are the criteria to distinguish between a compensable indirect taking (where there is no formal transfer of title) and a regulatory measure pursuing a legitimate public policy (which has an adverse effect on the foreign investor's property)? As investment tribunals have given different answers to this question, one can identify at least three distinct approaches. First, some tribunals have stressed adverse impact on the foreign investor's property as sufficient for a finding of indirect expropriation. Second, other tribunals have denied a finding of indirect expropriation by stressing that the host State measure at issue pursued a non-discriminatory, bona fide and legitimate public purpose. Third, sitting somewhere in between the two previous approaches, some decisions have stressed the relevance of both the measure's adverse effect on the foreign investment and the measure's public purpose, often complemented by recourse to a proportionality test. These tribunals have determined whether the host State measure constituted an indirect expropriation by balancing the investor's costs and the public policy benefits.

Rather than the existence of an inconsistent jurisprudence on the issue of the definition of indirect expropriation, what appears problematic in the context of the present discussion, is investment tribunals' incorrect or misleading use of precedents for purposes of justifying their legal findings. Two examples follow to illustrate this point.

The Tribunal in *Vivendi* v. *Argentina* was called upon to decide whether the actions of the Tucuman authorities (allegedly mounting a destructive campaign against the French investor operating a water services concession in the Argentinean province of Tucuman) constituted expropriation for purposes of Article 5 of the BIT between France and Argentina.[47] The tribunal took the view that, in determining the existence of a measure equivalent to expropriation, "the effect of the measure on the investor, not the state's intent, is the critical factor" (*Vivendi* v. *Argentina* 2007: para. 7.5.20), and particularly, the tribunal needs to enquire whether the foreign investor has suffered a substantial deprivation of value of its investment (*Vivendi* v. *Argentina* 2007: para. 7.5.10). Among the decisions referred to by the tribunal to support its finding on the definition of indirect expropriation, the tribunal made reference to the 2003 award in *Tecmed* v. *Mexico*. The *Vivendi* tribunal stated:

> In *Tecmed*, the tribunal held that a measure is equivalent to expropriation if: "the Claimant, due to [the actions of the Respondent] was radically deprived of the economical use and enjoyment of its investments, as if the rights related thereto . . . had ceased to exist. In other words, if due to the actions of Respondent, the assets involved have lost their value or economic use for their holder"
>
> (*Vivendi* v. *Argentina* 2007: para. 7.5.12)[48]

It is uncontested that the *Tecmed* tribunal did in fact emphasize the importance of the host State measure's adverse impact on the investment in order to determine whether the measure was indeed a measure equivalent to an expropriation. However, the *Tecmed* tribunal quite clearly also noted that this was *not* the exclusive criterion. In the very paragraph quoted by the *Vivendi* tribunal, the *Tecmed* tribunal had indeed specified that an enquiry over the adverse impact was only the *first* step in the determination of whether the measure was a measure equivalent to an expropriation.[49]

More fundamentally, the *Tecmed* tribunal had clearly set out the second step of the relevant test for a finding of expropriation. Quoting the case law of the European Court of Human Rights,[50] the *Tecmed* tribunal had stated as follows:

> in addition to the negative financial impact of such actions or measures, the Arbitral Tribunal will consider, in order to determine if they are to be characterized as expropriatory, whether such actions or measures are proportional to the public interest presumably protected thereby and to the protection legally granted to investments, taking into account that the significance of such impact has a key role upon deciding the proportionality.
>
> (*Tecmed* v. *Mexico* 2003: para. 122)

Ultimately, noting that the conduct of the Argentinean Province "struck at the economic heart of, and crippled, Claimants' investment", the *Vivendi* tribunal concluded that the claimants' concession rights had been expropriated in violation of the Treaty. One could well argue that, even without the reference to the *Tecmed* decision, the *Vivendi* tribunal would have taken the same approach towards the definition of indirect expropriation. However, it is difficult to determine with any certainty whether the *Vivendi* tribunal's misunderstanding or misuse of the *Tecmed* decision had an impact on the *Vivendi* tribunal's own conclusion on what constitutes the relevant test for a finding of indirect expropriation. Certainly, such misunderstanding or misuse has impacted on the clarity and strength of the decision's legal reasoning. More importantly, such abuse of precedents may undermine the internal and external legitimacy of the decision.

A second example of abuse of precedent may be found in the award in *CMS* v. *Argentina* where the tribunal had to determine whether emergency legislation implemented by Argentina in the midst of its economic crisis of 2001–2002 was a measure equivalent to expropriation for purposes of the Argentina–USA BIT. In a very concise analysis, the *CMS* tribunal first of all recognized that the issue of determining whether the emergency legislation constituted indirect or regulatory expropriation was not a "simple task" particularly because the legislation had had an important effect on the business of the claimant (*CMS* v. *Argentina* 2005: para. 260). The *CMS* tribunal then noted that the essential parameter applied by a number of tribunals, where indirect expropriation was at issue, is that of substantial deprivation of the economic benefit of the investor's property (*CMS* v. *Argentina* 2005: para. 262). The tribunal relied on a well-known dictum from the *Metalclad* v. *Mexico* award according to which indirect expropriation relates to incidental interference with the use of property which has "the effect of depriving the owner, in whole or in significant part, of the use or reasonably-to-be-expected economic benefit of property even if not necessarily to the obvious benefit of the host State."[51] Relying heavily on the award in *Pope & Talbot* v. *Canada*, the *CMS* tribunal found that the issues to be taken into account for reaching a determination of 'substantial deprivation' were not present in the present dispute. In particular, the CMS tribunal noted that "the investor is in control of the investment; the Government does not manage the day-to-day operations of the company; and the investor has full ownership and control of the investment" (*CMS* v. *Argentina* 2005: para. 263).[52] On the basis of these elements, the tribunal was persuaded that Argentina had not breached the standard of protection laid down in the Treaty for expropriation (*CMS* v. *Argentina* 2005: para. 264). While a later section will examine the internal consistency of the *CMS* tribunal reasoning on expropriation, our focus here is on the tribunal's apparent misuse of the decisions in *Metalclad* and *Pope & Talbot*.

While it is true that the *Metalclad* decision relied greatly on the host State measure's adverse effect on the investment, it also emphasized the relevance, for purposes of establishing an indirect expropriation, of the investor's legitimate or reasonable expectations.[53] However, the *CMS* tribunal did not incorporate that part of the *Metalclad* test in to its own legal standard for purposes of determining an indirect expropriation.

Moving on to the *CMS* tribunal use (or abuse) of the *Pope & Talbot* decision, it is true, as emphasized by the *CMS* tribunal, that the *Pope & Talbot* tribunal did look at the issues of 'ownership' and 'control' of the investment in determining whether the measure constituted 'indirect expropriation' (*Pope & Talbot* v. *Canada* 2000: para. 100).[54] However, the *Pope & Talbot* tribunal had crucially also looked at the issue of the extent of the Canadian measure's economic impact on the foreign investment. It was within that context that the *Pope & Talbot* tribunal had used the term "substantial deprivation". The *Pope & Talbot* tribunal had rejected the claim of expropriation also because the 'degree of interference' (or deprivation) was not 'sufficiently restrictive' (or substantial).

> Even accepting (for the purpose of this analysis) the allegations of the Investor concerning diminished profits, the Tribunal concludes that the

> *degree of interference* with the Investment's operations due to the Export Control Regime does not rise to an expropriation (creeping or otherwise) within the meaning of Article 1110. While it may sometimes be uncertain whether a particular interference with business activities amounts to an expropriation, the test is whether that interference is *sufficiently restrictive* to support a conclusion that the property has been "taken" from the owner.
> (*Pope & Talbot* v. *Canada* 2000: para. 102) [emphasis added]

Once again, the *CMS* tribunal's misunderstanding or misuse of the *Metalclad* and *Pope & Talbot* decisions undermines the clarity and strength of its decision's legal reasoning. The tribunal in *Metalclad* had not only relied on the adverse effect on the foreign investment but also on the existence of the investor's reasonable expectation. Similarly, the *Pope & Talbot* tribunal had not simply relied on whether the investor still owned and controlled its investment but more fundamentally on whether Canada's measure had substantially deprived the claimant of the value or benefit of its investment.

Lack of internal consistency

In adjudicating claims brought under investment treaties, investment tribunals often distinguish two distinct stages. At the first stage, the tribunal sets out the relevant standard following an interpretation of the text of the treaty according to the customary rules of treaty interpretation (interpretation stage). In the case of an expropriation claim, for example, the tribunal will determine the relevant standard in order to establish whether the measure at issue is a measure having effect equivalent to an expropriation: as seen above, the tribunal may chose inter alia the 'substantial deprivation of the economic benefit of the investor's property' as the relevant standard. At the second stage, the tribunal applies the standard enunciated at the interpretation stage to the facts of the case (application stage). Using the same example, the tribunal will enquire whether the specific host State measure at issue substantially deprived the investor of the value of its investment.

This section argues that a further failure in the legal reasoning of investment tribunals revolves around investment decisions' lack of internal consistency. A first type of internal inconsistency is when the tribunal's findings at the interpretation stage conflict with one another. A second type of internal inconsistency is when there is a lack of consistency between the legal standard enunciated at the interpretation stage and the standard actually applied to the facts of the case. Two examples follow to clarify these points.

As explained above, with regard to the issue of the definition of an indirect expropriation, the *CMS* tribunal adopted the standard of 'substantial deprivation of the economic benefit of the investor's property' and then emphasized certain issues (investor's control and ownership of the investment) to be taken into account in determining 'substantial deprivation'. As these elements were present in the instant case, the tribunal was persuaded that Argentina had not breached the standard of protection for expropriation (*CMS* v. *Argentina* 2005: paras 260–64).

There does not seem to be a very strong logical connection, or consistency, between the tribunal's finding that the relevant standard for an indirect expropriation is 'substantial deprivation of the enjoyment or economic benefit of the property', on the one hand, and the tribunal's finding that the elements upon which substantial deprivation should be determined are investor's ownership and control of the investment, on the other hand. Both 'ownership'[55] and 'control' do not really indicate whether or not the benefit or value of the property has been substantially deprived. Several of the claims based on indirect expropriation deal in fact with a host State measure that has left both the ownership and control of the investment in the hands of the investor, while the value of the investment has fully or substantially disappeared. In other words, ownership and control cannot really be used as the only proxies for determining whether the value of the investment has been substantially deprived by a host State measure.

It is difficult to determine whether the tribunal would have reached a different conclusion had it correctly examined Argentina's emergency legislation's adverse impact on the value of the claimant's investment. As noted in the previous section, the *CMS* tribunal did recognize that the issue of determining whether the emergency legislation constituted indirect or regulatory expropriation was not a simple task because the legislation had "had an important effect on the business of the claimant" (*CMS* v. *Argentina* 2005: para. 260). As the tribunal only focused on the issues of ownership and control, it never really examined whether that 'important effect' rose to the level of substantial deprivation.

A second example of internal inconsistency may be found in the award in *Metalclad* v. *Mexico*. There were two measures at issue in that case: (1) denial of a construction permit by a Mexican municipality and (2) an ecological decree issued by a Mexican state governor. It was uncontroversial that both measures had substantial adverse effect on the foreign investment (the hazardous waste landfill, which had been acquired and developed by the US investor, could not be operated). The *Metalclad* tribunal defined the notion of expropriation for purposes of Article 1110 NAFTA as follows:

> expropriation under NAFTA includes not only open, deliberate and acknowledged takings of property, such as outright seizure or formal or obligatory transfer of title in favour of the host State, but also covert or incidental interference with the use of property which has the effect of depriving the owner, in whole or in significant part, of the use or reasonably-to-be-expected economic benefit of property even if not necessarily to the obvious benefit of the host State.
>
> (*Metalclad* v. *Mexico* 2000: para. 103)

When the tribunal moved to apply the relevant legal standard (substantial deprivation of the reasonably-to-be-expected economic benefit) to the facts of the case, the tribunal appears to rely on a slightly different standard for each of the two measures under review.

In concluding that the first measure (denial of construction permit) amounted to an indirect expropriation, the *Metalclad* tribunal appears to add an additional element, which is not included in the tribunal's interpretation of the concept of 'expropriation', that is whether or not the Municipality had acted in compliance with Mexican law. The tribunal found:

> These measures [i.e. the denial of the construction permit], taken together with the representations of the Mexican federal government, on which Metalclad relied, and the absence of a timely, orderly or substantive basis for the denial by the Municipality of the local construction permit, amount to an indirect expropriation.
>
> (*Metalclad* v. *Mexico* 2000: para. 107)

There is only partial consistency between the legal standard enunciated by the tribunal in paragraph 103 and the legal standard applied in paragraph 107. As mentioned above, it was uncontroversial that the measure had a substantial adverse effect on the investment ('substantial deprivation' requirement). Furthermore, the tribunal found that the representations of the Mexican federal government (that there was no need of a municipal permit) had created legitimate expectations on the part of the foreign investor ('reasonably-to-be-expected' requirement). However, the tribunal's reference in its findings on paragraph 107 that the municipality had acted outside Mexican law ("and the absence of a [. . .] substantive basis for the denial") does not appear to be based on the legal standard enunciated by the tribunal at the interpretation stage.

In applying the legal standard set out at the interpretation stage to the second measure (the ecological decree), the tribunal seems to take away one of the elements of that legal standard, that is the 'reasonable expectations' requirement. The tribunal stated:

> Although not strictly necessary for its conclusion, the Tribunal also identifies as a further ground for a finding of expropriation the Ecological Decree issued by the Governor of SLP on September 20, 1997. This Decree covers an area of 188,758 hectares within the "Real de Guadalcazar" that includes the landfill site, and created therein an ecological preserve. This Decree had the effect of barring forever the operation of the landfill. [. . .]
>
> The Tribunal need not decide or consider the motivation or intent of the adoption of the Ecological Decree. Indeed, a finding of expropriation on the basis of the Ecological Decree is not essential to the Tribunal's finding of a violation of NAFTA Article 1110. However, the Tribunal considers that the implementation of the Ecological Decree would, in and of itself, constitute an act tantamount to expropriation.
>
> (*Metalclad* v. *Mexico*, Award 30 August 2000: paras 109 and 111)

Contrary to the legal standard enunciated generally by the tribunal, the tribunal here simply relies on the adverse effect of the ecological decree on the investment ("this decree had the effect of barring forever the operation of the landfill"). There is no consideration of whether the foreign investor could have reasonably expected that such a decree would not be issued by the Governor. Equally surprising, the *Metalclad* tribunal also did not employ the legal standard actually applied with regard to the first measure under review. In its finding that the ecological decree constituted indirect expropriation, the tribunal did not consider whether the ecological decree had been issued in conformity with Mexican law.

Minimalism

A further failure in the legal reasoning of investment tribunals undermining the transparency of investment decisions relates to the lack of adequate justification supporting tribunals' legal findings. Landau calls this failure 'a tendency towards minimalism':

> very little is often given away as to the tribunal's thinking. The flavour of such awards is one of minimalism – or the expression of no more than is strictly necessary for each proposition, in order to connect the final disposition to at least some of the parties' submissions. In some cases, reasons are given, but by way of short and compressed statements. In others, reasons are pared down in number to the fewest possible propositions. In others, conclusions are given, instead of any reasons at all.
>
> (Landau 2009: 22–23)

Once again, I will focus on a few examples dealing this time with the emergency exceptions under international investment law and the necessity test.

One of the (many) highly disputed issues in the investment arbitrations that have revolved around the emergency measures taken by Argentina following its economic crisis of 2001–2002 was Argentina's plea to be exempt from liability on the basis of the customary doctrine of 'necessity'[56] or the 'emergency clause' found in the underlying investment treaties.[57] The Argentine Republic argued in detail the severity that characterized the crisis affecting the country from 2000, which threatened in its view the very existence of the State and its independence. For example, the significant decrease of the Gross Domestic Product, consumption and investment during the crisis period, together with deflation and the reduction in value of Argentine corporations, resulted in widespread unemployment and poverty, with dramatic consequences in health, malnutrition and social policies.

One of the legal issues that Argentina needed to demonstrate for both the customary and treaty defences dealt with whether the measures adopted by Argentina were "the only way [. . .] to safeguard an essential interest" or "necessary for . . . the protection of its own essential security interests", respectively. This has also been referred to as the test of necessity (in the strict sense).

Five decisions, rendered in the last five years by five different investment tribunals hearing the complaints of five foreign investors allegedly adversely affected by Argentina's emergency measures, examined the customary and treaty emergency/necessity defences (*CMS*, *LG&E*, *Enron*, *Sempra*, *Continental*). The five tribunals took divergent interpretations on several issues, including the issue of the necessity test (i.e. the meaning of 'the only way' and 'necessary' in the customary and treaty defences). Once again, the problematic aspect that we wish to emphasize for purposes of the present analysis is not the lack of consistency; rather it is the lack of clear reasons underlying those decisions.

For example, the *CMS* tribunal failed to adequately explain their finding with regard to whether the measures under review were 'the only way' to deal with the economic emergency. The *CMS* tribunal found that only if it could be demonstrated that there were various ways to respond to the financial crisis, the wrongfulness of Argentina's conduct could be precluded. The tribunal acknowledged that the "views of the parties and distinguished economists are wide apart on this matter, ranging from the support of those measures to the discussion of a variety of alternatives, including dollarization of the economy, granting of direct subsidies to the affected population or industries and many others". After having emphasized that it was beyond its task to determine which of these policy alternatives would have been better, the tribunal concluded that "the measures adopted were not the only steps available" (*CMS* v. *Argentina* 2005: paras 323–324).[58] There was no discussion of whether the alternative measures suggested by the parties and their experts (i.e. the claimant and its experts) were indeed technically or politically feasible (letting aside the issue of whether they were more costly or less convenient). On the basis of its conclusion, one has to suppose that the tribunal believed that they were.

The *LG&E* tribunal does not fare much better when it comes to its reasoning underlying the decision that Argentina's emergency measures were indeed the only way to deal with the crisis for purposes of the customary defence of necessity. The tribunal recognized that the Argentine State faced an extremely serious threat to its existence, its political and economic survival, the possibility of maintaining its essential services in operation, and the preservation of its internal peace. In the view of the tribunal, in these circumstances, an economic recovery package was the only means to respond to the crisis (*LG&E* v. *Argentina* 2006: para. 257). The tribunal simply noted:

> Although there may have been a number of ways to draft the economic recovery plan, the evidence before the Tribunal demonstrates that an across-the-board response was necessary, and the tariffs on public utilities had to be addressed.
>
> (*LG&E* v. *Argentina* 2006: para. 257)

Another example of total lack of (or at best inadequate) reasoning may be seen in the decision by the *Enron* tribunal addressing the treaty exception found in Article XI of the US–Argentina BIT. The *Enron* tribunal did not actually interpret the term 'necessary' in Article XI as it simply conflated the treaty defence with the customary plea of necessity.[59] In the words of the *Enron* tribunal: "As the Tribunal has found above that the crisis invoked does not meet the customary law requirements of Article 25 of the Articles on State Responsibility, [. . .] there is no need to undertake a further judicial review under Article XI as this Article does not set out conditions different from customary law in this respect." (*Enron* v. *Argentina* 2007: para. 339). They provided no express reason why Article XI should be conflated into the customary necessity defence, particularly in light of the several different terms employed by the treaty provision compared to the text of Article 25 ILC.

The only explanation offered by the *Enron* tribunal for the 'confluence' appears to be that the Treaty exception does not provide for any of the specific conditions required for purposes of invoking the plea of necessity (*Enron* v. *Argentina* 2007: para. 334).[60] This is again quite unsatisfactory, as it is difficult to understand why a treaty interpreter (the investment tribunal in this case) cannot determine the required conditions for the applicability of the treaty exception from a perfectly legible provision.[61]

The failures in the reasoning of the above-mentioned tribunals in interpreting and applying the customary and treaty emergency defences may be contrasted with the more developed reasoning contained in the subsequent decision by the *Continental* tribunal. Borrowing heavily from the WTO jurisprudence interpreting a similar exception provision in GATT Article XX (for example, "measures necessary to protect public health"), the *Continental* tribunal first set out the 'applicable standard' for the necessity test in Article XI of the US-Argentina BIT (*Continental* v. *Argentina* 2008: para. 192).[62] The tribunal thus adopted a so-called 'reasonable less restrictive means' analysis according to which the adjudicator focuses on (1) whether there is an alternative measure that achieves the same level of benefit as the measure under review, where the alternative measure (2) results in less restrictive effects on foreign investment and (3) is reasonably available to the State in light of its administration and enforcement costs. If the alternative exists than the chosen measure will not be deemed 'necessary' and the host State may not rely on the treaty exception (Kurtz 2008: 51–52).

The *Continental* tribunal examined in details whether the various measures adopted by Argentina to tackle the economic crisis complied with the 'reasonable less restrictive means' test and found that all but one of the measures were indeed necessary.

Obviously, one can disagree with the tribunal's interpretation of the term 'necessary' in Article XI of the BIT and/or with its findings on the 'necessity' of the measures under review. That is not the point here. What we wish to emphasize is that the *Continental* tribunal gave *an* explanation for its legal and factual findings.[63]

Concluding remarks

Arbitration, as a method for the peaceful settlement of (international) disputes (whether between States or among merchants), has a long history dating back to ancient mythology (Born 2009: 8–57). It is without doubt that the users of arbitration today (particularly commercial subjects) value confidentiality as one of the key features of arbitration (Mistelis 2010: 6, 29–31). This is reflected in a general stance taken by the various international arbitration rules favouring confidentiality of arbitration proceedings (including arbitral awards). As international investment agreements are mostly silent on this issue, investment arbitration has initially developed on the basis of a presumption favouring confidentiality. However, as demonstrated above, the great majority of the (known) investment decisions are publicly available and there are a growing number of investment treaties (including the ICSID Convention) adopting a stronger approach with regard to the issue of external transparency of investment arbitration generally and investment awards, specifically.

Greater transparency of investment awards will inevitably lead (and has already led) to a greater scrutiny over the work of the arbitrators going beyond the four corners of the arbitral room. At least to the outsider, the legitimacy of investment arbitral tribunals is not very strong (partly due to the ad hoc nature of investment tribunals as well as the lack of full transparency of the arbitration process). Focusing on investment tribunals' reasoning, the analysis above has tried to identify certain basic failures that investment tribunals should avoid. These failures appear rather uncontroversial and fortunately are not widespread. However, I predict that future scrutiny will focus on the 'appropriateness' of the reasoning employed by investment tribunals in the exercise of their adjudicatory functions, raising (this time quite controversial) questions about the overall fairness of the entire system of international investment law.

Notes

1 Reader in International Economic Law, King's College London, federico.ortino@kcl.ac.uk. I wish to thank Shokouh Abadi for her research assistance.

2 See the Convention on the Settlement of Investment Disputes between States and Nationals of Other States signed in Washington in 1965, known as the 'ICSID Convention' since it established the International Centre for the Settlement of Investment Disputes (ICSID).

3 International Chambers of Commerce.

4 United Nations Commission on International Trade Law, 1976.

5 The London Court of International Arbitration, 1998.

6 The Stockholm Chamber of Commerce, 2010.

7 Rule 48(4), second sentence, read as follows: "The Centre may, however, include in its publications excerpts of the legal rules applied by the Tribunal".

8 Rule 48(4), second sentence, reads today as follows: "The Centre shall, however, promptly include in its publications excerpts of the legal reasoning of the Tribunal."

9 See next section below. Moreover, at times, domestic courts have caused an ICSID award to be made public following enforcement proceedings before such domestic court. (Schreuer 2001: 822).

10 The Tribunal made references to the decisions in *Amco* (1983); *Metalclad* (Award, 2000); *Loewen* (Decision on Jurisdiction, 2001).

11 "Additional copies certified true by the Secretary General shall be made available on request and at any time to the parties, but to no one else."

12 "The documents submitted to the Court, or drawn up by it in the course of its proceedings, are communicated only to the members of the Court and to the Secretariat and to persons authorized by the Chairman to attend Court sessions."

13 Article 1(5) provides for the relevant confidentiality safeguards: "Such authorization shall not be given unless the beneficiary has undertaken to respect the confidential character of the documents made available and to refrain from any publication in their respect without having previously submitted the text for approval to the Secretary General of the Court."

14 Article 20(7) provides as follows: "The Arbitral Tribunal may take measures for protecting trade secrets and confidential information."

15 Such a rule had been considered by the ICC but eventually rejected (Delaney and Magraw in Muchlinski et al. 2008: 739).

16 See http://www.iccwbo.org/court/arbitration/id5327/index.html.

17 However, the Paris Court of Appeal in *Aita* v. *Ojjeh* rejected an application to challenge an award on the basis that the mere application violated the principle of confidentiality.

18 See Preamble UNCITRAL Arbitration Rules. The term "international commercial arbitration" is broadly defined in the UNCITRAL Model Law on International Commercial Arbitration as follows: "The term 'commercial' should be given a wide interpretation so as to cover matters arising from all relationships of a commercial nature, whether contractual or not. Relationships of a commercial nature include, but are not limited to, the following transactions: any trade transaction for the supply or exchange of goods or services; distribution agreement; commercial representation or agency; factoring; leasing; construction of works; consulting; engineering; licensing; investment; financing; banking; insurance; exploitation agreement or concession; joint venture and other forms of industrial or business cooperation; carriage of goods or passengers by air, sea, rail or road." See note 1.

19 See Report of the UN Commission on International Trade Law at its 41st session (New York, June–July 2008), A/63/17, at para. 314.

20 Arbitration Rules of the Arbitration Institute of the Stockholm Chamber of Commerce, adopted by the SCC and in force as of 1 January 2007 (www.sccinstitute.com).

21 "The SCC Institute shall maintain the confidentiality of the arbitration and the award and shall deal with the arbitration in an impartial, practical and expeditious manner."

22 LCIA Arbitration Rules, adopted to take effect from 1 January 1998 (www.lcia.org).

23 Such duty of confidentiality applies also to "all materials in the proceedings created for the purpose of the arbitration and all other documents produced by another party in the proceedings not otherwise in the public domain". Such general duty of confidentiality does not apply when "disclosure may be required of a party by legal duty, to protect or pursue a legal right or to enforce or challenge an award in bona fide legal proceedings before a state court or other judicial authority". See Article 30.1 LCIA Arbitration Rules.

24 The award apparently rendered in December 2007 in *Archer Daniels Midland Company and Tate & Lyle Ingredients Americas, Inc.* v. *United Mexican States*, ICSID Case No. ARB (AF)/04/5, has not yet been made public. See www.naftaclaims.com.

25 Iran–US Claims Tribunal, Rules of Procedure, 3 May 1983. The Registry is responsible for supplying the public on request with copies of awards, decisions, and orders in accordance with the Tribunal's rules, charging a small fee for doing so.

26 See for example recent BITs that are silent with regard to the issue of transparency of arbitral awards (in parenthesis the type(s) of investor–State arbitration chosen by the contracting parties). 2004 Singapore–Jordan BIT (consent to ICSID arbitration); 2003 Japan–Vietnam BIT (consent to ICSID or UNCITRAL arbitration); 2003 Germany–China BIT (consent to ICSID arbitration); 2003 UK–Vanuatu BIT (consent to ICSID, ICC or UNCITRAL arbitration); 2003 Netherlands–Tajikistan BIT (consent to ICSID arbitration); 2004 India–Indonesia BIT (consent to ICSID or UNCITRAL arbitration); 2006 Switzerland–Azerbaijan BIT (consent to ICSID or UNCITRAL arbitration).

27 This obligation extends to (a) the notice of intent; (b) the notice of arbitration; (c) pleadings, memorials, and briefs submitted to the tribunal by a disputing party and any written submissions submitted pursuant to Articles 10.20.2 and 10.20.3 and 10.25; (d) minutes or transcripts of hearings of the tribunal, where available. Article 10.21.1.

28 *RDC* v. *Guatemala* is the first arbitration initiated on the basis of the CAFTA-DR.

29 Article 38.4. Available at http://www.international.gc.ca/trade-agreements-accords-commerciaux/assets/pdfs/2004-FIPA-model-en.pdf.

30 Article 38.4 expressly excludes the application of the provision in Article 38.3, which requires that "All documents submitted to, or issued by, the Tribunal shall be publicly available, *unless the disputing parties otherwise agree*, subject to the deletion of confidential information." [emphasis added]. Article 38.4 reads in full as follows: "*Notwithstanding paragraph 3*, any Tribunal award under this Section shall be publicly available, subject to the deletion of confidential information." [emphasis added]

31 Article 15.5 provides that "Each request for arbitration shall include information sufficient to present clearly the issues in dispute so as to allow the Parties and the public to become acquainted with them. All requests for arbitration shall be made publicly available by the Parties and by ICSID."

32 Article Eleven of the Schedule on investor–State dispute settlement of the 1998 BIT between Mexico and the Netherlands provides expressly for a broad duty of confidentiality. Article Eleven states as follows: "The final award shall only be published if there is an agreement in writing between the disputing parties."

33 However, this may soon change with regard to UNCITRAL rules following the on-going revision work with regard to transparency in investor–State arbitration.

34 Based on the data collected from the website Investment Treaty Arbitration (http://ita.law.uvic.ca/) as of 10 July 2008.

35 A decision is considered publicly available when the decision is available to the public in its entirety.

36 This section is based on the data collected from the website Investment Treaty Arbitration (http://italaw.com/) as of 10 August 2010.

37 Decisions rendered in the following five arbitrations remain not publicly available at the time of writing: *Binder* v. *the Czech Republic* (UNCITRAL), *European Media Ventures SA* v. *the Czech Republic* (UNCITRAL), *Pren Nreka* v. *the Czech Republic* (UNCITRAL), *Invesmart* v. *the Czech Republic* (UNCITRAL), *Georg Nepolsky* v. *the Czech Republic* (UNCITRAL). Decisions rendered in the following six arbitrations are on the contrary publicly available: *CME* v. *the Czech Republic* (UNCITRAL), *Lauder* v. *the Czech Republic* (UNCITRAL), *Nagel* v. *the Czech Republic* (SCC), *Saluka* v. *the Czech Republic* (UNCITRAL), *Phoenix* v. *the Czech Republic* (ICSID), *Eastern Sugar* v. *the Czech Republic* (SCC).

38 It appears that investment decisions are drafted either in English (the great majority), French or Spanish.

39 This may have a certain negative impact on the transparency of the arbitral decision particularly where the decision is a long one (at least in terms of number of pages) involving several factual and legal issues (for an example of a non-transparent decision, see the 2005 decision in *Methanex*).

40 *Compañía de Aguas del Aconquija S.A. and Vivendi Universal* v. *Argentina* (*Vivendi* v. *Argentina*), ICSID Case No. ARB/97/3, Decision on Annulment, 3 July 2002, at para. 64. Cf. *Azurix Corp.* v. *Argentina*, ICSID Case No. ARB/01/12, Decision on Annulment, 1 September 2009, at paras 53–56; *Enron* v. *Argentina*, ICSID Case No. ARB/01/3, Decision on Annulment, 2 August 2010, at para. 76.

41 *Patrick Mitchell* v. *Democratic Republic of Congo*, Decision on Annulment, 1 November 2006, at para. 21. Cf. *MINE* v. *Guinea*, Decision on Annulment, 22 December 1989, at para. 5.09 ("the requirement to state reasons is satisfied as long as the award enables one to follow how the tribunal proceeded from Point A to Point B

and eventually to its conclusion, even if it made an error of fact or of law. This minimum requirement is in particular not satisfied by either contradictory or frivolous reasons").

42 It is interesting how both annulment decisions in *Vivendi* and *Mitchell* refer to the same decisions (for example, *MINE* v. *Guinea*).

43 Article 25(2) of the ICC Rules of Arbitration states that "The Award shall state the reasons upon which it is based." Article 32(3) of the UNCITRAL Arbitration Rules states that "The arbitral tribunal shall state the reasons upon which the award is based, unless the parties have agreed that no reasons are to be given." Article 56 of the Statute of the International Court of Justice states that "The judgment shall state the reasons on which it is based".

44 "I cannot, I hope, be the only person who has sat down to write a judgment, having formed the view that A must win, only to find in the course of composition that there are no sustainable grounds for that conclusion and that on any rational analysis B must succeed."

45 It should also be noted that clearly-reasoned awards will allow host States to better implement changes in their investment treaty policies (and, for example, modify current treaties as well as shape future ones).

46 Article 5 UK Model BIT.

47 Article 5.1 of the France–Argentina BIT provides as follows: "The Contracting Parties shall not adopt, directly or indirectly, measures of expropriation or nationalization or any other equivalent measure having an effect similar to dispossession, except for public purpose and provided that such measures are not discriminatory or contrary to a specific commitment."

48 *Vivendi* v. *Argentina*, para. 7.5.12, quoting the *Tecmed* decision at paragraph 115. "The *Tecmed* tribunal also recognised that, although terms such as "equivalent to expropriation" or "tantamount to expropriation" (so-called indirect or creeping expropriation), do not have a clear or unequivocal definition "it is generally understood that they materialize through actions or conduct, which do not explicitly express the purpose of depriving one of rights or assets, but actually have that effect." *Idem*, at para. 7.5.13. See also *Vivendi*, at para. 7.5.24.

49 "To establish whether the Resolution is a measure equivalent to an expropriation [. . .], it must be *first* determined if the Claimant, due to the Resolution was radically deprived of the economical use and enjoyment of its investments." [Emphasis added] *Tecmed* v. *Mexico*, Award, 28 May 2003, para. 115.

50 See *Tecmed*, ibid, footnote 140 (ECHR, *In the case of Matos e Silva, Lda., and Others* v. *Portugal*, judgment of 16 September 1996).

51 "In the *Metalclad* case the tribunal held that this kind of expropriation relates to incidental interference with the use of property which has 'the effect of depriving the owner, in whole or in significant part, of the use or reasonable-to-be-expected economic benefit of property even if not necessarily to the obvious benefit of the host State.'". *CMS*, at para. 262.

52 "Substantial deprivation was addressed in detail by the tribunal in the *Pope & Talbot* case. The Government of Argentina has convincingly argued that the list of issues to be taken into account for reaching a determination on substantial deprivation, as discussed in that case, is not present in the instant dispute. In fact, the Respondent has explained, the investor is in control of the investment; the Government does not manage the day-to-day operations of the company; and the investor has full ownership and control of the investment."

53 "It was a crucial aspect of the tribunal's finding that Metalclad had relied on the representations of the Mexican federal government of its exclusive authority to issue permits for hazardous waste disposals" (Reinisch in Muchlinski et al. 2008: 448).

54 "The next question is whether the Export Control Regime has caused an expropriation of the Investor's investment, creeping or otherwise. Using the ordinary meaning of

those terms under international law, the answer must be negative. [. . .] The Investor's (and the Investment's) Operations Controller testified at the hearing that the Investor remains in control of the Investment, it directs the day-to-day operations of the Investment, and no officers or employees of the Investment have been detained by virtue of the Regime. Canada [. . .] does not take any other actions ousting the Investor from full ownership and control of the Investment."

55 It should be noted that 'ownership' is the principal element employed to determine whether a property has been *directly* expropriated. Accordingly, it should not play any role in determining whether a host State measure constitutes indirect expropriation.

56 Article 25 of the ILC Articles on State Responsibility is argued to embody the customary defense of 'necessity'. "1. Necessity may not be invoked by a State as a ground for precluding the wrongfulness of an act not in conformity with an international obligation of that State unless the act: (a) Is the only way for the State to safeguard an essential interest against a grave and imminent peril; and (b) Does not seriously impair an essential interest of the State or States towards which the obligation exists, or of the international community as a whole. 2. In any case, necessity may not be invoked by a State as a ground for precluding wrongfulness if: (a) The international obligation in question excludes the possibility of invoking necessity; or (b) The State has contributed to the situation of necessity."

57 Article XI of the BIT between US and Argentina provides: "This Treaty shall not preclude the application by either Party of measures necessary for the maintenance of public order, the fulfillment of its obligations with respect to the maintenance or restoration of international peace or security, or the protection of its own essential security interests."

58 Almost identical legal reasoning can also be found in the *Enron* award, at paras 308–309. Interestingly, this part of the *Enron* decision has subsequently been annulled by an ICSID ad hoc committee. "Further, even if the Tribunal did in fact satisfy itself that the "only way" requirement in Article 25(1)(a) was not met on the evidence before it, it is not apparent from the reasoning in the Award how or why the Tribunal came to that legal conclusion. Even if, contrary to all appearance, the Tribunal did apply the "only way" requirement in Article 25(1)(a), the Committee considers that the Tribunal failed to state reasons for its decision. This constitutes a ground for annulment under Article 52(1)(e) of the ICSID Convention." See *Enron* v. *Argentina*, ICSID Case No. ARB/01/3, Decision on the Application for Annulment of the Argentine Republic, 30 July 2010, at para. 378.

59 For an extensive analysis on this point see J Kurtz, 'Adjudging the Exceptional at International Law: Security, Public Order and Financial Crisis', *Jean Monnet Working Paper* (06, 2008).

60 "The expert opinion of Dean Slaughter and Professor Burke-White expresses the view that the treaty regime is different and separate from customary law as it is *lex specialis*. This is no doubt correct in terms that a treaty regime specifically dealing with a given matter will prevail over more general rules of customary law. Had this been the case here the Tribunal would have started out its considerations on the basis of the Treaty provision and would have resorted to the Articles on State Responsibility only as a supplementary means. But the problem is that the Treaty itself did not deal with these elements. The Treaty thus becomes inseparable from the customary law standard insofar as the conditions for the operation of state of necessity are concerned." *Enron*, at para. 334.

61 The *CMS* tribunal had taken an almost identical approach conflating the customary defence with the treaty defence. Interestingly, a subsequent ICSID ad hoc committee, while emphasizing the different nature and context of the two defences, did not annul the *CMS* award in part because both disputing parties (CMS and Argentina) had argued in their pleadings for such confluence. See *CMS* v. *Argentina*, Decision of the Ad Hoc

Committee on the Application for Annulment of the Argentina Republic, 25 September 2007, at paras 123–127.

62 The tribunal also rejected expressly the confluence approach adopted by the *Enron* tribunal whereby the tribunal looked at the customary concept of necessity for purposes of interpreting the treaty emergency provision. *Continental*, at para. 192.

63 Just the section on the 'necessity test' in Article XI of the Treaty comprised of 42 paragraphs (see 189–230). With regard to the pesification of the US dollar-denominated contracts and deposits, for example, the *Continental* tribunal noted inter alia as follows: "According to one of the most specific economic studies devoted to the issue, and discussed by the Parties at the hearing, '[re]denomination of dollar debts implied a substantial reduction of the real debt service burdens of dollar-denominated debtors. It was inspired by the realization that without redenomination Argentina would have to find a way to address massive economy-wide insolvency of dollar-denominated debtors, as well as huge relative price increases for energy and transport costs that were fixed by concession contracts in dollar terms.' Furthermore 'Argentina was in an unusually vulnerable macro-economic position as the result of the large fraction of domestic debts and transportation and utility concession contracts that were denominated in or indexed to the dollar, and the small fraction of its economy devoted to exports.' Thus de-dollarization seems to have represented, according to qualified observers, as almost a 'must' for Argentina, in order to devaluate effectively, avoid unbearable asymmetries in the allocation of the burden that devaluation entails and to stimulate the recovery. Finally, contrary to the Claimant's allegations, the de-dollarization of 2002 by Argentina was not without precedents in recent financial crises." *Continental*, at para. 213.

Bibliography

Bingham, T. (1988), "Reasons and Reasons for Reasons: Differences between a Court Judgement and an Arbitration Award", 4(2) *Arbitration International* 141.

Blackaby, N. (2002), "Public Interest and Investment Treaty Arbitration", in Kaufmann-Kohler, G. and Stucki, B. (eds), *Investment Treaties and Arbitration*, Zürich: Association Swiss de l'Arbitrage, Special Series No. 19.

Born, G. (2009), *International Commercial Arbitration*, Alphen aan den Lijn: Wolters Kluwer.

Buys, C. (2003), "The Tensions between Confidentiality and Transparency in International Arbitration", 14 *American Review of International Arbitration* 121.

Carbonneau, T. (1984–85), "Rendering Arbitral Awards with Reasons: The Elaboration of a Common Law of International Transactions", 23 *Columbia Journal of Transnational Law* 579.

Commission, J. (2007), "Precedent in Investment Treaty Arbitration: A Citation Analysis of a Developing Jurisprudence", 24(2) *Journal of International Arbitration* 129.

Delaney, J.F. and Magraw, D. (2008), "Transparency and Public Interest", in Muchlinski, P. et al. (eds), *The Oxford Handbook of International Investment Law*, New York: Oxford University Press.

Douglas, Z. (2006), "Nothing if not Critical for Investment Treaty Arbitration", 22(1) *Arbitration International* 27.

Egonu, M. (2007), "Investor–State Arbitration under ICSID: A Case for Presumption Against Confidentiality?", 24(5) *Journal of International Arbitration* 479.

Gaillard, E. and Banifatemi, Y. (eds) (2004), *Annulment of ICSID Awards*, New York: Juris Publishing.

IISD (2007), "Revising the UNCITRAL Arbitration Rules to Address State Arbitrations" (www.iisd.org).

Kingsbury, B. and Schill, S. (2009), "Investor–State Arbitration as Governance: Fair and Equitable Treatment, Proportionality and the Emerging Global Administrative Law", *Institute for International Law and Justice Working Paper* (Global Administrative Law Series).

Kurtz, J. (2008), "Adjudging the Exceptional at International Law: Security, Public Order and Financial Crisis", *Jean Monnet Working Paper*.

Landau, T. (2009), "Reasons for Reasons: The Tribunal's Duty in Investor–State Arbitration", in *ICCA Congress Series No.14*, Dublin Conference. Alphen aan den Rijn: Wolters Kluwer, pp. 187–205.

Mistelis, L. (ed.) (2010), *International Arbitration Survey: Choices in International Arbitration*, available at http://www.arbitrationonline.org/research/2010/index.html.

Muchlinski, P., Ortino, F. and Schreuer, C. (eds) (2008), *The Oxford Handbook of International Investment Law*, New York: Oxford University Press.

Newcombe, A. and Paradell, L. (2009), *Law and Practice of Investment Treaties: Standards of Treatment*, Alphen aan den Rijn: Kluwer Law International.

OECD (2005), *International Investment Law: A Changing Landscape*. Paris: OECD.

Reinisch, A. (2008), "Expropriation", in Muchlinski et al. (eds), *Oxford Handbook of International Investment Law*, New York: Oxford University Press.

Schreuer, C.H. (2001), *The ICSID Convention: A Commentary*, New York: Cambridge University Press.

Schreuer, C.H. (2004), "Three Generations of ICSID Annulment Proceedings", in Gaillard, E. and Banifatemi, Y. (eds), *Annulment of ICSID Awards*, New York: Juris Publishing.

Schreuer, C.H. and Weiniger, M. (2008), "A Doctrine of Precedent?", in Muchlinski, P. et al. (eds), *Oxford Handbook of International Investment Law*, New York: Oxford University Press.

Van Harten, G. (2007), "The Public-Private Distinction in the International Arbitration of Individual Claims Against the State", 56 *International and Comparative Law Quarterly* 371.

Rules and Conventions

Arbitration Rules of the Arbitration Institute of the Stockholm Chamber of Commerce, adopted by the SCC and in force as of 1 January 2007.

Iran–US Claims Tribunal, Rules of Procedure, 3 May 1983.

LCIA Arbitration Rules, adopted to take effect from 1 January 1998 (www.lcia.org).

Report of the UN Commission on International Trade Law at its 41st session (New York, June–July 2008), A/63/17.

The Convention on the Settlement of Investment Disputes between States and Nationals of Other States 1965 (ICSID).

UNCITRAL Arbitration Rules.

UNCITRAL Model Law on International Commercial Arbitration.

Cases

Archer Daniels Midland Company and Tate & Lyle Ingredients Americas, Inc. v. *United Mexican States*, (2007) ICSID Case No. ARB (AF)/04/5.

Azurix Corp. v. *Argentina*, ICSID Case No. ARB/01/12, Decision on Annulment, 1 September 2009.

Biwater Gauff v. *Tanzania*, ICSID Case No. ARB/05/22, Procedural Order No. 3, 29 September 2006.

CME v. *the Czech Republic* (UNCITRAL).

CMS v. *Argentina*, Award, 12 May 2005.

Compañia de Aguas del Aconquija S.A. and Vivendi Universal v. *Argentina* (*Vivendi* v. *Argentina*), ICSID Case No. ARB/97/3, Decision on Annulment, 3 July 2002.

Compañia de Aguas del Aconquija S.A. and Vivendi Universal S.A. v. *Argentina* (*Vivendi* v. *Argentina*), ICSID Case No. ARB/97/3, Award, 20 August 2007.

Continental v. *Argentina*, Award, 5 September 2008.

Eastern Sugar v. *the Czech Republic* (SCC).

Enron Corporation Ponderosa Assets L.P v. *Argentina*, ICSID Case No. ARB/01/3, Award, 22 May 2007.

Enron v. *Argentina*, ICSID Case No. ARB/01/3, Decision on Annulment, 2 August 2010.

Lauder v. *the Czech Republic* (UNCITRAL).

LG&E v. *Argentina*, Decision on Liability, 3 October 2006.

Metalclad v. *Mexico*, Award 30 August 2000.

Methanex v. *United States*, Final Award, 3 August 2005.

MINE v. *Guinea*, Decision on Annulment, 22 December 1989.

Nagel v. *the Czech Republic* (SCC).

Patrick Mitchell v. *Democratic Republic of Congo*, Decision on Annulment, 1 November 2006.

Phoenix v. *the Czech Republic* (ICSID).

Pope & Talbot, Interim Award, 26 June 2000.

RDC v. *Guatemala* (ICSID Case No. ARB/07/23).

Saluka v. *the Czech Republic* (UNCITRAL).

Sempra v. *Argentina*, Award, 28 September 2007.

Tecmed v. *Mexico*, Award, 28 May 2003.

Websites

http://www.iareporter.com/.

http://www.iccwbo.org/court/arbitration/id5327/index.html.

http://icsid.worldbank.org/ICSID/Index.jsp.

http://www.iisd.org/.

http://www.international.gc.ca/trade-agreements-accords-commerciaux/assets/pdfs/2004-FIPA-model-en.pdf.

http://ita.law.uvic.ca/.

http://www.lcia.org/.

http://www.naftaclaims.com.

http://www.sccinstitute.com.

http://www.transnational-dispute-management.com/OECD.

Treaties

1998 BIT between Mexico and the Netherlands.

2003 Germany–China BIT (consent to ICSID arbitration).

2003 Japan–Vietnam BIT (consent to ICSID or UNCITRAL arbitration).
2003 Netherlands–Tajikistan BIT (consent to ICSID arbitration).
2003 UK–Vanuatu BIT (consent to ICSID, ICC or UNCITRAL arbitration).
2004 India–Indonesia BIT (consent to ICSID or UNCITRAL arbitration).
2004 Singapore–Jordan BIT (consent to ICSID arbitration).
2006 Switzerland–Azerbaijan BIT (consent to ICSID or UNCITRAL arbitration).
France–Argentina BIT.
UK Model BIT.

7 International investment activities

Giving affected people greater voice and rights of recourse

Peter L. Lallas[1]

Introduction

While there are signs all around that we live in a "globalizing" age, there is also a long history of economic inter-connection among people which needs remembering. The pursuit of resources and opportunity in distant lands is woven deeply into our collective pasts – for better and for worse. Today, "international investment activity"[2] can foster not only much-desired improvements in economic well-being and development but, depending on how conducted, significant social and environmental harm. Mark Twain reportedly once said that history doesn't repeat itself, but it rhymes. As in the past, the effects of today's international investment activities may be borne most directly by local communities with little say over their design, arrival and operation.

International law plays an important role in this narrative, and in fostering cross-border economic activities. In the aftermath of World War II, a set of institutions and norms were developed to support a "liberal" international economic order, with a principal purpose to support and allow an expansion of international trade and investment activities among countries in line with certain core principles (e.g. non-discrimination).[3] Beginning in those years, many countries entered into bilateral and regional treaties and agreements to promote the establishment and protect various "rights" of international investors,[4] and the World Bank was established to finance and support post-War reconstruction and development activities. Through a legal lens, this overall (and very large) field has been called, conventionally, the "*law of international economic relations*."[5]

In recent decades, there have been significant efforts to expand the core purposes of this field of law to better integrate social, economic and environmental policy considerations in support of equitable and sustainable development. The World Bank, for example, has established an important set of operational policies and procedures, including social and envoirnmental safeguards, designed to promote better development results and prevent and mitigate undue harm to people and the envoirnment resulting from Bank-financed projects. Of particular relevance to the present article, it also has established corresponding mechanisms, including an "Inspection Panel", to empower project-affected people and communities to have greater voice and help hold the Bank accountable to these commitments. While significant challenges remain in this work, these are major developments.

A parallel effort to integrate environmental and social safeguards into normative structures governing international trade and (private) investment has been a difficult one. These efforts are based on a substantial, if often contested, body of analysis on the potential positive and negative impacts of international trade and investment agreements, and of the underlying activities they foster or promote.[6] They have also been driven by concerns that the expanding ability of private capital and investment to move across the globe has posed difficult challenges for the regulatory capacity of many countries, and that transnational private companies may operate beyond the easy reach of any single national legal system.[7]

The importance of this topic has, if anything, grown considerably in recent years. First, as both a cause and consequence of globalization, there has been a continuous expansion in international investment activity in the past two decades. By 2008, even in recessionary times, global foreign direct investment (FDI) inflows valued nearly 1.7 trillion dollars, nearly half of which (43 percent) went into developing countries and economies in transition. In parallel, there has been a striking change in the geography and directions of FDI, topped by increasing outflows from countries in Asia and other emerging economies and a marked rise in "South-South" FDI. Today it is estimated that there are "some 82,000 TNCs (transnational corporations), with 810,000 foreign affiliates . . . [which] play a major and growing role in the world economy."[8]

Second, there has been a veritable explosion in the number of bilateral and regional international investment agreements ("IIAs") around the world, which provide a number of legal protections for foreign investors and their investments. Recent United Nations Conference on Trade and Development (UNCTAD) data list a total of nearly 3000 such agreements (2676 of these are bilateral investment agreements, or "BITs"), a great majority of which have been developed within the past 20 years, spanning all regions of the world.[9] Of equal interest, the number of claims brought by private investors against party-Governments to such agreements, under the so-called investor–State dispute mechanisms of these agreements, rose to a total of 317 by the end of 2008.[10] In short, international investors have acquired, and are using, new legal rights under a growing number of IIAs to challenge government action, including regulatory measures, which may constrain or affect their international investments. There is a significant concern that this potential "de-regulatory" impact of IIAs is restricting the ability and space of governments to apply legitimate measures to protect against social and environmental harms from FDI.

Third, in the midst of all these negotiations and new legal instruments, some old realities persist. New IIAs provide expanding protections for international investors engaged in cross-border investment activities, which (developmentally) may bring new jobs or other benefits within the host countries. At the same time, these activities also continue too often to be associated with negative social, environmental and, ultimately, developmental outcomes for locally-affected people. These impacts take many forms, including economic, social and environmental loss resulting from large-scale logging and forest conversion, energy, mining and infrastructure projects, industrial-scale fishing, and other types of cross-border resource extraction and investment.[11] One recent illustration is so-called farmland acquisition or "farmland grabbing", a trend where foreign governments and investors are acquiring vast tracts of land, particularly in Africa, to boost their own food security, with potentially significant long-term implications for local populations.[12] Recent confrontations between indigenous peoples and governments in some countries, linked to laws and practices opening up their lands to outside investment, is another.[13] Often, the affected people are poor and vulnerable, with little voice or influence in major investment decisions that affect them.

The present chapter reviews the emerging international normative framework relevant to international investment activities, and its role in fostering and promoting these activities. It then considers the extent to which this framework also contains norms and provides a basis to identify and address the potential adverse social and environmental impacts that continue to be associated with such activities. The analysis shows that notwithstanding some attempts to the contrary in negotiations, IIAs themselves generally do not contain provisions designed to guard against such impacts; rather, these negative "side-effects" are addressed (where at all) through other instruments and initiatives.[14] This leads to a central issue: whether the normative framework relevant to FDI is fostering sustainable FDI, with transparency and accountability for locally affected people, or just FDI.

The final part of the discussion will focus, more specifically, on whether normative systems that do exist provide affected people with rights to seek recourse for harm that might arise from international investment activities. In particular, the question is not whether international investment activities can lead to adverse social and environmental impacts (they can), and not even whether there are norms somewhere in the system designed to address these impacts (there are, though their nature and scope matters, and varies). Rather, the focus here is on whether local people and communities affected by these actions have effective avenues to make their voices heard, seek recourse for harm, and hold those responsible accountable for their actions.

This question is posed in the light of an important development in some fields of international law in the past 30 years: the creation of new avenues of recourse and accountability to give non-State actors a greater role in asserting their rights set forth in relevant norms, and thus in having a stronger voice in decisions that affect them. As reflected by the practice of the World Bank Inspection Panel, for example, this can be referred to as "community-led accountability", or "bottom-up accountability", in which affected people and civil society are empowered to make international institutions and other actors answerable for meeting relevant norms to avoid social and environmental harm. One of its core strengths, in addition to giving voice to affected people, is that it engages the knowledge and expertise of local communities on matters that affect them. A second key principle is "recourse", i.e., that affected people have rights to bring claims to seek responsive action and remedies for harms they experience.

The analysis notes some leading examples of this emerging trend of relevance to international investment activities, including: the recourse and accountability mechanisms at international financial institutions (such as the Inspection Panel);

the public submission process of the North American Agreement on Environmental Cooperation; and the complaint process available to non-governmental organizations (NGOs), workers and others of the Organisation for Economic Co-operation and Development (OECD) Guidelines for Multinational Enterprises. The analysis also compares these mechanisms (available to affected people and civil society) with investor–State mechanisms under IIAs (available to foreign investors).

The working hypothesis of this chapter is that giving affected people an avenue for recourse and accountability under international law can provide an important means to identify and resolve adverse social and environmental impacts associated with international investment activities, in support of transparency and sustainability, and that important lessons may be gained through a review of mechanisms across different fields of international law. The discussion notes some of the achievements in this ongoing work, as well as challenges and opportunities.

The analysis also indicates that the nature and scope of existing mechanisms varies significantly. For example, there is a notable difference in terms of their legal "strength", with the investor–State mechanisms of IIAs at the top of that food chain. In addition, some normative systems applicable to FDI lack measures for bottom-up accountability and recourse entirely, and important opportunities may be available to extend the principles and lessons from this work. Seeking to do so, however, would raise several questions, including what might be an appropriate forum to receive grievances and complaints.

On this basis, the chapter poses a few open questions on actions that might be taken to better address potentially adverse social and environmental implications associated with private international investment activities, and give people a greater capacity to assert and protect their rights in relation to actions that affect them. High among these is the following: given that there are nearly 3000 IIAs with strong legal norms and rights of recourse to protect the interests of international investors, why do such agreements not contain similarly strong norms and rights of recourse to protect the interests of communities and the environment which may be affected by such investment activities? In the light of past experience in seeking reform in these areas, the paper also offers a cautionary note on the frustrations, and even dangers, of waking (or harassing) a sleeping giant.

Patterns of history and trends today: international "investment"

The flow of capital and investment across lands and borders may be on the rise in the modern, globalizing age, but it is a long pattern of history. For centuries, countries and peoples have taken extraordinary steps to expand, protect and support their economic interests on foreign soil, and to seek gains from the resources of foreign lands, indicating a kind of cyclical imperative of history that, as discussed below, is still with us today.

The benefits and the consequences for the affected populations and natural wealth of countries are complex and often high. Trade and economic exchange, like the movement and migration of peoples, are fundamental to the development and flowering of human civilizations, but there are also sadly countless abusive scenarios involving outside intervention leading to human rights abuses, exploitation and stripping of wealth. The late nineteenth and early twentieth century witnessed these same, age-old patterns; impulses of empire, colonization, exercises of political and economic hegemony for (among other reasons) economic and material gain.[15] In these cases, by their nature, affected local communities bore the impacts and had little means of recourse to defend their rights.[16]

In more recent decades, as the world has become more inter-connected with advances in technology, transportation, and communication, cross-border investments have continued and accelerated. Today, the age of globalization is characterized by, among other things, a large number of multinational enterprises from many countries with an expanded ability to move capital across borders and link in to multiple entry points for international trade in the goods and services which they produce or provide.

More particularly, global FDI has been growing strongly in recent years, reaching a value of $1.7 trillion in 2008, and there are many tens of thousands of transnational corporations carrying out operations in today's globalizing world.[17] In addition, the sources and directions of FDI flow have been expanding significantly, a reflection of emerging trends in the world all around us in terms of, among other things, sources and types of economic growth and activity. Data indicates that "developing countries are increasingly becoming a source of FDI flows", some 70 percent of which originates in so-called BRIC countries (Brazil, Russia, India and China).[18] There are particularly high levels of FDI within East and South-East Asia, significant rises in FDI to low-income African countries, including in infrastructure projects,[19] and significant increases into and out of Latin America and the Caribbean (with sub-regional variations).

Within these expanding levels of FDI, the natural resource "sector" is a significant area. The UNCTAD 2009 World Investment Report notes, for example, that "[n]atural resources and related activities continued to be the main attraction for FDI in South America," with particularly significant investment in sectors such as mining, oil and gas, and crops for bio-fuels.[20] Transnational corporations also are active in many other types of major investment operations in countries around the world, including in forests and logging, energy, agriculture, fisheries and so on.

In parallel to FDI, and sometimes in combination with it, international and national development organizations, such as the World Bank, also are major contributors to international investment activities, in support of broader developmental goals. In its fiscal year 2010, the World Bank reports lending and commitments in the form of grants, loans and investments of some $58.7 billion from the International Bank for Reconstruction and Development (IBRD) and the International Development Association (IDA) for 354 new operations in over 100 low and middle income countries.[21] Its private sector arm, the International Finance Corporation (IFC), committed over $18 billion in 2010, of which $12.7 was from its own account, investing in 528 projects.[22] According to recent figures, estimates and projections of the OECD, net official development assistance (ODA) from developed country donors in 2008 (for a wide range of purposes and uses) amounted to over $121 billion.[23]

While international and bilateral development aid flows remain at significant levels, the data indicate that private FDI flows over time are growing in relative value. This trend underlines the importance of assessing the needs and opportunities to address the social, economic and environmental impacts that these activities generate, and the extent to which affected communities have a voice and rights of recourse for harms that might result. The data further reflect an important shift in both the sources and directions of such investments, marked particularly by a rise in investment activities on the part of enterprises and financial institutions originating in countries of Asia and by a significant rise in so-called "South-South" investment (and trade) activity.[24]

Benefits

Many studies identify broad economic and other gains from expanded international trade and investment activities over the past 50 years. Developed and developing countries have, as a high priority, taken many steps[25] to attract international investment and capital as a means of creating economic growth, generating employment opportunities, providing needed goods and services (e.g. electricity, roads and transport infrastructure), diffusing technology and best practices, generating revenue for governments (e.g. through an increased tax base, royalty fees from licensed "concessions"), and products for export.[26]

These benefits of FDI, however, do not necessarily arise automatically. A recent review of a new detailed study on this subject[27] observes that the "academic debate on the investment-development nexus is longstanding and unresolved" and, when the discussion incorporates social and environmental concerns, "it is unsurprising that an academic consensus on the costs and benefits of FDI has failed to emerge."[28]

United Nations Secretary-General Ban-Ki Moon addresses this point in his introduction to the UNCTAD World Investment Report 2009, looking particularly at its analysis of TNCs and agriculture. The Secretary General comments on the importance of good policies and concerted efforts by all partners to help ensure that TNC activity generates benefits for local people and rural development:

> Greater involvement by TNCs will not automatically lead to greater productivity in agriculture, rural development or the alleviation of poverty and hunger. However, with the right policies in place, it can be used to bring about such gains, in particular by strengthening the capacities of local farmers. A concerted effort is required by all development partners to support and equip host-country governments, farmers, cooperatives and others to maximize the development benefits of TNC involvement.[29]

In addition to FDI, bilateral aid bureaus and international financial institutions (IFIs), like the World Bank, have made available significant financial and technical resources to support a range of investment and other operations in countries around the world. In keeping with the "public" nature of these institutions, these interventions have the stated purpose to reflect and support development priorities within borrowing countries, and help in the fight against poverty.[30] The World Bank and other international financial institutions (IFIs), for example, support investments in a wide range of areas, including (among others) health and nutrition programs, support for education, infrastructure development, social protection and labor, promotion of gender equality, and institutional reform and capacity building to help countries achieve improved governance, resource management, conservation, and social and economic development.[31]

It is also worth noting that in practice these two worlds, private and publicly-supported international investment, are coming into increasingly close contact. Many important cross-border investment activities are supported by multiple funding sources, and involve "partnerships" between public authorities and large corporations. In some cases, an IFI may provide guarantees against political or other risks to support and encourage engagement by private sector entities. In addition, public institutions like the World Bank Group provide financial and technical assistance both to governments (borrowers) and to the private sector in developing countries.[32]

Adverse impacts

As noted above, there are also other sides to these balance sheets. A range of studies and reports note the tensions and conflicts that sometimes surround international investment activities, and document instances where transnational investment activities have unfortunately contributed to a range of adverse social, environmental and economic impacts for local people and communities.

These impacts may include, among others: displacement of people resulting from major infrastructure operations, including dams, pipelines, and transport projects, sometimes without full and adequate measures to redress the resulting harms;[33] negative impacts on local peoples, the environment and livelihoods that may result from investments affecting natural resources, such as large-scale logging and conversion of forest-land to agriculture, spills and pollution resulting from on-shore and off-shore oil and gas drilling, and other activities;[34] social, cultural and environmental impacts arising from investments (e.g. mining, dams, plantations, tourism development) in the lands of indigenous peoples, or of other peoples living traditional lifestyles, and related harms to cultural properties and sacred sites;[35] and instances of human rights abuse.[36]

The costs of global environmental damage and depletion can also be reflected in broader economic terms. The Brundtland Report provided an early call to action on the two-way, downward spiral linkage between environmental destruction and poverty.[37] More recently, a study of the United Nations Environment Program (UNEP) finds that these types of impacts reached some US$6.6 trillion in the past year, or 11 percent of global GDP.[38] A recent news article on this Study highlights that this cost "amounts to 20 percent more than the $US5.4 trillion decline of pension funds in developed countries caused by the global financial crisis in 2007/2008." The Study is not limited to FDI, but does record that "the world's top 3,000 public companies were responsible for one-third of the damage, or US$2.15 trillion", nearly half of which is linked to utilities, oil and gas producers, industrial metals and mining.[39]

It should be highlighted that the "international" character of investment activities goes beyond the fact that they may be carried out by "foreign" companies (TNCs) or entities. Many investments are linked to and supported by consumption and demand in other countries: in other words, to the globalized economy. For example, a forest logging concession owned or operated by a TNC may be part of a larger economic "life-cycle" where trees are logged in the forests of one country, processed or manufactured into something else in another, and then sold on international markets to others.[40]

Similar global supply-and-demand chains exist in respect to other types of FDI, with potentially adverse local and sometimes global social and environmental impacts. These range from investments in hydro-electric plants (exporting the electricity) to oil palm and other cash crops (involving a wide range of commodity exports) to mining and energy investments (e.g. iron ore, gold and silver, oil and gas, etc.).[41] A recent Special Report on Forests in *The Economist* magazine notes that the "current onslaught" of forest loss is "mainly in the tropics", and writes that:

> Most tropical deforestation is the result of expanding commercial ranching and agriculture, driven by rocketing domestic and global demand for food, fibre and biofuel.[42]

These activities illustrate, among other things, the close relationship between many types of international investment activity and the assumptions and norms underlying an open international trading system. They also underline the complexity of these international economic systems, and the reality that they are driven by forces (market and otherwise) often well beyond the scope, control or knowledge of locally-affected people.

The phenomenon of farmland acquisition, or "farmland grabbing", provides a current and vivid illustration. In response partly to concerns over food security and rising food prices, there is evidence of a "growing trend for large scale investment in farmland across the developing world".[43] These investments have been originating in countries that are not self-sufficient in food production, as a means to ensure and expand the home-country access to agricultural lands and food security. Recent reports indicate that investors have been acquiring large tracts of land, particularly in Africa. As stated in an FAO Report from June 2010:

> The last three years have seen a surge of interest in international investment in developing country agriculture. Acquisitions of agricultural land in Africa have attracted most attention . . . The underlying driver for the recent spate of interest in international investment in food production appears to be food

> security and a fear arising from the recent high food prices and policy-induced supply shocks that dependence on world markets for food supplies or agricultural raw materials has become more risky . . . Current investments differ from the previous pattern of foreign direct investment in several respects: they are resource-seeking (land and water) rather than market seeking; they emphasize production of basic foods . . . for export back to the investing country.[44]

Some studies note potential development benefits in such transactions,[45] but there is also significant concern over the scale of these acquisitions and their potential impacts on local people and communities, including loss of arable land, who may have had little say in this rising phenomenon. The recent FAO report notes that the much publicized "land grab" is a form of investment which could be "least likely to deliver significant developmental benefits to the host country and . . . can provoke social, political and economic conflict." The Special Report on Forests of *The Economist* writes that:

> Foreign governments and investors are increasingly on the lookout to buy cheap, well-watered tropical land [citing examples]. And wherever there is such demand for tropical agribusiness, forests are being razed to meet it.[46]

This relatively new form of international investment activity is now the subject of high-level attention in a variety of international fora.[47]

The potential impacts of FDI in agriculture more generally are considered in the UNCTAD World Investment Report of 2009. Following a description of the potential benefits, the Report notes concerns about potential environmental, social and political repercussions. According to the Report, such investment can displace small farmers, lead to unfair distributions of economic benefits and, thus be at odds with host-country development objectives, concerns that are particularly high when TNCs own or control large areas of land.[48]

The types of impacts described above may arise in the context of public, as well as privately-financed, investment operations. The reports and findings of the World Bank Inspection Panel over the years are illustrative. The Panel has, on many occasions, found the Bank to be in compliance with its operational policies and procedures designed to safeguard people and the environment, and noted the importance and positive development benefits of Bank-financed projects. It has also, however, found many situations of non-compliance.[49]

In some instances, for example, the Panel found that some projects put a strong and steady focus on intended beneficiaries, but that other negatively affected communities were not "on the radar screen" and faced significant potential harms.[50] In others, the Panel found that projects affecting land use and natural resources failed to consider adequately the land tenure and livelihood rights and interests of local and indigenous communities in those lands, and failed recognize the full value (to local people) of such resources.[51] In still other investigations, the Panel made findings that affected people were not adequately consulted or engaged in project design or implementation, even though they faced direct and in some cases severe consequences (including displacement) as a result of the project operation.[52]

The expanded presence of outside investment in communities around the world, and the dependence these communities develop on these and other outside forces over which they have little or no control, can lead to another kind of consequence, more intangible but also perhaps more pervasive: a gradual loss of traditional practices and means for self-autonomy among communities, even a loss of culture. Before becoming President of the United States, Barack Obama, reflected on these themes in his book *Dreams from My Father*, recalling some of the traditional markets he knew as a child in Indonesia:

> I saw those Djakarta markets for what they were: fragile, precious things. The people who sold their goods there might have been poor, poorer even than folks out in Altgeld [the area in Southside Chicago where he had worked as a community organizer, which had been dramatically affected by loss of jobs due to the closing of a large steel plant]. They hauled fifty pounds of firewood on their backs every day, they ate little, they died young. And yet for all that poverty, there remained in their lives a discernible order, a tapestry of trading routes and middlemen, bribes to pay and customs to observe, the habits of a generation played out every day beneath the bargaining and the noise and the swirling dust.

He observes that the "absence of such coherence" is what "made a place like Altgeld so desperate", and makes the following reflection about the potential for loss of order, loss of culture in the two societies:

> I tried to imagine the Indonesian workers who were now making their way to the sorts of factories that once sat along the banks of the Calumet River [in Altgeld], joining the ranks of wage labor to assemble the radios and sneakers that sold on Michigan Avenue. I imagined those same Indonesian workers ten, twenty years from now, when their factories would have closed down, a consequence of new technology or lower wages in some other part of the globe. And then the bitter discovery that their markets have vanished; that they no longer remember how to weave their own baskets or carve their own furniture or grow their own food; that even if they remember such craft, the forests that gave them wood are now owned by timber interests, the baskets they once wove have been replaced by durable plastics. The very existence of the factories, the timber interests, the plastics manufacturer, will have rendered their culture obsolete; the values of hard work and individual initiative turn out to have depended on a system of belief that's been scrambled by migration and urbanization and imported TV reruns. Some of them would prosper in this new order. Some would move to America. And the others, the millions left behind in Djarkata, or Lagos, or the West Bank, they would settle into their own Altgeld Gardens, into a deeper despair.[53]

Issues of how benefits are distributed

There are also significant questions as to how the benefits of international investment activities are shared, including with respect to local communities and the host-country nation as a whole vis-à-vis foreign investors.

Beginning in the 1960s, for example, many developing countries initiated significant efforts to modify traditional "concession-based" contractual relationships between themselves, as host governments, and foreign investors in the natural resource extraction sector. A central purpose was to re-align the distribution of benefits of these investment activities, so that the host government and local communities would obtain a greater and more "equitable" share of these benefits, in exchange for making access to natural resources available. In the case of mining and mineral investments, for example, new types of concession agreements were negotiated which went beyond the royalty payments of traditional concessions and included provisions for equity sharing, management control, employment and training of nationals, and requirements on international investors to provide infrastructure and community services.[54]

A different illustration of this issue involves efforts in the past 20 years to ensure an equitable sharing of benefits in cases where international entities and investors seek to gain access to, and utilize, the expertise, knowledge and innovations of traditional and indigenous communities as a basis to develop medicines and treatments for illness on a commercial scale. The 1992 Convention on Biological Diversity addressed this issue directly in, inter alia, Article 8(j) which provides that Parties, as far as possible and appropriate, and subject to national legislation, shall:

> respect, preserve and maintain knowledge, innovations and practices of indigenous and local communities embodying traditional lifestyles relevant for the conservation and sustainable use of biological diversity and promote their wider application with the approval and involvement of the holders of such knowledge, innovations and practices and encourage the equitable sharing of the benefits arising from the utilization of such knowledge, innovations and practices.

The Parties to the Convention have issued a number of "decisions" relevant to the implementation of these provisions, and established a working group process to further advance both debate and implementation.[55]

More generally, the question of who benefits from internationally-based investment activities (e.g. the international investor, the central government, local communities) has been a major topic of discussion in international circles for many years. As noted above, serious tension and sometimes violent conflict has arisen where local communities believe that they have been marginalized and left outside of revenues generated by investment activities in their communities.[56]

In this larger context, and over the years, some operational policies and procedures of the World Bank, for example, contain certain provisions to ensure not only that projects avoid social and environmental harm, but that actions are taken to provide benefits to affected people and communities.[57] There is, in fact, an important debate now taking place regarding whether these types of provisions should be expanded.[58] The United Nations Conference on Trade and Development (UNCTAD) also has developed and sponsored extensive work on this topic since its creation, and on the impacts of international investment activities on development needs and rights of developing countries.[59] Some of its proposals and initiatives are noted later.

Factors relevant to the sustainability of international investment

In short, as described above, international investment activities can bring both benefits and harms to locally affected populations. Set forth below are a few observations on factors that might be relevant in shaping outcomes in particular circumstances, as a basis for the discussion of the relevant normative framework which follows.

One major concern is that some host countries may lack adequate capacity and resources to regulate against potentially adverse social and environmental impacts of international investment activities, particularly those that operate at a large scale and may shift operations from one place to another. Host countries may find it equally difficult to promote means to ensure that locally affected people "fairly share" in the benefits of such activities. Lack of capacity and resources has been a core concern of international discussions for many years on how to promote more equitable and sustainable patterns of development, and to ensure that economic, social and environmental policies are mutually-reinforcing in support of this objective.[60] The arrival of large-scale investment operations into a country lacking capacity and resources to regulate and guard against its potential social and environmental risks is a matter of high, ongoing importance.[61]

A second concern is that countries may feel the need to compete against each other in order to attract needed international investment, and thus feel an incentive either to relax the level of stringency of their own environmental and other laws and regulations ("downward harmonization", also referred to as the "pollution haven" issue) or fail to effectively enforce these laws and regulations.[62] Similarly, there may also be "competition" between providers of public and private capital, in which at least some host-countries might look more favorably to sources of funding that come without corresponding social and environmental safeguard requirements.[63]

This last point is a topic of much discussion in international development circles, where there is both systematic study[64] and considerable "corridor talk" on the question of whether "high" social and environmental safeguards applied to project operations create what some refer to as a kind of "transaction cost" that can delay project activities and/or increase their cost, particularly vis-à-vis alternative sources of capital not subject to such norms. From another perspective, representatives of local communities around the world have expressed that they feel at the mercy of international investors who, if confronted with strong levels of social and environmental protection policies, or by community efforts to reduce impacts and improve benefit sharing, may simply move to another community or country and take with them the benefits (jobs, etc.) that they have created.[65] These dynamics are seen by many as creating a downward harmonization pressure on those institutions (or societies and communities) applying more stringent standards.

A fundamental counter-point to these pressures is that social, environmental and other safeguards, including those on financial integrity, are a core asset to ensure positive development outcomes and avoid potentially serious harm to affected people and the environment. This is, of course, a kind of first-principle of ideas about sustainable development, in the light of interrelationships between the goals and practices of economic development, social progress and development, environmental protection, equity and the fight against poverty. The decisions by these institutions to adopt and integrate these elements into their mandate and operations also serve to reflect their basic beliefs and values, by and for the people they serve.

In practice, there may be "ground truth" to each set of perspectives: safeguards are fundamental to sustainable and equitable development and the overarching mission of development institutions, they need to be of high quality in supporting these objectives, and they face downward pressures, with quite real implications for affected people and the development process. In addition, in these complex settings, both perception and reality matter.

A third major concern is the potential for corruption in transactions surrounding some international investments, with implications for both the nature and beneficiaries of such investments.[66] This issue has been taken up by, among other entities, the OECD Anti-Bribery Convention and its Guidelines for Multinational Enterprises,[67] and by the World Bank as a central challenge in promoting positive development results and making progress in the fight against poverty.[68] A related concern is that some large transnational companies "control such huge resources, more than what many (or most) governments are able to marshal, that they are thus able to have great policy influence in many countries."[69]

A fourth concern, at the focal point of this chapter, is that local people and communities may have little voice or input in decisions regarding the arrival, establishment and conduct of international investment operations, even though they may be significantly affected. This concern is considered in detail later.

There are, as well, a range of other factors that bear on the sustainability of international investment activities. A few of particular relevance to the present analysis are noted below.

First, it bears repeating that international investment can bring not only jobs, development benefits and economic opportunity where it takes place, but also new and sometimes best practices, processing methods and technologies to a host country and local communities. Thus, the stories of negative impacts described above, which are crucial to understand and address, should not be viewed as suggesting an overall assessment of the role played by international investment in efforts among countries to achieve positive and sustainable patterns of development.

Second, while obvious, it is important to note that the nature and outcomes of investment operations vary according to investor, situation, context and multiple other factors. International investment activities, even those that do generate impacts, are likely to be only one of possibly many inter-locking factors in relation to impacts experienced by affected people.

For example, studies and experience indicate that a major culprit behind continuing environmental loss from investment activity (domestic or foreign) is that the full value of affected natural resources is not recognized. Building on principles of sustainable development from the Bruntland Report to the Rio Declaration to the Millennium Ecosystem Assessment to present day, *The Economist* Special Report on Forests describes, in the words of one its sub-articles, how "Forests are disappearing because they are undervalued." The article notes that the extensive and in many ways incalculable values of forests, including ecosystem services[70] and contributions to livelihoods of forest dependent communities, often are not recognized or "priced" on markets. Rather:

> Forests are usually valued for their main commercial resources, timber, which is why they are so wantonly logged and cleared.[71]

In this context, it is also important to stress that local and domestic enterprises may be engaging in the same types of activities as "international" investors, with similar or larger impacts on social, economic and environmental conditions within a country and individual communities. This is true in all countries, rich or poor.

The case of mountaintop coal mining in the US provides an illustration. A summary analysis by Robert F. Kennedy Jr. (in 2009) notes the thousands of tons of explosives being used each day "to blow up Appalachia's mountains and extract sub-surface coal seams". The explosives have "demolished 500 mountains . . . buried hundreds of valley streams under tons of rubble, poisoned and uprooted countless communities, and caused widespread contamination to the region's air and water". The author contends that a central enabling cause of these destructive activities is a failure to enforce existing federal laws, including the US Clean Water Act. The analysis further suggests that, far from creating jobs, the increased mechanization of used in these mining operations has "shrunk" the number of employed West Virginia miners from 46,000 in 1966 to fewer than 11,000 today. This translates not only to loss of employment but less reinvestment by workers into their own communities. Rather, it is argued, the companies "extract more coal annually, but virtually all the profits leave the state for Wall Street . . . Coal is not an economic engine in the coalfields. It is an extraction engine." These are US-based coal companies acting within the territory of the US, the "coal barons".[72]

This example illustrates both of the types of impacts that can be wrought by large-scale investment operations, and the care which is needed when making distinctions between domestic and internationally-based investment activities. It also underscores the point that in a world of changing international relationships and governance structures, the question of who fits where into this globalized system, and the balances between benefits and costs, is complex.

Commentaries about investment patterns in Africa suggest another case in point. Dr. Maathai notes that a new set of actors and dynamics have taken a center stage in international investment activities on the continent. Today in Africa, she writes, countries from Asia "have been assuming a larger role in African affairs" and have "begun to form bilateral arrangements offering African nations development aid and construction assistance on the one hand, and seeking access to oil and mineral deposits to fund [their] own exponential growth on the other."

She describes the debate about these new developments, including that business is being carried out in places "that turn a blind eye to human rights and environmental destruction." On the other hand, she writes that "it can be argued that Africa benefits from these new sources of investment", noting trade agreements and construction of needed hospitals, roads and even soccer stadiums.[73] Other studies and reports also note the benefits that countries in Africa may receive from such investments.[74]

Dr. Maathai further observes, however, that like any "would-be Great Power", the powerful nations today are "seeking to advance their interests, acquire needed resources, find new markets for their products, and exert their influence in regional and global policymaking". In sharp terms, she states:

> In the past, people entered Africa by force. These days, they come with similarly lethal packages, but they are camouflaged attractively to persuade Africa's leaders and peoples to cooperate. Of course, such packages are eye-catching to many African governments, not least because they may be free of "conditionalities", such as respect for human rights, protection of the environment, and promotion of equity.[75]

These observations paint a picture of both continuity and change in the overall landscape of international investment activities. In one sense, new patterns of international investment activity may be reflective of the age-old drive to seek gains from resources and economic relationships in distant lands. In another, both the actors and the mechanisms are in a process of change and perhaps re-alignment. Indeed, the international community is in the midst of a significant evolution in terms of the relative economic and political situation among countries, which is being reflected not only in the directions of international investment activities but also in ongoing reforms to international governance structures that have been largely in place for many decades.

Finally, it must also be stressed that each individual country sets its own priorities and objectives for economic and other forms of development, and the role and desirability of foreign investment in this context. Among other things, this implies that countries and societies will themselves determine levels of regulatory control to guard against "adverse" social and environmental impacts of business and investment operations, and indeed how to judge such impacts in the first place vis-à-vis the country's own basic development and other priorities.

Accordingly, within the framework of international law, there will likely be many different views among countries and interested stakeholders about the balance of costs and benefits of particular types of investment activities, and how best to promote opportunities for development and sustainability. The role of national systems also is highlighted in the commitment of the international community to the principle of "country ownership" in recent discussions on aid effectiveness, calling for the use (and building capacity) of country-borrower systems to manage development and safeguard against potential harm from externally-supported aid/development projects.[76]

This need not be seen, however, as a barrier to further international work and cooperation to address these issues, or more specifically to explore ways to give affected people and communities' greater voice and rights of recourse in response to actions that affect them. Indeed, as described below, such work is ongoing in a variety of fora.

International norms governing transnational investment activities

The discussion which follows provides a general overview of the international normative framework that governs, or perhaps more accurately, that is relevant to transnational investment activities, with a particular focus on private foreign direct investment (FDI).

Post World War II roots

In the aftermath of the downward economic spiral and depressions of the 1930s, and the war which followed, a number of countries joined together to establish not only the United Nations but also a fundamentally new set of norms and institutions to govern international trade and economic relationships. These latter arrangements were founded upon, among many other elements, three main pillars: (1) a new rules-based system to guide international trade (the GATT, now converted and expanded into the WTO); (2) the International Bank for Reconstruction and Development (the World Bank, designed to promote economic reconstruction and international development); and (3) the International Monetary Fund (the IMF, designed to promote international financial stability).

Leaving aside the public-funds support for international development of the World Bank, this original post-War framework did not create an explicit normative structure to govern international investment activities. The original trading rules of the GATT had some skeletal provisions relating to investment, but as Professor Jackson describes these were focused on situations where "restrictions on foreign investors had the effect of discouraging the importation of foreign goods" and thus could be in violation of GATT obligations on national treatment and other "trade-related" obligations.[77]

Instead, a separate legal track was developed on investment activities. This consisted, initially, of the re-negotiation of so-called "Friendship, Commerce and

Navigation" treaties to put a greater emphasis than before on the objective of promoting a secure and enabling environment for international investment activities. Professor Jackson writes that, among other factors, "[t]his change in emphasis was a direct reflection of the increased foreign investment role of American business firms after World War II".[78]

Beginning especially in the 1970s, these were followed by the negotiation of a large number of Bilateral Investment Treaties (BITs, also referred to as IIAs) and other instruments, including NAFTA.[79] Professor Jackson writes that the so-called BIT program, as conceived of by the US, was developed in large measure to protect the rights of US investors in cases of expropriation by host governments, particularly in response to claims by developing countries "that customary international law no longer required that expropriation be accompanied by prompt, adequate, and effective compensation, if indeed it ever had."[80] Professor Jackson observes that the BITs, at least at their inception, focused on protecting existing US investments in the territory of other States, but did not have as a goal the promotion of future investment, as this "would have been inconsistent with the US policy of letting the market direct investment flows and could have raised opposition to these treaties on the part of labor groups concerned about the loss of jobs".

During these same years, many developing countries viewed matters from a decidedly different perspective, and stood on the other side of this negotiating "equation". As reflected in debates leading up to the declaration of a New International Economic Order in the UN General Assembly in 1974, many of these countries viewed TNC investment activities with mistrust and were concerned over their impacts.[81] In this context, they "imposed widespread controls, restrictions and conditions on FDI entry and operations",[82] and sought to ensure that disputes (e.g. over issues of expropriation by the host government over a foreign investor) would be decided solely by domestic courts of that State.[83]

This "North-South" divide occurred at a time when FDI flows from North-to-South were a far greater proportion of overall FDI than they are today. The debates reflected an important philosophical difference in terms of relevant norms: a free-market, liberalized system on the one hand, geared toward protecting the "rights" of foreign investors to establish and operate in other countries; versus a more interventionist, regulatory model on the other, focused more on asserting the sovereign control of the host country government.[84]

In the 1980s and 1990s, this situation evolved significantly, and the North-South divide began to dissipate. During those years, many developing countries adopted a more favorable view toward foreign investment and its potential to bring economic and other benefits.[85] Martin Khor touches on these questions, writing in 2000:

> The last few decades have also witnessed a significant shift of perspective in many developing countries toward foreign investment. In the 1960's and 1970's there was considerable reservation and mistrust by governments of many developing countries, as well as many development economists.

> towards foreign investment. Starting with the 1980's, however, there has been a growing tendency for viewing foreign investment more positively. A new orthodoxy came into being, that as a form of foreign capital, investments are superior to loans because investments (unlike loans) would not land the host country in a debt crisis . . . In reality, there are benefits and costs accompanying foreign investment. The task for policy makers and analysts alike is to ascertain the determinants of the benefits and costs, and attempt to devise policies to increase the benefits and reduce the costs, with the aim of ensuring that there are net benefits.[86]

An OECD Policy Brief in 2001 reflected similarly on this policy evolution, noting that the policy environment for international investment:

> has generally become more favourable and countries now compete actively for such investments. Today, [multinational enterprises] are an integral part of the international economy, as agents for beneficial investment flows and for diffusion of technology and as an important source of tax revenues. At the same time, public concerns remain about their activities and many initiatives are under way that aim to address these concerns.[87]

There are now many indicators of strong interest among countries in attracting foreign investment. The UNCTAD 2009 World Investment Report notes a number of policy incentives and other measures by many countries in Africa and Asia designed to create a more favorable and enabling environment for foreign investors.[88]

As these debates continued to evolve, and as FDI flows from developing countries continued to expand, renewed energies were put into the negotiation of a new generation of bilateral and regional investment treaties. As noted previously, these international investment agreements, or IIAs, now number nearly 3000, cross-extending to countries throughout the world.[89] As such, they form an increasingly important, but somehow surprisingly "below-the-radar-screen", part of the international normative landscape governing transnational investment activities.

The discussion below notes briefly some key features of these agreements, with a focus on an early and important example, the Investment Chapter (Chapter 11) of the North American Free Trade Agreement (NAFTA) between Canada, Mexico and the US.[90]

As will be described, a key thrust of these agreements has been to provide a more secure and favorable environment for overseas investment activities of foreign investors, as well as strong rights of recourse for investors to ensure that host country governments abide by the protections for investors contained in these agreements. By comparison, the agreements themselves tend to contain very little to regulate or otherwise address the potential negative social and environmental impacts that may result from such activities.[91]

NAFTA Chapter 11 and other, similar investment agreements

The negotiation of the Chapter 11 (on Investment) of the North American Free Trade Agreement (NAFTA) took place in the early 1990s. In many ways, the negotiation provided not only a continuation and expansion upon earlier Bilateral Investment Treaties (BITs, herein also referred to as IIAs), but also a kind of early testing ground for the inclusion (or not) of new provisions to address the environmental and social implications of international investment activities.

Basic obligations supporting the rights of foreign investors

As finally negotiated, the investment provisions of the NAFTA build upon, and expand beyond, earlier bilateral investment treaties to which the United States was a party.[92] At their core, they consist of a number of binding substantive obligations designed to protect and secure the rights of investors of one Party against certain types of actions by the host government Party, supported by strong and legally binding procedures to ensure adherence to these obligations and provide means of recourse in the event of non-compliance.

The basic protections for investors consist of several "disciplines" upon how Party-governments treat foreign investors in their territory. Among others, these include requirements: not to discriminate against foreign investors (including as compared to similarly situated national investors); not to nationalize or expropriate the investments of foreign investors, except under strictly laid out conditions (including compensation); and to accord to foreign investors treatment in accordance with customary international law, including "fair and equitable treatment" and "full protection and security".[93]

The agreement also contains other provisions that in some sense respond to earlier and historical debates about whether foreign investors may be obliged by the host-government to share the benefits of their enterprises with local communities, e.g. through obligations to purchase or give preference to local goods or services, to transfer technology, or to achieve a given level of domestic content. These provisions are in the form of a general restriction against the imposition of such "Performance Requirements" by the host government, with certain specified exceptions. On the other hand, the agreement also clarifies that these provisions do not prevent a party from conditioning the receipt of an advantage to the investor "on compliance with a requirement to locate production, provide a service, train or employ workers, construct or expand particular facilities, or carry out research and development, in its territory."[94]

Perhaps the most remarkable feature of NAFTA Chapter 11 is its dispute settlement system. In addition to providing a strong, compulsory and legally binding State-to-State arbitration system, the agreement established an "investor–State" dispute settlement mechanism. This latter mechanism confers specific legal rights of standing upon private investors of the Parties to file a claim for arbitration against a Party government to NAFTA, alleging harm as a result of violation by that government of one or more of the substantive obligations (noted above), and empowering arbitrators to award monetary damages as redress for these harms.[95] This mechanism, and some of the reasons behind its creation, is considered in more detail below.

Potential social and environmental effects

At the time these provisions were being negotiated in the early 1990s, the more general issue of the relationship between trade and environment virtually exploded as a topic of international law and policy debate. As described in many writings during and after that time, there was a growing awareness that the rules of international trade in particular, and the still amorphous process of globalization more generally, had potentially profound implications (for better and for worse) for the environment and the achievement of national and internationally-defined objectives for environmental protection.[96]

These debates penetrated into a variety of international negotiations at the time, including those surrounding international investment agreements like NAFTA Chapter 11.[97] One prominent concern related to the potential "(de-)regulatory effects" of these agreements. In particular, there was significant concern especially among representatives of environmental agencies and interested NGOs that the disciplines in these agreements upon how governments treat foreign investors might be interpreted in a way that would unduly restrict the ability of governments to adopt and apply needed health and environmental measures vis-à-vis such investors.[98]

In addition, and of particular relevance to the present chapter, there was also a debate over whether the protections afforded foreign investors by NAFTA Chapter 11 would foster international investment that could be socially or environmentally disruptive (as well as beneficial) and, if so, what types of responsive measures should be developed.

One aspect of this concern was whether NAFTA Chapter 11 would produce a so-called "pollution haven" effect. This refers to the possibility that as trade relations among the countries become more liberalized, they might have an incentive to relax the level of stringency of their own environmental and other laws and regulations, or fail to effectively enforce those laws, to attract investment and enhance their ability to stay competitive.

This possibility was analyzed in a stand-alone chapter of the US Environmental Review of the NAFTA,[99] and was raised as a concern by many in civil society who were following these early trade and environment debates. In the end, the issue was raised in the negotiations among the Parties, and led to the inclusion of the following provision as NAFTA Article 1114.2:

> The Parties recognize that it is inappropriate to encourage investment by relaxing domestic health, safety or environmental measures. Accordingly, a Party should not waive or otherwise derogate from, or offer to waive or otherwise derogate from, such measures as an encouragement for the

> establishment, acquisition, expansion or retention in its territory of an investment of an investor. If a Party considers that another Party has offered such an encouragement, it may request consultations with the other Party and the two Parties shall consult with a view to avoiding any such encouragement.[100]

Importantly, while this provision does require that parties consult on this issue, it is not otherwise framed as a binding legal obligation and is not, in any case, made subject to the investor–State dispute settlement provisions of NAFTA Chapter 11 (noted above).

A second question was whether NAFTA Chapter 11, and similar investment agreements, would contribute to changes in investment flows among Parties, and corresponding environmental and social effects (so-called "structure and scale effects").[101] A particular point of concern was the possibility that these agreements would further promote large-scale cross-border investment activities that might be beyond the capacity of host countries to properly regulate.

There has been considerable debate on the question of a "causal" linkage between international investment agreements and changes in investment flows.[102] A typical difficulty in this research is to separate out any effects "traceable" to the agreements as compared to multiple other factors that may play a role, including often variable macro- and micro-economic conditions and considerations among many others.[103] It has also been pointed out that international investment activities (and impacts) have been occurring long before modern-age investment agreements were ever negotiated.

Recent studies, nevertheless, are indeed finding a linkage between IIAs and flows of FDI to developing countries. In summarizing one of its recent reports, UNCTAD states:

> A new report discusses international investment agreements (IIAs) as a tool to boost FDI. The study concludes that – within their limited role as foreign investment determinants – IIAs can influence a company's decision where to invest. This impact is generally stronger in the case of preferential trade and investment agreements than with BITs. However, IIAs need to be embedded in broader FDI policies, covering all FDI determinants and carefully balancing the costs and benefits of such agreements.[104]

Moreover, as noted above, a basic objective of these agreements is to promote and foster international investment through creation of a more favorable environment for foreign investors.

During the negotiation of NAFTA Chapter 11, there was debate within the US inter-agency team about whether to include in NAFTA Chapter 11 itself stand-alone substantive obligations to address the possible linkage between NAFTA and changes in the structure and scale of cross-border investment activities. On the US side, at the initiative of involved officials and negotiators from the US Environmental Protection Agency, various options were considered, including a provision which would require actions to address potential environmental effects linked to large-scale investment activity that might be fostered by the agreement.

These types of options ran into resistance, however, on three principal arguments: that there was not a clear linkage between the agreement and new investment activity, or potential harms from such activity; that such provisions might lead to special restrictions on the actions of foreign investors, which would be "discriminatory" (i.e. extra restraints) as compared to the way domestic investors were treated; and that there was no precedent for such agreements in earlier BITS or other instruments. In the end, rather than establishing an affirmative duty to address potential impacts, the final negotiating process led to a provision as follows:

> Nothing in this Chapter shall be construed to prevent a Party from adopting, maintaining or enforcing any measure otherwise consistent with this Chapter that it considers appropriate to ensure that investment activity in its territory is undertaken in a manner sensitive to environmental concerns.[105]

In the broader sense, however, the overall NAFTA "package" certainly did not ignore these types of environmental and social safeguard issues. In particular, and among other things, Canada, Mexico and the US negotiated two agreements in parallel to NAFTA that contain important provisions relevant to these concerns. Indeed, the concern that Parties might relax standards to attract investment, or fail to effectively enforce their own environmental (and other) laws and regulations was a major factor in the decision of the Parties to negotiate and conclude separate "side agreements" to NAFTA on both environment and labor issues.

The environmental side agreement, known more formally as the North American Agreement on Environmental Cooperation, contains general requirements relevant to environmental protection and enforcement in the three Parties. These include obligations to ensure that their laws and regulations provide for high levels of environmental protection, to strive to continue to improve those laws and regulations, and to ensure that enforcement procedures are available under its laws to remedy violations. The agreement also sets forth a cooperative work program on environmental concerns of mutual interest, supported by the creation of a Council of Ministers (representing the Parties), an independent Secretariat, and both national and joint advisory bodies.[106]

In addition, and of particular relevance to the present chapter, the environmental side agreement contains a "public submission" process under which non-governmental organizations and other members of the public may request the independent Secretariat to prepare a "factual record" to determine whether or not a Party is acting in compliance its obligations to effectively enforce its environmental laws. Like the World Bank Inspection Panel and the investor–State mechanism of NAFTA Chapter 11, this process embodies a new and innovative basis for non-State actors to engage on matters of international law. It is noted in more detail below.

The (never adopted) Multilateral Agreement on Investment at the OECD

In the mid-1990s, members of the OECD initiated the negotiation of a new multilateral agreement on investment, the MAI. This agreement was conceived as going beyond the WTO agreement on Trade Related Investment Measures (TRIMs), and in fact used many provisions of NAFTA Chapter 11 as a basic model.

The dynamics of this negotiation are worth noting. Initially, many European countries appeared supportive, partially with the hope that it would provide an improved and more integrated framework not only to support the legitimate rights of transnational investors, but also to establish new norms and obligations to help ensure that such investment would be conducted in a socially and environmentally sustainable way. Views in the US were mixed, with some hoping to expand the NAFTA model to yet a broader range of countries, and others worried about the implications of doing so, particularly in light of the swirling issues about the possible use of an investor–State mechanism to challenge legitimate and needed domestic health and environmental measures.

As it turned out, however, with strong inputs and critiques of civil society, many came to the conclusion that the agreement, if adopted, would tend strongly to reinforce and expand the rights of international investors (compare NAFTA) to a much broader range of countries, with little on the other side of the ledger in terms of new norms and means to address the potential social and environmental implications of such investment activity.[107] Maartje van Putten, a former member of the European Parliament and the World Bank Inspection Panel, wrote:

> An earlier attempt to control FDI via the so-called Multilateral Agreement on Investment (MAI) in the [OECD] was abandoned in 1998 when a majority of the European Parliament voted against it. I also voted against it. We were strongly lobbied by NGOs and trade unions stressing that the MAI was mainly about the rights of foreign investors, not about their duties. Special concern was expressed about the position of poor nations that could not handle powerful investors taking over their entire financial systems when entering their fragile markets.[108]

Other international investment agreements

As noted previously, there are now nearly 3000 bilateral and regional investment agreements worldwide. A recent survey of these agreements by the OECD indicates that they generally continue to focus on a fairly standard set of issues linked to investment promotion and economic cooperation and development.[109] They include obligations and disciplines of the type noted previously, as well as investor–State dispute settlement mechanisms, designed to protect the rights and interests of foreign investors.[110]

Similarly, the UNCTAD database service on Bilateral Investment Treaties summarizes the purposes and provisions typically embodied in these agreements:

> Bilateral investment treaties (BITs) are agreements between two countries for the reciprocal encouragement, promotion and protection of investments in each other's territories by companies based in either country. Treaties typically cover the following areas: scope and definition of investment, admission and establishment, national treatment, most-favoured-nation treatment, fair and equitable treatment, compensation in the event of expropriation or damage to the investment, guarantees of free transfers of funds, and dispute settlement mechanisms, both state-state and investor–State.[111]

A more recent study by UNCTAD also notes the concern about the potential "de-regulatory" implications of these agreements, stating that:

> It is now open to discussion whether IIAs have become too one-sided in that expansive interpretations of the scope of coverage and protection offered by such agreements have led to fears that the host country's national policy space and the right to regulate have been unduly curtailed in ways that might adversely affect genuine policy objectives (citing to earlier studies).[112]

The OECD survey noted above also addresses the question of whether IIAs contain any social and environmental safeguard provisions designed to protect against possible negative impacts associated with international investment activities. It reports that most governments "do not use international investment agreements as a means for pursuing their environmental, labour and anti-corruption objectives", or even more broadly their "sustainable development objectives". Rather, according to the survey, governments rely on other domestic and international policies and process to address these concerns.

A recent UN survey of States on issues of human rights and transnational corporations indicates that very few States report having tools, policies or programs designed specifically to address corporate human rights challenges, and that a larger number rely on CSR initiatives such as soft law instruments like the OECD Guidelines on MNEs or voluntary initiatives such as the UN Global Compact. With respect to IIAs, it is noted that "[v]ery few explicitly consider human rights criteria in their export credit and investment promotion policies or in bilateral trade and investment treaties, points at which government policies and global business operations most closely intersect."[113]

In short, the following points may be highlighted: (1) IIAs contain a number of strong provisions and mechanisms designed to protect the interests of foreign investors and their investment activities; (2) it is increasingly recognized that these raise at least the potential of having a "de-regulatory" effect upon the space of the host-country to apply regulations to address adverse impacts associated with such investments; and (3) even though these IIAs provide a close "point of intersection" between government policy and global business, they generally do not include norms and rights of recourse to safeguard against potential social and environmental effects of investment. Rather, this task is "left" to other instruments and initiatives, outside the IIAs.

Other norms and instruments to address impacts of international investment

The discussion below provides a brief review of some of the other norms and instruments that have a role in addressing social and environmental impacts of international investment activities.

Corporate social responsibility (CSR) and related norms and initiatives

In recent years there has been a flurry of activity in developing or enhancing non-binding norms and initiatives aimed to foster and promote responsible corporate behavior with respect to, inter alia, social, environmental, labor and human rights matters. Some are sponsored by international organizations and take on the form of "soft law"[114] international instruments and commitments, others by private associations, foundations and non-governmental organizations. They include, among many others, the UN Global Compact, the OECD Guidelines for Multinational Enterprises (MNEs), the ILO Tripartite Declaration of Principles concerning Multinational Enterprises and Social Policy, the Global Sullivan Principles of Social Responsibility, the Equator Principles (for private international financial institutions), the Bhopal Principles on Corporate Accountability (Greenpeace), and Human Rights for Companies (Amnesty International).[115]

There are also important draft and new proposals, including (draft) Norms on the Responsibilities of Transnational Corporations and Other Business Enterprises with Regard to Human Rights, ISO Guidance on Social Standards and brand new Voluntary Guidelines prepared by the UN Food and Agriculture Organization on the issue of farmland acquisition, or farmland grabbing, noted earlier in this chapter. The UNEP Principles for Responsible Investment is established "to help investors achieve better long-term investment returns and sustainable markets through improved analysis of environmental, social and governance issues."[116] The UNEP Finance Initiative is a public-private partnership between UNEP and the global financial sector, with the aim to help banks, insurers and investment firms "understand the impacts of environmental, social and governance issues on financial performance and sustainable development, and to embed best sustainability practice in financial institution strategies and operations."[117]

As seen by even a brief listing, these initiatives set forth a wide range of soft law or voluntary norms and guidelines on core issues relating to the social, environmental and economic implications of international investment activities. The relevant websites record many important stories and achievements, and it has also been noted that these instruments are likely to play a key role in further defining corporate responsibility for human rights in a more legally binding sense.[118]

There are, at the same time, significant questions regarding these initiatives. In respect to their sheer number, the *OECD Observer* notes that:

> The global landscape of international initiatives to promote responsible business practice has become increasingly – and perhaps confusingly – crowded

> over the last decade. A diverse array of voluntary instruments has emerged, including hundreds of corporate codes of conduct, certification and labeling schemes, model codes, and sectoral initiatives, all designed to assist private and civil society organizations as they try to assess and respond to such issues as sustainable development, climate change or poverty alleviation.[119]

In addition, many commentators have raised important questions as to whether these voluntary norms are effectively applied or, rather, are used primarily as a public relations exercise. One recent analysis writes as follows:

> In order to meet social expectations for corporate actions, firms will often publicize isolated projects and philanthropic activity but neglect to report on the totality of their activities. Is it enough that corporations are at least doing some good voluntarily? Does this have the potential of deflecting critical attention to other activities of the corporation?[120]

In a stinging commentary in the aftermath of the recent BP oil spill in the Gulf of Mexico, and on the lack of regulatory control or accountability of activities in the financial sector contributing to the recent international financial crisis, Chrystia Freeland wrote:

> As crude poured into the Gulf of Mexico . . . corporate social responsibility might seem a perverse target. Surely we need more corporate responsibility, not less. But many of the business disasters of the past 24 months have been facilitated by the mini-industry of corporate social responsibility . . . The problem with CSR is that it muddies the waters . . . CSR, and the humanitarian philosophy behind it, asks us to believe that the interests of an individual company and those of the wider community are fully aligned. They aren't – a truth too many regulators forgot in recent years.[121]

One key question in this context is the extent to which companies, including TNCs, may be held accountable to apply (or comply with) the norms and guidelines to which they subscribe. Because of their non-binding nature, the relevant instruments generally do not contain specific mechanisms for enforcement or to allow affected people to seek recourse for non-compliance and harm.

In this regard, a recent survey of the UN reports on issues of accountability in respect to the application of instruments and initiatives of corporate social responsibility. On the issue of human rights, most responding firms indicated that they have "internal reporting systems" to monitor their human rights performance, and that "sustainability reporting has risen exponentially." But, according to the Report, "quality has not matched quantity" and "without independent external assurance of some sort these systems lack credibility, especially for companies with questionable performance records." Where "self-regulation is most challenged", writes the report, "is in its accountability provisions."[122]

The Report mentions, at the same time, some notable efforts in recent years "to enhance accountability for compliance".[123] One important example is the system under the OECD Guidelines on Multinational Enterprises for civil society to bring complaints to "National Contact Points" regarding transgressions of the Guidelines by TNCs.

The OECD Guidelines on Multinational Enterprises (MNEs)

The OECD Guidelines date back to 1976, and were significantly revised in 2000. They are among the earliest international initiatives establishing non-binding norms to promote "responsible behavior" by multinational corporations engaged in international investment activities.

The Guidelines consist of "recommendations addressed by governments to multinational enterprises", and in particular multinational enterprises "operating in or from their territories." In terms of normative content, they contain general policies as well as specific sections on topics ranging from information disclosure to environment to employment to combating bribery. They were expanded in a number of areas in the year 2000, with new recommendations relating to the elimination of child and forced labor, human rights, and measures on environmental performance and information disclosure, and new chapters on combating corruption and consumer interests.[124]

The OECD system also establishes a mechanism under which members of the public may submit enquiries or complaints with national government contact points about specific instances of business conduct that may not be in line with the Guidelines. This complaint system is described in Section IV, below.

National and international law

Beyond instruments of CSR, it is important to recognize the basic role played by national and international law in addressing the potential impacts arising from international investment activities. Some countries have adopted specific laws on corporate liability, including for crimes and torts committed abroad,[125] and countries over the years have more generally developed laws, regulations, programs and institutions to address environmental, social and other types of policy issues and priorities. As noted previously, however, there remain significant differences in capacity among countries in applying these frameworks to potential impacts arising from transnational investment activities.

There is, as well, a wide body of international law and instruments, including treaties and other instruments to address concerns of human rights, labor rights, environmental protection and harm, and other matters of concern in relation to the potential impacts of FDI and TNC activity as noted in this chapter. These laws and instruments also provide a fundamental basis and means to address these policy areas and concerns. Unlike IIAs and the CSR-related initiatives noted above, however, they tend not to focus per se on responsibilities or systems of accountability for transnational investors. And, as noted earlier, these instruments notwithstanding, international investment activity continues to generate harms as well as benefits for local communities around the world.

Initiatives at the World Bank and other international financial institutions

Over the years, the World Bank and other international financial institutions have developed an important body of norms and policies to help ensure that the projects they finance avoid or minimize adverse social and environmental impacts, and to support and enhance positive outcomes for local and affected people.

The safeguard policies of the World Bank[126] include, inter alia, policies on Indigenous Peoples, Involuntary Resettlement, Cultural Properties, Environmental Assessment, Natural Habitats, Forests, Pesticides, and Dam Safety.[127] These policies are accompanied by a number of other important policies and procedures to improve the Bank's decision-making process and ultimate development outcomes, including Access to Information, Project Appraisal, Supervision (of project implementation), and Economic Analysis of Investment Operations.

These operational policies and procedures contain a number of procedural and substantive provisions to help avoid and reduce social and environmental harm that may arise in the context of Bank-financed operations, and the Bank requires itself to comply with these policies during project design, preparation and implementation. Ultimately, the application of these policies is intended to support the overall mission of the World Bank as a development organization to help reduce poverty.[128]

As noted previously, the World Bank has established an independent Inspection Panel which is available to people affected by Bank-financed operations who believe that they are, or might be, harmed as a result of non-compliance by the Bank with its safeguard and other policies and procedures. The Inspection Panel and other similar mechanisms at other international financial institutions, and at the International Finance Corporation of the World Bank, are considered in more detail below.

The evolving role of non-state actors in international law

The discussion above indicates that there exist a variety of norms (of varying scope and strength) relevant to the potential impacts of FDI and TNC operations. A key question, however, is the extent to which there is accountability to ensure that these norms are applied, particularly to those who might be adversely affected.

This section provides a brief overview of an important evolution under international law on the role of non-State actors in the law and policy process. It focuses, in particular, on one aspect of this trend: the creation of formal new mechanisms enabling people and civil society organizations to seek recourse and accountability for decisions and actions that affect them at the international level, above and beyond those available as a matter of domestic law.[129] The discussion is intended to provide a reference point for possible lessons that might be applied to the current normative framework governing private transnational investment activities.

Overview – steps along the road

Under traditional doctrines of international law, nations and in particular their government representatives are the "subjects" of international law, the actors on its stage. Traditionally, nation-States, not individuals make international law,[130] take the lead in its implementation and enforcement,[131] possess its rights and are subject to its obligations.

There is, however, a steady march beyond this traditional view. Indeed, one of the notable developments in international law over the past 30 years has been the expanded role and participation of non-State actors, and the development of formal legal means to support and enable this participation. This gives them, in effect, a legal "status" as actors on this stage.

Professor Louis Sohn signaled this evolution in a seminal article in 1982.[132] The analysis traces back to post-World War II Nuremburg trials in which *individuals*, and not just States, were made directly subject to substantive obligations under international law (crimes against humanity). It also notes, inter alia, human rights treaties which create rights and avenues for persons subject to human rights abuses to bring their concerns directly to an international level, without having to rely upon or await intervention by their government.

The 1992 Rio Summit marked an important milestone in this evolution.[133] The Summit, among many other things, highlighted the role of major non-State groups in this "work among nations" (youth, workers, NGOs, farmers), and adopted an important new set of principles on issues of transparency, public participation and the right of communities "to know" about environmental toxics and problems to which they might be exposed.[134] Indeed, the Summit itself served as testament to this growing role and influence, as it was attended by thousands of members of these groups, and reflected a growing practice among at least some international organizations of having decision-meetings open to public observers.

In the years since the Rio Summit, there have been significant advances in this trend. The creation of the World Bank Inspection Panel in September 1993, for example, represented a pioneering means for affected people (non-State actors) to seek recourse and accountability from the World Bank in cases where the Bank is not following its own policies designed to avoid harm to people and the environment and support poverty reduction and sustainable and equitable development. In subsequent years, other international financial institutions have followed this example and developed their own recourse and accountability mechanisms. These and other examples of mechanisms which provide a forum for non-State actors to raise complaints within the framework of international law are considered later.

In the years following Rio, civil society has played an increasingly important role in international law and policy work.[135] In many (but not all) fields, international organizations adopted more open rules and procedures relating to participation by civil society organizations in international meetings and treaty negotiations.[136] Aided by these rules, and building on longstanding efforts and campaigns on a range of social, environmental, labor and development issues,[137] civil society has played a critical role in catalyzing support for, helping to frame, and then participating in the development of, a number of important new international agreements negotiated during these years, including the International Treaty on Land Mines, the UN ECE Convention on Access to Information, Public Information in Decision Making, and Access to Justice in Envoirnmental Matters (the Aarhus Convention), the Stockholm Convention on Persistent Organic Pollutants, the Kyoto Protocol to the Framework Convention on Climate Change, and many others.

More recently, the Rome Agreement establishing an International Criminal Court, and other ad hoc International Tribunals, was established, with authority to bring charges against individuals for violation of internationally-defined crimes. These new instruments reinforce this now longstanding evolution to encompass non-State actors within the framework of rights and obligations established under international law, and may be seen as direct descendants of some of the early precedents, like the Nuremburg trials, noted by Professor Sohn.[138]

Stages of the International law and policy process

Viewed thematically rather than chronologically, this steady evolution in the role of non-State actors under international law is to some degree manifested in two principal stages of the international law and policy process. The first may be termed the "design and development" stage. This includes, for example, expanded participation by non-State actors in the process to conceive, initiate and negotiate international treaties (e.g. supported by expanded provisions for participation in rules of procedure governing treaty negotiations).

The second may be termed the "implementation and enforcement" stage. This includes, for example, expanded participation by non-State actors in the systems of implementation and enforcement of international law (e.g. non-compliance procedures such as that under the Montreal Protocol and the Aarhus Convention; dispute settlement procedures such as those embodied by the investor–State mechanism of NAFTA Chapter 11, making individuals subject to criminal proceedings under international tribunals, such as the International Criminal Court).

In some cases, as in the World Bank Inspection Panel, the two are joined: the concept is to enable affected people to seek recourse for harms caused by non-compliance (hence, implementation and enforcement), but the system also enables claims by "potentially affected" people submitted at the stage of project design and appraisal, and is intended to create an incentive at the outset to ensure policy-compliant projects (hence, design and development).

This "dual" purpose is an integral feature of "recourse and accountability mechanisms" like the Inspection Panel based on "community-led accountability" or "accountability from below". Indeed, the growing experience and use of these mechanisms is suggestive of the need, perhaps, for a kind of "special category" within the frames of international law.

"Dimensions" of accountability

From another perspective, this ongoing evolution toward greater voice and participation by non-State actors under international law can be reflected in terms of the different means available to enhance the accountability of international organizations to those affected by their actions, what One World Trust refers to as the "dimensions" of accountability.

This framework on accountability is set forth in the 2006 assessment carried out by One World Trust on accountability among international organizations, including transnational companies and intergovernmental organizations like the World Bank. The Report notes, as suggested in the present chapter, that the actions and decisions of these organizations "can have a profound effect on people's daily lives". In this context, they pose the question "but how do we hold these organisations to account for their actions?"[139]

Reflecting the analysis set forth above, the study suggests that "state based accountability is inadequate" and "new tools are needed at the local, national, and global level to make transnational actors more accountable and transparent to affected individuals and communities"[140] They divide these tools into four core "dimensions" of accountability: transparency, participation, evaluation, and complaint/response mechanisms.

This fourth dimension, complaint and response mechanisms, is of particular relevance to the present analysis. The Report notes that such mechanisms are designed to give voice and provide avenues of recourse for affected people and communities, and goes on as follows:

> Without an effective complaint and response mechanism in place, there is little that stakeholders can do to prevent abuses of power should other accountability mechanisms fail. A rigorous complaint and response mechanism will provide an incentive . . . to ensure that other accountability mechanisms are consistently implemented and adhered to in all areas of their work and that, should they fail, the organization will take action to address them.[141]

Selected mechanisms: themes of recourse and accountability

The discussion below highlights three mechanisms that reflect, in varying ways, the themes of recourse and accountability for locally-affected people outlined above. These are: the Inspection Panel of the World Bank and similar mechanisms at other IFIs; the public submission process of the NAAEC; and the public complaint system under the OECD Guidelines on Multinational Enterprises (MNEs). It then draws a comparison between these systems and the investor–State mechanisms of IIAs.

A full analysis of these mechanisms is beyond the scope of this chapter. Rather, the discussion highlights a few key features that affect their functioning and effectiveness. Particular attention is given to the Inspection Panel as an entry-way for the follow-on discussion.

The World Bank Inspection Panel and similar mechanisms

The World Bank Inspection Panel was established by the Bank's Board of Executive Directors in 1993 as an independent accountability mechanism of the World Bank. The Panel provides a forum for people who believe that they have been, or might be, harmed by World Bank financed projects to request an independent investigation of their concerns.

In particular, in response to a request for investigation by two or more project-affected people, the Panel has the authority to investigate whether World Bank Management has complied with the Bank's own operational policies and procedures, and if not, whether such non-compliance is or might lead to harm to affected people. As noted above, these operational policies and procedures (the relevant underlying norms) include safeguard policies (described above) designed to ensure that Bank financed operations avoid and minimize social and environmental harm, and promote benefits.

The Panel reports its findings directly to the Bank's Board of Executive Directors, and in response Bank Management is required to develop and submit to the Board recommendations and an action plan to address Panel findings on non-compliance and harm. In short, the Panel provides an independent vehicle for project affected people to bring their complaints and concerns to the highest decision-making levels of the Bank. The Panel's findings, and the Bank response, are made publicly available, both for purposes of transparency and as a means to bring "sunshine" onto questions of compliance by the World Bank.[142]

WHY THE PANEL WAS CREATED

The reasons behind the creation of the Panel are instructive to questions raised in the present chapter. The Panel was created in response to both external and internal criticisms of the World Bank in the 1980s and early 1990s. From the outside, rising concerns were voiced by civil society and communities affected by Bank-funded projects that some of these projects were resulting in major adverse social and environmental harms to affected people, and were leading to "development disasters."[143]

A core critique in these years was that while the Bank had already established important social and environmental safeguard policies, it was failing to comply with these policies – and there was little or nothing that affected people could do to alter these negative outcomes. The people adversely affected by these projects often were poor and vulnerable, already at high risk of being left out of the development process. There was, moreover, a strong sense of outcry and concern about the continuing potential for problems in the future if the Bank was not held more accountable for abiding by its own safeguard policies.[144]

In this context, the Panel was created as a mechanism of both accountability and recourse. In terms of the former, the Panel process enables affected people to see that the Bank is held accountable (also defined as "answerable") for adhering to its own policies and procedures (the norms against which accountability are judged). It also is premised on the recognition that local communities have knowledge and expertise which is critical to the achievement of positive development outcomes. In terms of recourse, the process is designed not only as a check on compliance, but also to lead to responsive actions for the affected people in response to Panel findings of non-compliance and harm.

THE PANEL PROCESS

Once the Panel receives and registers a request for inspection that is within its mandate, the Panel follows a two stage process. The first stage, is the eligibility and recommendation phase. During this phase, Bank Management is required to respond to the request for inspection within 21 working days, and the Panel then has 21 working days to make its findings on whether or not the request meets certain technical eligibility criteria, and whether to recommend that a full investigation be conducted (which goes to the Board for approval on a non-objection basis).[145] During this "eligibility" phase, the Panel normally visits the affected people and the project area, and there may also be opportunities for problem-solving efforts between the Requesters and Management to address issues raised by the Request, in advance of a possible investigation.

In cases where the Panel goes to full investigation, the Panel hires expert consultants to assist in its fact-finding process, carries out on-site field visits to meet with requesters, government officials, Bank staff, and others, has access to and reviews all relevant Bank documentation relating to the project, and carries out detailed interviews with Bank staff. The mandate is to carry out a full, impartial fact-finding process and follow the facts wherever they may lead, as a basis for the Panel's findings on non-compliance and harm.

The Panel submits its final Investigation Report to the Board, and Bank Management has six weeks to develop its response and recommendations to address the Panel's findings. The Board of Executive Directors considers the Bank Management Response and Action Plan, and whether any additional steps are needed. Following the Board meeting, the Panel's Investigation Report and the Management Response become public, and the Panel makes a return visit to the Requesters to inform them of the results of the investigation. The Panel does not have a mandate to monitor implementation of action plans agreed between Bank Management and the Borrower, although in some cases it has been requested to play a follow-up fact-finding role by the Board. Bank Management typically reports back to the Board at specified intervals on progress in implementing the Action Plan and addressing the underlying issues of non-compliance and harm.[146]

IMPORTANT CHARACTERISTICS

The Panel consists of three members of different nationalities, chosen on the basis, inter alia, of their independence, integrity and exposure to issues in developing countries. The Panel is supported by a small permanent Secretariat which reports only to the Panel, and provides support and advice in the carrying out of its responsibilities.

For purposes of the present analysis, several observations are worth making about the Panel and the Panel system. First, the Panel does not act as a "court" or even a formal arbitration body with the power to render a binding and enforceable judgment. Rather, it is an independent fact-finding body that has the authority to make findings on compliance and harm. As noted above, the "remedies" in response to such findings need to be developed by Bank Management, for consideration and approval (with or without amendment) by the Board.

Second, while the Panel from its inception has had a strong focus on examining issues of compliance and harm, it also has taken increasing actions in recent years to promote problem-solving efforts during the early stage of the Panel process, as described above. These actions have been taken to enhance early action to address harm, in the interests of the affected people and all concerned.

Third, the Panel's work is predicated on three "I's"; independence, impartiality and integrity, and its founding Resolution and procedures contain many structural features designed to protect and support these characteristics. The Resolution creating the Panel begins by stating, for example, that there is established an "independent" Inspection Panel, and includes a number of specific provisions to ensure that Panel members are structurally independent.[147] The Panel is completely independent of Bank Management (which it investigates), and reports directly to the Board of Directors as a whole. The Panel administers and controls its own budget independently, based on levels provided from its first year in operation (with upward adjustments over time for cost), and its resolution specifically provides that "the Panel shall be given such resources as are necessary to carry out its responsibilities."[148]

ACCESSIBILITY AND ISSUES OF AWARENESS

As a bottom-up accountability mechanism, the Inspection Panel is intended to be readily accessible to affected people. Requests can be submitted in any language, need not be long, and are not required to cite specific provisions of Bank policy as a basis for their claim. Rather, what is important is to provide some basic explanations about the nature of the issues and alleged harm, as well as to indicate whether attempts have been made to resolve issues first with Bank Management.[149]

There remains, however, a marked lack of awareness about the availability of the Inspection Panel among communities that might be affected by projects financed by the World Bank. This is true notwithstanding the fact that the Panel has been in existence for 17 years, and despite ongoing efforts to build awareness. The Inspection Panel is re-doubling its efforts to address this problem, and the Board of Directors also has called upon Bank Management to do more to build awareness of the Panel at its end.

INVESTIGATIONS, IMPACTS AND EFFECTIVENESS

Over the years, the Panel has received 77 Requests for Inspection, and has carried out full investigations in just under half of these cases. These investigations have involved a range of Bank-financed projects raising a wide range of social, environmental and other types of issues and impacts, including large-scale infrastructure (dams, pipelines, irrigation and drainage systems, transport, landfills), land use planning, regulatory reform in natural resource and other sectors, among many others.

The recent publication *The Inspection Panel at 15* provides an extensive up-to-date review and retrospective on the work of the Panel, the nature and scope of its investigations and work, Bank policies most frequently raised in Requests for Inspection, and the types of impacts and outcomes that have resulted from the Panel's work.[150] The outcomes of the process occur at various levels, including: (1) the project level (e.g. changes or adjustments to projects, both during design and implementation, to address Panel findings on issues of non-compliance and harm); (2) the sector-level (e.g. lessons drawn from Panel cases relevant to other similar Bank-financed projects, e.g. involving forests, indigenous peoples, land administration, infrastructure); (3) the corporate level (e.g. the Panel's existence provides an incentive to promote proper application of Bank policies. The Panel also contributes to corporate learning through the analysis and record of its findings and analysis in specific cases, and it acts as a "check-and-balance" for the Bank's Board of Executive Directors to provide them an independent, technically-based analysis of what is happening with projects on the ground in response to the concerns of locally-affected people, in support of the Board's fiduciary responsibilities for the organization).

There are, as well, ongoing challenges in the work of the Panel. One of these, noted above, is the lack of public awareness of its existence to project-affected people who may wish to seek recourse and accountability. A second is the challenge of finding an effective way to combine opportunities for early problem-solving with its responsibilities to act as an accountability and recourse mechanism for instances of non-compliance by Bank Management with Bank policies and procedures. Others challenges are noted in *The Inspection Panel at 15* referred to above.

MECHANISMS AT OTHER IFIS

As noted previously, since the creation of the Inspection Panel, other international financial institutions have created their own independent accountability mechanisms (IAMs) for project affected people. These institutions include: the International Finance Corporation at the World Bank, the Inter-American Development Bank, the Asian Development Bank, the African Development Bank, the European Investment Bank, and the European Bank for Reconstruction and Development, among many others.

The IAMs at these other institutions have, in some cases, developed or been endowed with new approaches or authorities to carry out their responsibilities. For example, some have developed a formal function for "problem solving" or "dispute resolution" in parallel to their functions of examining issues of compliance with relevant policies. These systems may utilize independent, expert mediators to assist in finding solutions to problems raised by local communities. Also, and by comparison to the Inspection Panel, several of these mechanisms have explicit authority to monitor actions taken by the institutions in response to their investigations.

At the June 2012 United Nations Summit on Sustainable Development in Rio de Janeiro, the IAMs cooperated to present an analytical paper and trends of their work over the past twenty years describing the basic features. The paper provides an important overview of how these mechanisms work, what the record of their work indicates about issues of development and sustainability in relation to activities financed by international financial institutions, and what lessons might be taken for the application of their principles of citizen-driven accountability to other institutions and fields of work.

The public submission process of the NAAEC

A second example of a mechanism which provides rights to non-State actors, of relevance to the present analysis, is found in the North American Agreement on Environmental Cooperation (NAAEC), also known as the Environmental Side Agreement to NAFTA. When it came into force in January 1994, the NAAEC created a new mechanism, the "public submission" process, as part of overall "package" of actions and initiatives to address interrelated trade and environment issues linked to NAFTA and the environment. Under this approach, non-governmental organizations from any of the three NAFTA parties can submit a claim to the Secretariat of the Commission on Environmental Cooperation (CEC) alleging that a NAFTA Party is failing to effectively enforce its own environmental laws, and request the Secretariat to prepare a "factual record" on the matter which would be made publicly available.

One of the reasons for creating this system was the policy concern that closer economic integration under the NAFTA could lead to perverse incentives for the parties to relax their levels of environmental protection to attract investment. In more positive terms, it was recognized that measures to help ensure effective enforcement of environmental laws at high levels of protection would promote sustainability as the three economies became more closely linked.

The NAAEC public submission process gives the NAAEC independent Secretariat responsibility to review a submission to see if it meets certain criteria specified in the agreement.[151] On the basis of its review, and its related review as to whether the submission warrants a response from the involved government-Party,[152] the Secretariat shall inform the Council of Ministers, representing the three NAFTA parties, as to whether a Factual Record should be prepared (with supporting reasons) addressing the issues raised in the submission. The Secretariat shall prepare a Factual Record if the Council instructs it to do so by two-thirds vote.[153]

In preparing a Factual Record, the Secretariat shall consider any information furnished by a Party and may consider other relevant information as noted in Article 15. The Agreement contains additional provisions regarding comments by Parties, publication and other aspects of the process. These procedures do not require any specific response actions by the concerned Party. Rather, the intent is to enable the development of an independent, publicly available record as to the facts surrounding whether a Party is meeting its obligation under the agreement to effectively enforce its own environmental laws, in response to concerns of interested non-governmental stakeholders.[154]

A core reason behind the development of this public submission process was to give a greater voice and role to non-governmental organizations as a check on whether the government-Parties were meeting their own requirements regarding enforcement of environmental laws. This concept, again a concept of "accountability from below", built on years of experience at the national level within the Parties of the critical role played by NGOs in this field, including through domestic-law avenues such as rights to bring "citizen suits" to ensure government agencies were carrying out their obligations.

Another critical question during the negotiations involved the independence of the Secretariat. Negotiators from environmental agencies, and stakeholders from civil society and NGOs, stressed that establishing such independence was essential to the entire premise and credibility of the system. It was noted, in particular, that if the Secretariat were not independent, and was subject to pressure and influence by the government-Parties in carrying out this work, then both the relevance and the integrity of the process and its results would be compromised.

In the end, the agreement specified that the Secretariat would be "independent". Still, as in the case of other accountability mechanisms, how this is achieved and maintained in practice is of great significance. In the absence of specific structural safeguards, pressures can be applied from many directions: e.g. through decisions by the Parties on budget and resources, on work programs, and on how to engage and respond to the public submission process itself. A recent article by the former Director of the Enforcement Unit at the NAAEC Secretariat offers an important perspective on the public submission process over the years, including significant difficulties and issues faced in this work.[155]

The complaint process of the OECD Guidelines on MNEs

A third example is found in the OECD Guidelines on Multinational Enterprises (MNEs). As noted previously, these Guidelines contain norms of conduct for multinational enterprises in a wide range of areas, including human rights, environmental protection, labor rights, and many others.

In terms of accountability, the Guidelines are accompanied by a mechanism enabling members of the public to submit enquiries or complaints with "national contact points" established by governments about "specific instances" of business conduct that may not be in line with norms set forth in the Guidelines. Under this procedure, National Contact Points (NCPs) are called upon to respond to concerns raised by, inter alia, members of the public about implementation of the Guidelines in relation to specific instances of business conduct. Such concerns may be raised by other NCPs, the business community, employee organizations, other NGOs, the public or other governments.

When an NCP receives a concern or complaint about a specific instance, it makes an initial assessment of whether the issues raised merit further examination, and responds to the party or parties raising them. When they do, the NCP offers "good offices" to help the parties resolve the issue, and will consult with the parties where relevant. In carrying out this role, the NCP will seek advice from relevant authorities and representatives of the business community, employee organizations, other NGOs and relevant experts, and consult with the NCP in the other country or countries concerned. The NCP will also offer and, with the agreement of the involved parties, facilitate access to non-adversarial means to address the issues raised, such as conciliation or mediation.

If the parties do not reach an agreement on how to address the issues raised, the NCP will "issue a statement, and make recommendations as appropriate, on the implementation of the Guidelines." The Guidelines also state that if issues arise in countries that do not adhere to the Guidelines, the NCP will "take steps to develop an understanding of the issues involved, and follow these procedures where relevant and practicable."[156]

According to the Guidelines, NCPs are to operate in accordance with "core criteria of visibility, accessibility, transparency and accountability." In terms of their institutional structure, "adhering countries have flexibility in organizing their NCPs, seeking the active support of social partners, including the business community, employee organizations, and other interested parties, which includes non-governmental organizations."[157] NCPs are required to report annually, to the OECD Committee on Investment, on the nature and results of their activities, including implementation activities in specific instances. The Committee considers these reports and carries out certain other responsibilities relevant to this process, as set forth in the Guidelines.

Recent reports provide important information and details on the functioning of the NCP and specific instance process. The Report of the Chair on the 2008 Annual Meeting of NCPs (June 2008), for example, reviews NCP activities, the use of the specific instance procedure, and some emerging trends:

> [a]though there has been a slight decline in the number of specific instances raised over the 2007–2008 implementation cycle of the Guidelines, the NCPs' reports show continued support for the specific instances facility. There were 27 cases raised for a total of 182 requests since the June 2000 Review. Of these, 136 specific instances have been considered by NCPs. The trend of searching for amicable solutions is continuing, resulting in efforts to better co-ordinate and consult on cases involving multiple requests. However, some questions remain for further discussion.[158]

The Report notes some "innovations" in NCP structure and procedures. In Egypt, for example (which became the 40th adherent country in July 2007) it notes that the NCP is a Senior Manager from its Ministry of Investment, assisted by an Advisory Committee with representatives from several ministries, economic, legal and financial experts, and the Egyptian Trade Union Federation. In the

Netherlands, it notes that the Dutch NCP "now consists of an independent chairman and three independent members who all possess backgrounds in the various stakeholder groups of the NCP's work."

The Report also highlights certain suggested steps to improve the operation of the Guidelines and the NCP system in the future. These include, among others: peer learning among NCPs; actions to enhance public awareness about the existence of the Guidelines and the NCP system; and actions to build the skills or resources of NCPs in mediation and conciliation functions, including by third parties. In addition, the Report notes a suggestion to invite governments to take appropriate action to address resource constraints faced by some NCPs in fulfilling their duties.

A separate Report, "Specific Instances Considered by National Contact Points" (October 2008) provides a table of data about each specific instance considered by NCPs to date, listing NCP concerned, issue dealt with, date of notification, host country, guidelines chapter (i.e. the relevant norm), status, final statement (whether issued) and comments.[159] Just recently, the 42 Governments adhering to the OECD MNE Guidelines for Multinational Enterprises have agreed on Terms of Reference (TOR) for an update to these Guidelines. On the issue of accountability and the NCP process, these TOR state as follows:

> Mindful that the NCP mechanism is the most unique feature of the Guidelines and that procedural provisions set the frame for the implementation of the Guidelines, the update should consider how the implementation procedures adopted in 2000 could be further improved to enhance awareness, visibility and a more widespread and effective use of the Guidelines, including in non-adhering countries. This consideration should take due account of the experience, challenges and lessons learned during the past nine years of implementation of the Guidelines, proposals made by business, trade unions and NGOs, and the recommendations formulated by the UNSRSG for non-judicial redress mechanisms, including on institutional issues and the functioning of the NCP mechanism.[160]

This new initiative presents a potentially significant opportunity to strengthen the foundations for both "voice" and "bottom-up accountability" in the context of the Guidelines.

The investor–State mechanism of NAFTA Chapter 11

As noted above, the investor–State dispute settlement mechanisms under IIAs also provide a system of rights to recourse for non-State actors under international law. In contrast to the systems noted above, however, it does not address concerns about the potential adverse impacts of international investment activities on locally affected people or the environment. Rather, it is available to protect the rights and interests of foreign investors making the investments.

The investor–State mechanism under NAFTA Chapter 11 is illustrative. This mechanism gives private investors legal standing to file a claim for arbitration against a Party government to NAFTA, alleging harm as a result of violation by that government of one or more of the substantive obligations. It also empowers arbitrators to award monetary damages as redress for these harms.[161]

The procedures governing investor–State proceedings are set forth in Section B of Chapter 11, which provide in some detail the process by which investors may submit claims for arbitration, the conditions for submission of a claim, the place of arbitration, the governing law and the manner by which such arbitration is conducted. Article 1135 (Final Award) provides that the Arbitral Tribunal may award monetary damages plus interest and/or restitution of property. The text also contains explicit provisions on finality and enforcement of an award, including the timing by which an award is to be rendered. In other words, the mechanism is designed to be both specific and strong enabling recourse for the claimant investors. Under these provisions, private investors have filed some 40 claims for investor–State arbitration. The arbitral decisions, and related information, are reproduced at the websites of the Parties and elsewhere.[162]

During background discussions on the US side, it was argued that this investor–State mechanism was needed to ensure effective implementation of the provisions of the agreement protecting the interests of foreign investors. It was argued, in particular, that reliance on even an admittedly strong State-to-State arbitration system was not sufficient to achieve this objective, as State Parties may be reluctant for a variety of reasons to initiate arbitration actions to address instances of non-compliance. Among other things, it was contended that the State Parties would be far more cautious as part of their calculations to maintain overall diplomatic relationships, and to lessen the possibility of being on the receiving end of a complaint by another party. Some negotiators on the US side also expressed the view that there was no reason to believe that an investor–State mechanism would lead to a large number of new challenges by investors against government regulations of private investment.

Viewed through the passage of time, the creation of a "private right of action" for investors to bring claims against governments, with strong provisions for remedies, is perhaps one of the strongest examples found in international law of conferring rights of recourse and redress to non-State actors. It is now found in the nearly 3000 IIAs (and counting) that have been negotiated in multiple directions among countries around the world. As noted previously, however, these investor–State mechanisms are available for actions by private investors to protect their rights as set forth in these agreements. They are not, by comparison, available to people and members of the public who may be adversely affected by the activities of such investments, nor generally do they impose duties upon investors (or governments) to reduce or prevent such harms.

Observations

The discussion above suggests a few important basic themes and issues for further consideration.

First, and perhaps most fundamentally, these mechanisms reflect the new trend under international law to give a greater role to non-State actors to seek accountability and recourse for decisions that affect them. As described, this is premised on the recognition that traditional patterns of State-based or "top-down" accountability are not sufficient, by themselves, to ensure adherence to relevant norms of conduct, and on the recognition that people have basic rights to have a voice in, and effective avenues of recourse to address, actions that may cause them harm.

The availability of these mechanisms, however, varies. The Inspection Panel is premised on the foundation of giving voice and avenues for recourse to locally affected people and communities. The CEC public submission process and the complaint process of the OECD Guidelines on MNEs provide a venue for complaints from civil society and non-governmental organizations. The investor–State process, by comparison, is available only to private investors whose rights are protected against certain government-Party actions as specified in the relevant obligations.

Beyond this, a few specific factors are noted below that may be helpful in considering these mechanisms and in drawing the relevant cross-comparisons. The analysis does not intend to pass judgment on how these factors should play out in any particular venue (e.g. international investment agreements, the OECD Guidelines on MNEs and/or other non-binding CSR initiatives), but rather provide a framework for further consideration.

The first factor relates to the *relevant norms* of the system. This is a critical aspect of any recourse and accountability mechanism, because it is against these relevant norms which accountability and recourse may be sought. Important considerations in this regard include: the extent to which the norms are legally binding; their overall scope vis-à-vis the issues of concern; their level of specificity, and practicality in terms of their application; and the extent to which they include substantive as well as procedural elements.

It is not within the scope of this chapter to examine these considerations; rather, they are posed as factors for consideration. One additional point worth noting is that two of the mechanisms noted above rely on new sets of norms and procedures established at the international level, specifically the Inspection Panel process (judging compliance with World Bank operational policies and procedures) and the investor–State mechanism (judging compliance with obligations created under NAFTA Chapter 11). This is also the case with the OECD Guidelines on MNEs which are established as new norms of conduct at the international level, agreed upon by adhering governments.

By comparison, the CEC public submission process, while creating a new obligation and process at the level of international law (to effectively enforce national environmental laws), essentially imposes a new regime to secure (or at least check) compliance by Parties with their domestic (environmental) laws. As described previously, this approach arose out of particular concerns that the trade and investment liberalizing features of NAFTA might create an incentive for countries to relax the enforcement of their laws, and more generally on the view that additional means to support the enforcement of such laws was an important overall ingredient to ensure that new patterns of trade and economic activity that might be linked to NAFTA would be carried out sustainably and not generate environmental problems.

A second factor may be referred to as the *characteristics of the mechanism*. This refers to elements such as mandate, independence in operation, transparency, and level of resources. In mechanisms such as the Inspection Panel and the CEC public submission process, for example, the discussion signals the importance of independence, particularly from the entity being investigated. As noted above, there have also been some recent innovations in the structure of some NCPs under the OECD MNE Guidelines system, notably the establishment by the Netherlands of an "independent" chairman and three independent members with backgrounds in relevant stakeholder groups.

The discussion of the Inspection Panel and CEC public submission process also point to the importance of independent control over an adequate resource base. This highlights an important challenge: the need for adequate resources will be an important question in the transferability of lessons and practices of these mechanisms to other settings. The reflections in the Report by the Chair of the 2008 Annual Meeting of NCPs about issues of budget and resource constraints faced by NCPs is a reminder that this concern cuts across the relevant mechanisms.

A third factor can be referred to as effectiveness, including in particular in terms of providing effective response and recourse to the concerns raised by affected people. This is a broad topic and, again, not assessed in the current chapter.

One aspect, however, is noted: the process by which a mechanism seeks to achieve remedies and corrective measures. The mechanisms noted above each have their own particular features and mandates in this regard. In the context of private investment activities and FDI, the strongest (legally) is reflected in the power of arbitral tribunals under the investor–State system of NAFTA Chapter 11 and other IIAs to issue binding decisions, with the possibility of monetary awards. The NCP system, by comparison, puts non-adversarial problem solving at the core of its approach, and has provisions to make the findings of NCPs publicly available, but is not a system leading to compulsory and binding arbitration and remedies. The CEC public submission process involves the preparation of a factual record, with provisions to be made for public release; it does not prescribe responsive actions; rather, this is a matter to be taken up by the Party investigated in light of the overall process.

In terms of investment activities supported by IFIs, the Inspection Panel is illustrative. It uses, by comparison, a system of findings on compliance and harm which then trigger a required response by Bank Management to address such findings, reviewed by the Board. The Panel system and other IAMs also makes increasing use of opportunities for early problem-solving to address concerns raised by affected people early in the Panel process.

A fourth set of factors revolves around issues of *accessibility and other practical issues* and challenges that relate to the development and effective use of recourse and accountability mechanisms. As suggested by the discussion above (see, e.g. case of Inspection Panel and OECD NCP system), one practical concern is lack of awareness about the existence of recourse mechanisms on the part of affected and interested people. A second critical concern is the level of resources that might be needed for such a mechanism to function effectively, and resource constraints affecting either affected people in accessing the system or the entities responsible for carrying out its basic responsibilities.

Lastly, it should be emphasized that each of the mechanisms described above is designed within a specific framework and context, according to the institutional framework and other *context-specific* factors in which it is developed. Thus, while a cross-consideration of mechanisms may be useful at various levels, the context-specific nature of the various mechanisms needs to be kept strongly in mind.

Conclusion

The analysis presented in this chapter is part of a conversation about issues facing local people around the world in the face of the modern age of globalization. In particular, the question is posed as to what has been (and might yet be) done, within the context of international law, to give local communities and people a greater voice in cross-border investment activities that can bring to them both benefits and harm.

An important theme running through the chapter is that the international legal framework which governs (or relates to) cross-border investment activities has, over the years, built in many provisions and mechanisms to protect and secure the rights of investors engaged in cross-border investment, and to create a positive and more favorable environment for such investment. The investor–State mechanisms of international investment agreements are an impressive example: they give private investors a legal right under international law to bring claims to an international tribunal against governments (Parties), to protect their rights and seek monetary awards for non-compliance. They also provide an instructive illustration of the broader trend under international law to give greater legal rights to non-State actors, but in this case limited to a very narrow sub-set, private investors given specific rights under the relevant agreements.

The availability of this investor–State mechanism may itself be extended more broadly. As described above, in the 1990s there was an attempt to negotiate a multilateral agreement on investment within the framework of the OECD which, at least under initial drafts, would have included strong protections for the rights of foreign investors and an investor–State mechanism. There have also been discussions in recent years about possibly developing a multilateral investment agreement within the framework of the WTO. Even if negotiations do not expand into these broader settings, for strategic or other reasons, the number of bilateral and regional IIAs has been growing dramatically.

The present chapter began with a basic question: given that there are nearly 3000 IIAs with strong legal norms and rights of recourse to protect the interests of international investors, why do such agreements not contain similarly strong norms and rights of recourse to protect the interests of communities and the environment which may be affected by such investment activities? If for the investors, at nearly 3000 and counting, what about for the potentially affected people and communities?

The discussion above notes some of the explanations for this seeming asymmetry, including: that these issues are addressed by various other instruments; that putting such responsibilities on "foreign investors" under IIAs could put them at a disadvantage vis-à-vis similarly situated domestic investors; that the linkage between IIAs and social and environmental harms resulting from investment activity is contested and may not be readily apparent.

A final explanation, illustrated by the negotiations over the OECD MAI, is the wariness that many advocates of social and environmental policy objectives have about the further negotiation of any IIAs based on the existing model. This stems, in particular, from the concern over the potential "de-regulatory" effect of these agreements, i.e. that their "disciplines" to protect the right of foreign investors could be interpreted to constrain national regulatory authorities from applying needed environmental, social and other regulations to those investors. This concern is amplified by practical experience over many years of policy negotiations in the fields of trade, investment, labor rights and environmental protection, the sense that the power structure favors the former, that seeking greater policy integration could even backfire; the fear of arousing a sleeping giant.

And yet the reality is that these IIAs continue to be negotiated to help secure important rights for investors, but without corresponding responsibilities, let alone accountability mechanisms, to help ensure that their investment avoids social and environmental harm and is, more broadly, positive and helpful from an overall development perspective. This, it is said, is left to other instruments and initiatives, including those relating to Corporate Social Responsibility.

These other instruments and initiatives are important in scope and nature, but (with some exceptions) often are based on a model of voluntary commitment and "self-regulation", without external or independent mechanisms to hold investors accountable for putting them into practice. This stands in sharp contrast to the strong level of accountability and recourse provided to foreign investors under the investor–State mechanisms of IIAs, and to the bottom-up accountability mechanisms created over the years at the World Bank and other international financial institutions.

These latter examples, and new trends in international law noted above, suggest the importance of giving greater voice and rights of recourse to people who may be affected by international investment activity, and in particular FDI. The analysis suggests, as one possibility, to include norms and accountability into IIAs themselves, to help ensure that the international legal system effectively secures not only the rights and interests of international investors, but the rights and interests of people and communities who might be negatively affected by their activities. More generally, the idea is to help visualize how we (collectively) might put into practice these basic principles of "bottom-up accountability", so that affected people have a voice and right of recourse over actions that affect them, in the context of the ever-expanding cross-border investment activity of today's world.

Notes

1 The views and opinions expressed in this chapter are those of the author in his personal capacity, and do not reflect official positions.

2 In the present analysis, this term generally encompasses both foreign direct investment (FDI) by, inter alia, transnational corporations (TNCs), and investment activities financed or supported by international financial institutions (e.g. infrastructure development). There are, however, significant differences among these, and the scope and definition of "foreign investment" under international law continues to evolve. See UNCTAD Series on Issues in International Investment Agreements II: 2011. The principal focus of this chapter is FDI.

3 This new legal framework is often referred to as the "Bretton Woods" system due to the role played in its establishment by an international conference in Bretton Woods, New Hampshire in 1944. At its core, it was founded on the original General Agreement on Tariffs and Trade (GATT, now incorporated within the legal framework of the World Trade Organization), the World Bank, and the International Monetary Fund.

4 These included, initially, a series of newly negotiated "Friendship, Commerce and Navigation Treaties", followed by Bilateral and Regional Investment Treaties and other instruments (described below). See Jackson, Davey and Sykes, Jr. 2008: 198–199; UNCTAD World Investment Report 2009.

5 See Jackson et al. 2008; Ruggie 1982 (describing various factors behind and within the development of this new legal order, including the relative power and political interests among countries in the post-War era).

6 The potential positive and negative impacts of international investment activities are noted in this chapter. The extent to which trade and investment agreements promote – versus simply govern – these activities is a point of debate, addressed below.

7 See van Putten 2008: 7–14, which offers an instructive review of this issue, and differing perspectives on how the role and authority of countries as nation-states has been affected by the process of globalization, including the increased mobility of capital and transnational corporations.

8 World Investment Report 2009. By comparison, total FDI inflows were $58 billion in 1982 and $207 billion in 1990.

9 *Idem.*; see also World Investment Report 1996: 147.

10 World Investment Report 2009: 34.

11 Studies and examples are noted in the discussion below, including linkages back to the role played by consumption patterns in wealthier/consuming countries.

12 See, e.g. *Financial Times* 2009: 4 and discussion in text.

13 See, e.g. Gamboa et al. 2008.

14 These include other international instruments addressed to social and environmental issues, systems of Corporate Social Responsibility (CSR) and domestic law. See, e.g. International Investment Law 2008 (observing that governments generally rely on other domestic and international policies and processes to pursue environmental, labor and sustainable development objectives).

15 See, e.g. Maathai 2009:26 , noting the "legacy of woes" left by colonizers and oppressors, both from outside and within. The colonizers were not only competing against each other for geopolitical dominance, but "seeking new sources for the raw materials they needed to expand their industrial economies"; UNCTAD World Investment Report 2009 (describing early histories of foreign investment in agriculture,

including colonial expansion into developing countries "largely motivated by the search for natural resources, combined with cheap labor by indentured workers or slaves"); Hochschild 2000 (colonization history of the "Belgian Congo").

16 See, e.g. Maathai 2009 (colonial administrations could confiscate the most valued assets of the local population, and that the affected communities lacked any means of redress or redistribution).

17 This figure compares with some $58 billion in 1982 and 207 billion in 1990, with over 40% going to developing countries and economies in transition. See World Investment Report 2009 and 1995, supra. See also Wheeler 2009 (noting that "[O]ver the past decade, 30% of global FDI went to the developing world").

18 Wheeler, *idem*. The UNCTAD World Investment Report 2009 (at p. 53) notes, for example, that FDI outflows from South, East and South-East Asia reached $186 billion in 2008, fuelled by the relatively high economic growth, accumulation of foreign currency reserves through trade surpluses, greater competitiveness of firms in these economies, and often supportive government policies.

19 UNCTAD notes that these investments in Africa, for example, "play a crucial role in the financing of infrastructure in African LDCs, such as Angola and the Democratic Republic of Congo."

20 *Idem*. See also FAO 2008 ("[c]urrent estimates indicate that the biofuels industry will continue to grow, with output of global ethanol and biodiesel projected to more than double between 2007 and 2017").

21 World Bank Annual Report 2010. The IBRD is the International Bank for Reconstruction and Development, which is the part of the World Bank group which lends to middle income and creditworthy low income countries. The IDA is the part of the World Bank group which provides interest-free, long-term loans (known as credits) and grants to governments of the 79 poorest countries which have no or little capacity to borrow on market terms.

22 IFC Annual Report 2010.

23 OECD DAC Secretariat Simulation using 2008 dollars. It is emphasized that there are many different methodologies for calculating and imputing aid volumes, many different types of purposes and uses, and much room for debate about what actually constitutes aid (e.g. OECD excludes military aid and makes various other assumptions and distinctions for different types of aid). See also UN statistical service aggregates data on ODA flows in support of Millennium Development Goal 8, to Develop a Global Partnership for Sustainable Development.

24 The UNCTAD World Development Report 2009: 15–16 notes that "the share of developing countries in global outward FDI, and in FDI to both developed and LDCs has increased. Developing-country TNCs now account for a larger share of outward FDI than ever before."

25 See, e.g. UNCTAD 2009 World Investment Report: 48–49 (noting a number of policy incentives and other measures by many countries in Africa and Asia designed to create a more favorable and enabling environment for foreign investors; observing by comparison, a tendency toward more "State control" in parts of Latin America and the Caribbean). See also OECD Policy Brief, June 2001.

26 These and other types of potential benefits of TNC activity are noted and reviewed in some detail in the UNCTAD World Investment Report 2009. In the case of FDI in agriculture, for example, it is noted (with certain caveats) that TNC investment has been observed to help "improve labour productivity" and "efficiency in production" especially in traditional export-oriented commodities, to provide effective channels for technology transfer and dissemination, and provide a "missing ingredient" that can assist developing countries "to exploit their comparative advantages, access foreign markets, build export competitiveness and expand agricultural exports." World Investment Report 2009: 134–162.

27 Gallagher et al. 2007.
28 Tienhaara 2009 (reviewing new book of Gallagher and Zarsky, supra). There is also concern that the benefits of foreign investment in terms of job creation and development in a receiving (host) country can correspond to an "outsourcing" and loss of jobs away from the investor's country of origin.
29 UNCTAD World Investment Report 2009 (Introduction).
30 The overarching mission of the World Bank, for example, is to work toward a "world free of poverty". Evaluations and commentaries on international development and aid work is available in a wide variety of scholarly books, articles and reports (beyond the scope of the present chapter).
31 See, e.g. World Bank Annual Report 2011. For example, health and nutrition investments include initiatives to strengthen health systems, improve sanitation and combat diseases such as malaria and HIV/AIDs; education programs support teacher training, primary school enrolment and attention to marginalized populations.
32 See www.worldbank.org; www.ifc.org (describing the role, mission and activities of the International Finance Corporation, or IFC).
33 See Clark et al. 2002 (recounting history of proposed Narmada dams in India); Cernea et al. 2008; Modi 2009; Inspection Panel Investigation Report on the Mumbai Urban Transport Project 2007.
34 Ibid. See also World Bank Inspection Panel Investigation Reports on forest-related projects in DRC and Cambodia (describing, inter alia, pressures being placed upon forests by large-scale logging on forest-land of high importance and value to local and indigenous communities, and the difficulties faced by these communities in having an effective voice to influence these events); and Investigation Reports on energy and hydro-power projects in West Africa, Uganda and Argentina/Uruguay at www.inspectionpanel.org; UNEP et al. "Freshwater under Threat"; Fuller 2009 (describing plans and potential impacts of a series of new dams supported by foreign investment on the Mekong River, expected to provide electricity largely for export); Gamboa et al. 2008 (impacts of foreign investor energy investments on indigenous communities and forests in Peru). UNCTAD World Investment Report 2009 (noting various types of adverse social, environmental and political impacts within a host country that can result from FDI). The recent BP spill in the Gulf of Mexico has highlighted dramatically the risks and negative effects that can arise from oil and gas drilling operations – a reality in many regions of the world from the Gulf of Mexico to the Niger Delta to the forests in Peru.
35 See, e.g. UNHCR 2010 (describing how actions to encourage foreign investment and increase exploitation of natural resources, through a large number of licenses to forestry and oil companies "have had a particularly negative impact on indigenous communities living in the Amazon basin"); Gamboa et al. 2008 (impacts of foreign investment in energy and gas in Peru, particularly on isolated and vulnerable indigenous peoples); Acción Ecológica 2002 (describing legacy of "scars", "devastation", "water contamination" and "social tragedies" for indigenous peoples left by 30 years of multinational company oil investment in Ecuador, and ongoing pressure to open up additional areas to FDI).
36 See, e.g. Horta 2002 (describing stark negative impacts on poor rural communities and indigenous peoples of an oil and pipeline project); National Geographic documentary film on oil exploration in the Niger Delta (describing the serious toll of such operations on local populations, and issues relating to the sharing of benefits); Beltran et al. 2005 (noting history of links between multinational oil companies operating in the developing world and armed forces in the host countries, and instances of serious abuses – forced labor, rape, murder of community activists – in various countries).
37 Brundtland 1987 (describing poverty as both a cause and effect of environmental destruction, and providing enormous foundation and insights for the Rio Earth

Summit and following years of international cooperation on issues of environment and development). See also below.

38 UNEP "Putting a Price on Global Environmental Damage"; Genasci 2010.

39 *Idem*. (UNEP Report, Genasci).

40 See, e.g. Inspection Panel Reports on forest-projects in DRC and Cambodia, op. cit. See also Greenpeace 2009 (examining links between cattle ranching, international trade and consumption worldwide).

41 See, e.g. Fuller 2009 (Mekong River dams, electricity to be exported); *Washington Post* 2010 (large-scale investments by foreign investors into iron ore mines to supply steel mills in the home country to produce products sold throughout the world); Horta 2002.

42 *The Economist* 2010 (citing examples).

43 See, e.g. *Financial Times* 2009: 7.

44 FAO 2010.

45 See, e.g. World Bank 2010: preface, 16–17, "Rising Global Interest in Farmland: Can it Yield Sustainable and Equitable Benefits?" (stating that "When done right, larger-scale farming can provide opportunities to poor countries with large agricultural sectors and ample endowments of land"; noting also that large scale land acquisition can neglect existing land rights and deprive local communities of arable land, contributing to serious conflict).

46 *The Economist* 2010 (noting, inter alia, recent foreign investments to build and renovate thousands of kilometers of roads in Congo, reportedly linked to an interest to cultivate oil palm there "on a massive scale"). See also Global Witness at farmlandgrab.org.

47 See Reports noted above; World Bank Report reproduces a set of "Principles for responsible agro-investment" formulated by FAO, the World Bank, IFAD, UNCTAD and other partners.

48 World Investment Report 2009.

49 See, e.g. *The Inspection Panel at 15 Years: Participation and Accountability at the World Bank* (2009).

50 Ibid. See, e.g. Inspection Panel Investigation Report, Pakistan National Drainage Program Project, 2006. The project was developed to finance a national drainage system in Pakistan to alleviate problems of flooding and salinization along the Indus River valley (due to past irrigation programs). While it supported the needs of affected upstream farmers (the intended beneficiaries), it contributed to a significant increase in flooding risks and saline contamination of important waters and fisheries for downstream people – impacts that had not been accounted for or addressed prior to the time of the Inspection Panel's involvement.

51 See, e.g. Inspection Panel Investigation Reports in the cases of Democratic Republic of Congo Forest Operations (2005), and Cambodia Forest Management and Concession Project, 2006.

52 See, e.g. Inspection Panel Investigation Reports on Mumbai Urban Transport Project, 2005 (an urban transport and road improvement project in the city of Mumbai, India, which led to the involuntary resettlement of over 100,000 affected people), and on the Honduras Land Administration Project, 2007 (a project involving, inter alia, support for land regularization and titling activities within Honduras, including in lands of the Garifuna peoples). More detailed summaries of these and other Inspection Panel cases are contained in the Annual Reports of the Inspection Panel (see www.inspectionpanel.org) and in *The Inspection Panel at 15*, supra.

53 Obama 1994, 2004: 182–183.

54 See Smith and Wells 1975.

55 See www.cbd.int, Article 8(j) working activities.

56 One illustration is the ongoing tension and conflict in the Niger Delta relating both to the impacts of oil and gas drilling operations on local communities and the question of the sharing and distribution of the revenues of these operations. See, e.g. O'Neill 2007.

57 See, e.g. OP 4.12 on Involuntary Resettlement (in addition to provisions to avoid or minimize involuntary resettlement where feasible, and to compensate and assist people to improve or at least restore former living standards and livelihoods, the policy states that resettlers should be "provided sufficient investment resources and opportunities to share in project benefits"); OP 4.10 on Indigenous Peoples (indigenous peoples development plans in context of Bank-financed operations affecting indigenous peoples).

58 The recent Report of the World Bank Independent Evaluation Group (2010) on Safeguard Policies has helped bring renewed attention to this issue. One question that has been raised in discussions is the extent to which the provision of "positive benefits" should be addressed through policy norms vis-à-vis program operations. See also Herbertson et al. 2010 (recommending that Bank norms should go beyond the paradigm in its policies of "do no harm" and explicitly consider human rights into all its investment decisions).

59 See www.unctad.org.

60 See, e.g. Brundtland 1987 which highlighted these issues as well as the interrelationship between poverty and environmental loss; the 1992 Rio Earth Summit on Environment and Development, including the Rio Declaration and Agenda 21 which call for action (including financial assistance and technology transfer) to address problems of lack of capacity and resources in developing countries to address global environmental problems. The need to address lack of capacity also is embedded in many operational policies and procedures of the World Bank, as well as many of the projects and operations that it supports.

61 See, e.g. UNCTAD World Investment Report 2009, noting that the environmental impact of TNC participation in agricultural production depends on, inter alia, host country rules and regulations with respect to these impacts, and that "the nature and scale of many of the production activities in which they are involved make the question of their environmental impact particularly relevant." See also van Putten 2008 Chapter 1 (addressing issues and noting various studies on globalization, FDI, and the diminishing control of the State).

62 See discussion in Section III, below.

63 See Maathai 2009, The Challenge of Africa (the "eye-catching" nature to host governments of economic cooperation packages proposed without conditionalities, quoted below).

64 These and other issues relating to the safeguard policies of the World Bank are addressed in the recent report of the World Bank's Independent Evaluation Group (IEG), noted op. cit.

65 Based on discussions, observations and field encounters of author in his work as part of the World Bank Inspection Panel.

66 In 1996, former World Bank President James Wolfensohn decried the "cancer of corruption" and its effects on efforts to advance the development of developing countries, and in recent years the World Bank has established a number of means and procedures to address this issue as part of its development work. See also Maathai 2009 (describing issues of corruption and accumulation of wealth by some leaders and their inner circles).

67 See www.oecd.org.

68 *Idem.*

69 Khor 2000: 5 (commenting as well that "the large corporations have taken over a large part of decision making even in the developed countries"). The political and economic influence of large transnational investment companies is another "pattern of history" (e.g. early trading companies, oil companies, large scale agriculture industries).

70 As described in the 2005 Millennium Assessment, these include protection against flooding and erosion, provision of fresh water, regulating and contributing to the Earth's

water and carbon cycles, contributions to livelihoods of forest dependent peoples, and being shelter and home to plants, wildlife and biodiversity.

71 *Idem.* See also Report of the Inspection Panel on DRC Forest projects, supra (finding that initial studies greatly undervalued the value of non-timber resources in the forests of DRC, with major adverse implications for the forest peoples, biodiversity, and other values).

72 Kennedy 2009.

73 Maathai 2009: 109–110.

74 *Financial Times* Editorial 2010.

75 *Idem.* More recently, Dr. Maathai highlighted the issue of leadership to the problems facing Africa: "Decolonization began 50 years ago. The principal cause of poverty can be found in the ruling class which has thought to enrich itself and not to govern." Maathai 12 July 2009: 9.

76 The Paris Declaration on Aid Effectiveness (2005), the Acra Agenda For Action (2008), and the Busan Partnership for Effective Development Co-operation (2011). In terms of substantive outlook vis-à-vis FDI, there have also been important evolutions in views over the years. For example, while there was originally a notable and fairly well-defined "North-South" dynamic to this debate, in which countries of the "global South" fought against undue influence and impacts by transnational companies of the North, and worked to establish new norms and principles to re-align the international economic order, there has been a significant evolution in these views and related circumstances over time. This subject is addressed in the next section.

77 Jackson et al. 2002: 1136.

78 Ibid.:198.

79 *Idem.* See also UNCTAD World Investment Report 2009 (and discussion below).

80 Jackson et al. 2002: 198 (noting the 1974 Charter of Economic Rights and Duties of States adopted by the UN General Assembly in 1974, providing that "compensation for expropriation was to be measured by the law of the expropriating State."). See discussion on this topic below.

81 See e.g. Kohr 2000; UNCTAD World Investment Report 1996: 133.

82 *Idem.*

83 *Idem*, reflecting tenets of the "Calvo Doctrine".

84 *Idem.*

85 See e.g. Khor 2000 at 72. In parallel, a new approach (and narrative) was forming on issues of trade and development. Taking into view the apparently successful export-led growth and development strategy followed by a number of countries in Asia in the 1980s, developing countries entered in increasing numbers into the WTO trading system with the aim to enter forcefully in the give-and-take negotiation of terms of trade that reflected their interests, rather than "stand apart" from this system and rely on principles of special and more favorable treatment that, in the end, were not leading to the hoped-for results. See also Bhagwati 1988.

86 Khor 2000: 72.

87 OECD Policy Brief, June 2001.

88 UNCTAD World Investment Report 2009: 48–49. It observes, by comparison, a tendency toward more "State control" in parts of Latin America and the Caribbean.

89 They have also been considered, though not yet adopted, as potential models for new agreements at a broader regional level (e.g. OECD) and multilateral (e.g. WTO) level.

90 Some of the discussion below is drawn from the author's own experiences in the policy discussions and negotiations of NAFTA Chapter 11, as a newly arrived staff attorney addressing international law matters for the US Environmental Protection Agency.

91 See, e.g. Garcia-Bolivar 2009 ("To some extent it has been left for granted that the sole purpose of the international law of foreign investment is to promote and protect foreign investments").

92 Indeed US negotiators referred to a "model" BIT as a point of reference during deliberations as part of the negotiating process, while allowing for the possibility to alter and go beyond this model.
93 NAFTA Chapter 11, Article 1106. The text of NAFTA and related information is available at the website of the NAFTA Secretariat at www.NAFTA-sec-alena.org.
94 See NAFTA Chapter 11.
95 See NAFTA Chapter 11, Section B.
96 See, e.g. Lallas et al. 1992. For many in the US, at least, a triggering event was a 1991 determination by an arbitration panel under the GATT in the so-called "Tuna-Dolphin" case, finding that provisions of the US Marine Mammal Protection Act that prohibited the import of tuna from Mexico caught in a way that involved incidental trapping and killing of dolphins. This put a focus on what became an early and leading concern in the trade and environment debates, namely that the rules of international trade could come into conflict with the ability of governments to take needed measures to protect health, the environment and natural resources. This became referred to as the potential "regulatory effects" of trade (perhaps more aptly, the "de-regulatory effects"). See also Lallas 1993 (suggesting a typology of different types of environmental impacts of trade).
97 These included the negotiation of NAFTA between the Mexico, Canada and the US and the negotiation of the Uruguay Round of Multilateral Trade Negotiations, an OECD working group on trade and environment, and the WTO Committee on Trade and Environment established in 1994 at the conclusion of the Uruguay Round negotiations.
98 In particular, there was concern that the prohibitions against direct or indirect expropriation, or measures "tantamount" to expropriation, could be applied by foreign investors, under investor–State procedures, to challenge health and environmental measures as a form of "regulatory takings" for which compensation is due.
99 Review of US–Mexico Environmental Issues 1992 (hereinafter NAFTA Environmental Review).
100 NAFTA, Article 1114.2.
101 NAFTA Environmental Review, supra. See also Economic Globalization and the Environment, OECD, 1997; Jones 1998; Lallas 1993.
102 Studies on the effects of NAFTA on FDI flows, sponsored by the North American Commission on Environmental Cooperation, found some evidence that NAFTA increased FDI flows, but the evidence was considered "inconclusive" in terms of growth effects, and it was noted that "country-specifics matter." Crosby 2005.
103 Guisinger 1996, indicating that "[v]ery little is known about repercussions of foreign direct investment liberalization on host economies . . . The link between investment liberalization and macroeconomic performance has received scant attention from researchers." Quoted in Khor 2000: 72. See also Garcia-Bolivar 2009. ("in real terms, the impact of IIAs has been uncertain") and Gallagher et al. 2007.
104 UNCTAD, *The Role of International Investment Agreements in Attracting Foreign Direct Investment to Developing Countries*, 2009.
105 The original draft proposal of this provision, considered among US policymakers and negotiators, did not contain the words "otherwise consistent with this chapter". In addition, an earlier tabled version referred to being otherwise consistent with the "non-discrimination" provisions of the chapter. Although the earlier versions were proposed and preferred by environmental policymakers, they did not win the day in the negotiating process. The final change came very late in the process.
106 See North American Agreement on Environmental Cooperation at www.cec.org. See generally Magraw 1994; Charnowitz 1994.
107 The author participated in discussions and negotiations relating to the OECD MAI while working at the US EPA.

108 van Putten 2008.
109 OECD, International Investment Law 2008.
110 *Idem*. See also UNCTAD World Investment Report 2009 at 34–35.
111 UNCTAD, at www.unctad.org.
112 UNCTAD Series on Issues in International Investment Agreements II 2011.
113 Ruggie 2007.
114 Soft law refers to non-binding instruments that generally express apolitical-level commitment but are not legally binding in nature. These instruments have been developed to express commitment and expectations for future work (e.g. in the form of a non-binding Declaration an Action Plan), including in cases where the will to enter into legally-binding commitments is not at hand; they may also form a basis for subsequent development of legally binding norms at the international level, whether through treaty negotiation or as customary international law ("hard" law).
115 See, e.g. Kravchenko and Bonine 2008, Chapter 9 (Corporate Accountability).
116 This initiative is established by the UNEP Finance Initiative and the UN Global Compact, with more than 800 signatories from 45 countries, managing over $22 trillion of assets. See www.unep.org.
117 See www.unep.org.
118 See, e.g. Ruggie 2007.
119 *OECD Observer* 2009. See also Coulter et al. 2009 (noting the "proliferation of voluntary codes and voluntary principles and polices for corporations and other business", but adding that "few observers today believe that corporate performance . . . in developing countries in respecting human rights and protecting the environment is adequate").
120 Kravchenko and Bonine 2008: 379–380.
121 Freeland 2010 (citing other examples from the financial and other sectors).
122 Ruggie 2007.
123 Ruggie 2007 (noting the OECD MNE Guidelines and other initiatives to promote transparency, participation and status reviews, adding that these arise "in specific operational contexts, not in any overarching manner").
124 OECD Policy Brief, June 2001.
125 See, e.g. Kravchenko and Bonine 2008.
126 In this context, World Bank refers to the IBRD and IDA, which generally provide financial support directly to governments (borrowers) to develop and implement projects and other operations in support of their critical development needs. Other entities of the World Bank Group, including the International Finance Corporation and MIGA, have a separate set of "Performance Standards" to address the social, environmental and other implications of their operations. By comparison to IBRD and IDA, these latter entities finance or provide guarantees directly to private sector companies, in accordance with a number of specifically established criteria.
127 These policies, which have been developed and revised over a period of many years, are reproduced on the World Bank website, www.worldbank.org.
128 See www.worldbank.org.
129 The discussion focuses on new, "formal" means by which members of the public participate in the international law and policy process, but also notes the crucial and expanding role over the years of civil society and NGOs "outside" the "formal" structures of the system – in the function of "watchdogs" and outside monitors, sounding the alarm, representing the interests of affected communities and environmental or other public interests that otherwise may lack advocates in the process, and as providers of critical information about issues, problems and practices affecting their areas of concern (whether human rights, labor, environmental, locally-affected communities, or many others).
130 As reflected in Article 39 of the International Court of Justice, international law consists of treaties (negotiated by *governments*), customary law (derived from the

actions and statements of *governments* taken under a sense of legal obligation), and general principles of law (derived from legal precepts and practices widely followed in the *laws of nations*). The scholarly writings of commentators – i.e. non-State actors – are viewed as a "secondary source" of international law, for example to be considered in by international tribunals in their analysis of questions and interpretation of international law.

131 Under treaty systems, for example, Parties (i.e. governments) develop and implement programs of cooperation to advance the purposes of the treaty through decisions taken at Meetings of Parties once a treaty is in force. The dispute settlement systems of treaties also traditionally are available as between Parties (governments).

132 Sohn 1982.

133 United Nations Conference on Environment and Development, Rio de Janeiro, June 1992.

134 See the Rio Declaration, including Principles 20–22 and Agenda 21, Chapters 23–32, both adopted at the Rio Summit.

135 See, e.g. Brown Weiss 1995 (marking this evolution, highlighting aspects of NGO and public participation in the field). See also discussion below.

136 See, e.g. Lallas 2000/2001.

137 *Idem.*

138 It is worth noting another comment made by Professor Sohn: that these and other mechanisms of international law are shaped by those with the most influence and power (citing Victor Hugo, law is made by the powerful). Just as it has been observed that the post-World War II international economic order was designed seemingly in line with the interests of those having the greatest voice in its development, the words of Robert McNamara (who just recently passed away) serve as a reminder that the same can be said about the establishment of other mechanisms, like tribunals to judge war crimes. In the documentary *The Fog of War*, as described in a recent retrospective of his life, McNamara recalls his supporting role in military headquarters in US firebombing attacks on cities during World War II, and his conversation with General Curtis E. LeMay of army air forces: "Lemay said, 'If we'd lost the war, we'd all have been prosecuted as war criminals.' And I think he's right. He, and I'd say I, were behaving as war criminals." He then asked, without being able to answer "What makes it immoral if you lose and not immoral if you win." See *International Herald Tribune* 2009.

139 One World Trust 2006 at 6.

140 *Idem.*

141 Ibid.: 50

142 The notion here is that "sunshine" or the "spotlight of public opinion" themselves can generate important additional incentives to encourage or induce compliance, and to take appropriate actions in response to findings of harm or potential harm. See, e.g. Brown Weiss et al. 2009.

143 One particularly high-profile project was the Bank's financing of proposals to build dams on the Narmada River in India. Local community and civil society organizations mobilized in protest against the large-scale displacement and other potential impacts of the project, and a Commission eventually appointed by the Bank (the "Morse Commission") found that the Bank had, indeed, failed to comply with its own core social and environmental safeguard policies in respect to the project.

144 In the early 1990s, there were also important internally-generated critiques about aspects of World Bank operations, including low success rates in achieving project objectives and the so-called "culture of approval" which failed to give adequate consideration to, inter alia, to the proper application of Bank safeguard policies. See, e.g. Clark et al. 2003; *The Inspection Panel at 15 Years* 2009.

145 See 1999 Clarifications, paragraph 9; 1993 Resolutions establishing the Panel, paragraph 9. These include, in brief, that: the requesters are two or more people in the

territory of the borrower (in some cases, they may act through representatives); they allege harm or potential harm as a result of Bank non-compliance with its operational policies and procedures; they assert that they have contacted Bank Management prior to coming to the Panel in an attempt to resolve their concerns, and are not satisfied with the results of these efforts; the project is not about procurement (handled by another Bank mechanism); the project is not yet closed (more than 95% disbursed); and the Panel has not made a previous recommendation on the project or, if it has, that there are new circumstances and evidence to justify an investigation.

146 For a more detailed description and discussion of the Panel process, including some of the issues and challenges faced over the years, see *The Inspection Panel at 15*, supra (and the references and studies cited and reviewed therein), at *www.inspection-panel.org*. See also Brown Weiss et al. 2009 and the Inspection Panel website at www.inspectionpanel.org.

147 For example, Panel members serve fixed and non-renewable five-year terms, and can never work for the World Bank following the end of their tenure as a Panel member. Candidates for Panel member positions cannot have worked in any capacity for the Bank in the two years prior to the time of entry onto the Panel.

148 1993 Resolution Establishing the Panel, paragraph 11. The discussion below owes a particular debt of gratitude to former Chairperson of the Inspection Panel, Edith Brown Weiss, who played a leading role in initiating what are now annual meetings among IFI recourse and accountability mechanisms to exchange views and experiences, and subsequently presented a set of criteria that could be used as a basis for self-assessment by accountability mechanisms for discussion during these meetings.

149 There are a few other basic requirements reflected in informational brochures developed by the Panel, including that the Request is submitted in writing and is signed. Panel procedures also allow for Requesters to keep their identities confidential, for example if they fear a possibility of reprisal as a result of filing a claim with the Panel.

150 This and other information is also available at www.inspectionpanel.org.

151 NAAEC, Article 14.1.

152 NAAEC, Article 14.2.

153 NAAEC, Article 15.1 and 15.2.

154 For an analysis at the time of features and innovations of the NAAEC and the public submission process, and some of the key issues faced during its negotiation, see Magraw, 1994.

155 See Garver 2008 (concluding that "[i]t is clear that environmental mechanisms in the NAFTA package have not met their promise or potential, and yet they are being duplicated with little analysis or meaningful modification." See also information on the public submission process at the CEC website, www.cec.org.

156 OECD Guidelines for MNEs, Part C, Implementation in Specific Instances.

157 *Idem*.

158 Report by the Chair of the 2008 Annual Meeting of NCPs, p. 3.

159 Specific Instances Considered by National Contact Points, 10 October 2008.

160 Terms of Reference for an Update of the OECD Guidelines on MNEs, at www.oecd.org. The TOR also address, among other things, topics of climate change, human rights, and due diligence by companies in light of circumstances along their supply chains (drawing on discussions with Professor Ruggie).

161 See NAFTA Chapter 11, Section B.

162 See, e.g. website of the Office of the Legal Adviser of the US Department of State, at www.state.gov.

Bibliography

Acción Ecológica (2002), *Informe de la Campaña en Contra de la Construcción de la OCP.*, June 2002.

Beltran, B. and Oldham, J. (2005), "Shaking off *El Norte*: Oil Multinationals Privatize the Military in Ecuador", *Synthesis/Regeneration 38*, Fall 2005, available at http://www.greens.org/s-r/38/38–05.html (visited 9 June 2012).

Bhagwati, J. (1988), *Protectionism*, Cambridge, MA: The MIT Press.

Brown Weiss, E. (1995), *New Issues in International Environmental Law.*

Brown Weiss, E., Lallas, P. and Herken, A. (2009), *The World Bank Inspection Panel: Participation and Accountability*, Tokyo/New York/Paris: UNU publication.

Brundtland Commission (1987), *Our Common Future*, Oxford: Oxford University Press.

Cernea, M. and Mathur, H. (eds) (2008), *Can Compensation Prevent Impoverishment*, Oxford: Oxford University Press.

Charnowitz, S. (1994), "The NAFTA Environmental Side Agreement: Implications for Environmental Cooperation, Trade Policy, and American Treatymaking", 8 *Temple International and Comparative Law Journal* 257.

Clark, D., Fox, J. and Treakle, K. (eds) (2003), *Demanding Accountability: Civil Society Claims and the World Bank Inspection Panel*, Lanham, MD: Rowman and Littlefield.

Crosby, A. (remarks), "Trade and Environment in North America 2005", Third North American Symposium on Assessing the Environmental Effects of Trade, Investment, Growth and the Environment.

Coulter, R., Crippa, L. and Wann, E. (2009), *Principles of International law for Multinational Development Banks: The Obligation to Respect Human Rights*, Helena, MO/Washington, DC: Indian Law Resource Center.

Economist, The (2010), "Seeing the Wood, A Special Report on Forests", 25 September.

Financial Times (2009), "Tokyo's G8 Initiative Aims to Halt 'Farmland Grabbing' in Developing Nations", 26 May, p. 4.

Financial Times (2009), "The World Must Learn to Live and Farm Food Sustainably", 6 July, p. 7.

Financial Times (2010), "Scramble for Africa", Editorial, 25 August.

Freeland, C. (2010), "The Real Corporate Responsibility", *Washington Post*, 18 July, p. A.19.

Fuller, T. (2009), "Dams and Development Threaten the Mekong", *New York Times*, 18 December.

Gallagher, K. and Zarsky, L. (2007), *The Enclave Economy: Foreign Investment and Sustainable Development in Mexico's Silicon Valley*, Cambridge, MA: The MIT Press.

Gamboa, C., Cueto, V. and Davila, J. (2008), *El Estado Peruano cumplio con Camisea*, DAR.

Garcia-Bolivar, O. (2009), "*International Law of Foreign Investment at Crossroads: The Need to Reform*", presented at Second Biennial General Conference of the Asian Society of International Law, University of Tokyo, August 2009.

Garver, G. (2008), "Tooth Decay", 25 *Environmental Forum* 34.

Genasci, L., "Environmental Damage Costs 11 Percent Global GDP", posted on 10 October 2010 at genascihk.worldpress.com.

Global Witness, "The Food Crisis and the Global Land Grab", available at farmlandgrab.org.

Greenpeace, "Slaughtering the Amazon", posted in June 2009 at http://www.greenpeace.org.

Guisinger, S., OECD-organized workshop on FDI and the MAI in March 1996, Quoted in Khor 2000.

Herbertson, K., Thompson, K. and Goodland, R. (2000), *A Roadmap for Integrating Human Rights into the World Bank Group*, Washington, DC: World Resources Institute.

Hochschild, A. (2000), *King Leopold's Ghost*, New York: Mariner Books.

Horta, K. (2002), "Rhetoric and Reality: Human Rights and the World Bank", 15 *Harvard Human Rights Journal* 227.

International Finance Corporation (2000), *Annual Report*, Washington, DC: International Finance Corporation.

International Herald Tribune (2009), "Robert McNamara dies: architect of Vietnam War", 7 July.

Jackson, J., Davey, W. and Sykes, A. Jr. (2002), *Legal Problems of International Economic Relations, 4th edition*, St. Paul, MN: West Publishing Group.

Jones, T. (1997), "Globalisation and Environment: Main Issues", in OECD, *Globalisation and Environment: Preliminary Perspectives*, Paris: OECD.

Kennedy, R.F. Jr. (2009), "A President Breaks Hearts in Appalachia", *The Washington Post*, 3 July.

Khor, M. (2000), "Globalization and the South: Some Critical Issues", *UNCTAD Discussion Paper No.147*.

Kravchenko, S. and Bonine, J. (2008), *Human Rights and the Environment: Cases, Law and Policy*, Chapter 9 (Corporate Accountability), Durham, NC: Carolina Academic Press.

Lallas, P. (1993), "NAFTA and Evolving Approaches to Identify and Address 'Indirect' Environmental Impacts of International Trade", 5 *Georgetown International Environmental Law Review* 519.

Lallas, P. (2000/2001), "The Role of Process and Participation in the Development of Effective International Environmental Agreements: A Study of the Global Treaty on Persistent Organic Pollutants (POPs)", 19 *UCLA Journal of Environmental Law and Policy* 83.

Lallas, P., Esty, D. and van Hoogstraten, D. (1992), "Environmental Protection and International Trade: Toward Mutually Supportive Rules and Policies", 16(2) *Harvard Environmental Law Review* 271.

Maathai, W. (2009), *The Challenge for Africa*, New York: Pantheon Books.

Maathai, W. (2009), "Decolonization began 50 years ago. The principal cause of poverty can be found in the ruling class which has thought to enrich itself and not to govern", quoted in *Corriere della Sera*, 12 July.

Magraw, D. (1994), "NAFTA's Repercussions: Is Green Trade Possible", *Environment Magazine*, March 1994 issue.

Modi, R. (ed.) (2009), *Beyond Relocation: The Imperative of Sustainable Development*, Thousand Oaks, CA: Sage Publications.

National Geographic documentary film on oil exploration in the Niger Delta, available at www.nationalgeographic.org.

Obama, B. (2004), *Dreams from My Father*, New York: Three Rivers Press.

OECD (1997), *Economic Globalisation and the Environment*, Paris: OECD.

OECD (2001), *Policy Brief*, June.

OECD (2008), OECD-*DAC Secretariat Simulation of DAC Members' Net ODA Volumes in 2008 and 2010: in Constant 2008 USD million*, available at www.oecd.org/dataoecd/47/56/42458719.pdf.

OECD (2008), *International Investment Law: Understanding Concepts and Tracking Innovations*, Paris: OECD.

OECD (2009), *OECD Observer*, 9 May.

O'Neill, T. (2007), "Curse of the Black Gold: Hope and Betrayal in the Niger Delta (continued)", *National Geographic*, available at www.nationalgeographic.org.

One World Trust (2007), *2007 Global Accountability Report*, London: One World Trust.

Review of US–Mexico Environmental Issues, conducted by US Government interagency task force coordinated by the Office of the US Trade Representative, February 1992 ("NAFTA Environmental Review").

Ruggie, J. (1982), "International Regimes, Transactions, and Change: Embedded Liberalism in the Postwar Economic Order", 36(2) *International Organization* 379.

Ruggie, J. (2007), "Business and Human Rights: Mapping International Standards of Responsibility and Accountability for Corporate Acts", Report of the Special Representative of the Secretary-General (SRSG) on the issue of human rights and transnational corporations and other business enterprises, UN Doc. A/HRC/4/035, 9 February.

Smith, D. and Wells, L.T. Jr. (1975), *Negotiating Third World Mineral Agreements: Promises as Prologue*, Pensacola, FL: Ballinger Publishing Co.

Sohn, L. (1982), "The New International Law: Protection of the Rights of Individuals Rather than States", 32 *American University Law Review* 1.

Tienhaara, K. (2009), "Book Review: Gallagher and Zarsky (2007), *The Enclave Economy: Foreign Investment and Sustainable Development in Mexico's Silicon Valley*, Cambridge, MA: The MIT Press, 9(1) *International Environmental Agreements: Politics, Law and Economics* 85.

United Nations Conference on Trade and Development (UNCTAD) (1996), *World Investment Report 1996*, Geneva: UNCTAD.

UNCTAD (2009a), *World Investment Report 2009*, Geneva: UNCTAD.

UNCTAD (2009b), *The Role of International Investment Agreements in Attracting Foreign Direct Investment to Developing Countries*, Geneva: UNCTAD.

UNCTAD (2011), *Series on Issues in International Investment Agreements II, Scope and Definition*, Geneva: UNCTAD.

United Nations Environment Program (UNEP) and Asia Institute of Technology (2009), *Freshwater under Threat: South East Asia*, Nairobi: UNEP.

UNEP Finance Initiative and Principles for Responsible Investment (2010) , "Putting a Price on Global Environmental Damage", available at http://www.unpri.org/files/uop_press_release_final.pdf.

United Nations Food and Agriculture Organization (FAO) Committee on Commodity Problems (2010), "Foreign Investment in Developing Country Agriculture – Issues, Policy Implications and International Response", Rome, 14–16 June, available at http://www.responsibleagroinvestment.org/rai/sites/responsibleagroinvestment.org/files/OECD_RAI%20Issure_Policy%20Implications.pdf.

United Nations Food and Agriculture Organization (FAO) (2008), *Report*, Rome: FAO.

United Nations High Commissioner on Refugees (UNHCR) (2010), *World Directory of Minorities and Indigenous Peoples – Peru*, Geneva: UNHCR.

United Nations Statistical Service.

van Putten, M. (2008), *Policing the Banks*, Montreal: McGill-Queen University Press.

Washington Post (2010), "The Other Superpower", 14 February.

Wheeler, G. (2009), (former) Managing Director, the World Bank, "Thoughts on the Outlook for Foreign Direct Investment and Political Risk", Address at the MIGA/Financial Times Global Political Risk Summit, London, 3 December, available at http://web.worldbank.org/WBSITE/EXTERNAL/NEWSZ/0,,contentMDK:22411494~pagePK:34370~piPK:42770~theSitePK:4607,00.html.

World Bank (2010a), *World Bank Annual Report 2010*, Washington, DC: World Bank.

World Bank (2010b), *Rising Global Interest in Farmland: Can it Yield Sustainable and Equitable Benefits?*, Washington, DC: World Bank. (This report of the World Bank reproduces a set of "Principles for responsible agro-investment" formulated by FAO, the World Bank, IFAD, UNCTAD and other partners.)

World Bank (2011), *World Bank Annual Report 2011*, Washington, DC: World Bank.

World Bank Independent Evaluation Group (IEG) (2010), *Safeguards and Sustainability Policies in a Changing World*, Washington, DC: World Bank.

World Bank Inspection Panel (2009), *The Inspection Panel at 15 Years: Participation and Accountability at the World Bank*, Washington, DC: World Bank, available at www.inspectionpanel.org.

World Bank Inspection Panel Investigation Report, *Cambodia Forest Concession Management and Control Pilot Project*, 2007, available at www.inspectionpanel.org.

World Bank Inspection Panel Investigation Report, *DRC Transitional Support for Economic Recovery Credit and Emergency Economic and Social Reunification Support Project*, 2007, available at www.inspectionpanel.org.

World Bank Inspection Panel Investigation Report, *Honduras Land Administration Project*, 2007, available at www.inspectionpanel.org.

World Bank Inspection Panel Investigation Report, *Mumbai Urban Transport Project*, 2007, available at www.inspectionpanel.org.

World Bank Inspection Panel Investigation Report, *Pakistan National Drainage Program Project*, 2006, available at www.inspectionpanel.org.

Index